OPEN ROAD'S BEST OF

Belize

by Charlie Morris

**Open Road Travel Guides – designed for the
amount of time you *really* have for your trip!**

Open Road Publishing

Open Road's new travel guides.
Designed to cut to the chase.
You don't need a huge travel encyclopedia – you need a
selective guide to steer you right. If you're going on vacation
for a few weeks or less, get a guide that brings you the *best* of
any destination for the amount of time you *really* have for
your trip!

Open Road – the guide you need for the trip you want.

The New Open Road *Best Of* Travel Guides.
Right to the point.
Uncluttered.
Easy.

Open Road Publishing
P.O. Box 284, Cold Spring Harbor, NY 11724
www.openroadguides.com

The author has made every effort to be as accurate as possible, but neither
she nor the publisher assumes responsibility for the services provided by
any business listed in this guide; for any errors or omissions; or any loss,
damage, or disruptions in your travels for any reason.

About the Author
Charlie Morris is also the author of *Open Road's Best of Costa
Rica, Open Road's Best of Honduras,* and *Switzerland Guide.*

Photo credits on page 8.

CONTENTS

Maps

PHOTO CREDITS

1. INTRODUCTION

Belize is a true tropical paradise, a place where you can explore the wonders of the wilderness while never straying far from the comforts of civilization. All the attractions of Central America are here: palm-shaded Caribbean beaches, azure seas, coral reefs, and vast expanses of uninhabited forest where clear rivers wind lazily past mysterious Mayan ruins, observed only by the monkeys and the birds.

Belize's relative prosperity and English-speaking population make traveling here a breeze. Crime and aggressive hustlers are far less of a problem than in many other tropical destinations. Tourist facilities are well developed: you'll have no problems getting around the country by bus, small plane or rented car, finding excellent accommodations, from modern luxury resorts to charming budget lodgings, and enjoying delightful local or international cuisine.

Belize is one of the world's **top ecotourism destinations**. The rain forests hold an amazing array of flora and fauna (Belize has more

species of birds than the entire continent of North America), from playful monkeys to gaudy toucans to elusive wild cats. The seas teem with tropical fish. There's a vast variety of landscapes, from sandy beaches to coastal mangrove swamps to mountains carpeted with lush greenery.

But the greatest asset of this peaceful and serene country is her people, a fascinating mix of Creoles, Mestizos, Garifuna, Mayans and Mennonites. Belizeans are some of the friendliest folks you'll meet anywhere. They've built a strong nation that has avoided the civil wars and poverty that have plagued some of her neighbors, and are doing an excellent job of preserving their priceless natural treasures.

The activities are endless. With the **world's second-longest barrier reef** and three coral atolls, Belize has the finest diving in the Western Hemisphere. Fishing is spectacular, from tarpon and snook in the lagoons to bonefish and permit on the grass flats to billfish offshore. The many beautiful rivers offer everything from kayaking to cave tubing. The forested mountain landscapes are full of caves, and are perfect for hiking, birding, horseback riding and mountain biking.

Of course, many travelers also enjoy more sedate pursuits, such as sipping a cool drink while basking on a beautiful beach, and the opportunities for doing that in Belize are second to none.

2. OVERVIEW

Belize has a huge variety of things to see and do for such a small country. You can explore the rain forest-clad mountains and relax on pristine Caribbean beaches, all on the same trip. Ancient Mayan temples tell mysterious stories about the country's previous inhabitants, while today's residents make beautiful music and art. There are fun activities for all interests and all levels of strenuousness. If you want to see the flora and fauna of the rain forest on foot, on horseback or by boat, or if you want to explore the ocean diving, snorkeling, fishing or kayaking, you can find the trip of a lifetime here. Along the way, you'll find attractive and comfortable accommodations, exotic cuisine and charming local crafts.

As a travel destination, Belize is a country in transition. Long an off-the-beaten path destination for backpackers and birders, the country is quickly becoming a center for mega-tourism. Last year, gargantuan cruise ships disgorged nearly a million wide-eyed day-trippers to the shiny new **Tourism Village** in Belize City, and **Ambergris Caye** is evolving into a major upscale resort. As yet however, there is nothing in Belize to match the crassness of tourist centers such as Nassau or Cancun. Mass tourism is concentrated in a few areas of the country, and there are still vast areas where you can spend days without seeing another tourist.

The Northern Cayes
Off the coast of Belize lies a sprawl of small islands called cayes (pro-

nounced "keys"). The largest and northernmost of these is called **Ambergris Caye**, and it's the country's top tourist destination. Here you'll find lodgings for every taste and budget, from backpacker favorites to luxury resorts, as well as a huge selection of tour operators offering diving, snorkeling, fishing, and boating trips, and some lively nightlife. **Caye Caulker** is a bit more laid back, a lazy place where old gringos go to seed and eat cheap lobster. Hard-core divers and fishermen head for a handful of colorful lodges on some of the smaller cayes.

Belize City & Northern Belize

Most visitors don't linger long in **Belize City**, the country's business capital, but the region has some don't-miss attractions. The **Belize Zoo** and the **Baboon Sanctuary** offer glimpses of the country's animals for the whole family. The Mayan ruins of **Lamanai** and **Altun Ha** are hidden in remote jungles teeming with wildlife. Birders come from all over the world to cruise the lagoons of **Crooked Tree Wildlife Sanctuary**.

Cayo & Western Belize

This is ground zero for ecotourism and adventure travel. Dozens of jungle lodges in all price ranges cater to every interest, including birding, hiking, caving, river tubing and horseback riding. **Mountain Pine Ridge** is a unique ecosystem, and the locale of many caves and waterfalls. This region has the country's highest concentration of Mayan ruins, including Belize's largest, **Caracol**. Just across the border in Guatemala is the largest known Mayan site in the world, **Tikal**.

Southern Belize

Fewer tourists venture to the south, but that's starting to change as people begin to realize how much this region has to offer. Offshore are some of the most pristine dive sites in the country, on the barrier reef and around **Glover's Reef Atoll**. A short way inland, **Cockscomb Basin** and **Mayflower Bocawina** are two of Belize's nicest and easiest to visit nature reserves. The friendly **Garifuna** people have a unique culture and a fascinating musical scene going on in their coastal villages.

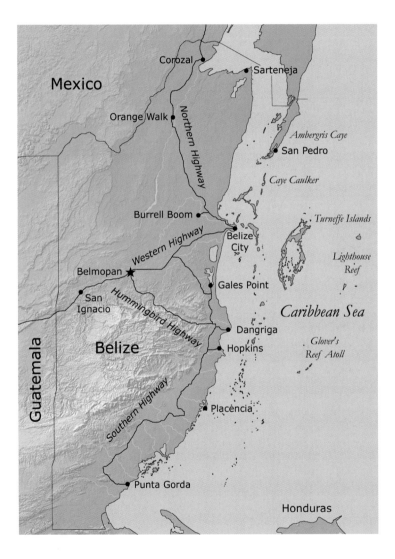

Diving

Belize has the most spectacular **coral reefs** in the Western Hemisphere – the world's second-longest barrier reef and three idyllic 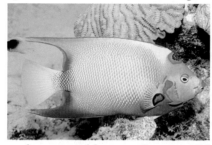 coral atolls. A rainbow of coral and tropical fish awaits you. A very well developed dive industry makes it easy to plan the dive vacation of a lifetime. Many reefs are in shallow water just a short way offshore, so the wonders of the undersea world are easily accessible to **snorkelers** too. Even if you've never snorkeled before, you simply must give it a try before you leave Belize.

Fishing

Belize has a huge variety of fishing opportunities. Inside the atolls are vast expanses of sand **flats**, perfect territory for bonefish, permit and tarpon. Silver kings that average 40-80 pounds will trash your tackle with astonishing leaps into the air. The **reefs** hold snapper, grouper and jacks – you might bring home a couple of yellowtail snapper for the grill. **Offshore** anglers battle with blue and white marlin, sailfish, wahoo, dorado, tuna, kingfish and shark. The **rivers and lagoons** are stiff with snook.

Canoeing & Kayaking

Belize's lazy rivers are made for canoeing. You won't find much whitewater, but you will find lovely clear pools surrounded by jungle greenery and melodious birds. A kayak is an excellent way to explore the lagoons and mangrove wetlands of the coast, or the grass flats out on the coral atolls.

Horseback Riding

The best way to explore some of Belize's rugged terrain is on horseback, and riding is a very popular way to enjoy the rain forest. You'll find extensive equestrian centers near Belmopan and Mountain Pine Ridge. You can take a horseback tour or rent horses in most regions of the country.

Spelunking

The **Chiquibul** cave system is one of the largest systems of caverns in the Western Hemisphere. There are caverns and caves suitable for both novice and expert cavers. At a couple of locales, you can go cave tubing. Floating through caves on an inner tube is an unforgettable experience, and one of the most popular activities in Belize. Caves were sacred places to the ancient Mayans, who called the underworld **Xibalba**, and you can visit several caves where skeletons and artifacts of the ancient ones can be seen.

Observing the Animals

The greatest thrill in Belize is the chance to see wild animals going about their daily business in the forest. If you spend some time in one or more of the parks and preserves, your chances of seeing some critters are good. However, some animals are much more easily seen than others, and some visitors have unrealistic expectations.

White-nosed coatis (locally known as quash) are frequently seen, and they are friendly and fun. Monkeys are everyone's favorites, and they are pretty common (a little too common, say the owners of stolen sunglasses and hats). Belize has two species: spider monkeys and howler monkeys, whose cries boom through the forest. We'd all love to see a wild cat,  and Belize has five species: pumas, jaguars, ocelots, margays and jaguarundis. Outside of a zoo or rehabilitation center however, you're unlikely to spot one of these secretive, nocturnal predators.

If you really want to see some of the rarer forest denizens, visit one of the more remote parks, walk quietly, and take your hikes in the early morning or just before dusk. I highly recommend hiring a local guide, who can show you animals (and plants) that you would never see on your own.

Wildlife

The Belizean government has long seen the value of protecting their wilderness areas, and has created an impressive system of **national parks and nature reserves** throughout the country. Belize has a wide variety of different climates and ecosystems, and the parks have been planned to preserve at least a sample of each one. Visitors can expect to see lovely flowers, butterflies, hummingbirds, colorful parrots and macaws, coatis, monkeys, agoutis, crocodiles and iguanas. The lucky may see anteaters, peccaries, tapirs, ocelots, manatees or whales.

Bird Watching

With over 550 (and counting) bird species available for viewing,

it's impossible for even the most hard-core birder to visit Belize without adding significantly to their life list. Multicolored **parrots** and **toucans**, along with a wide assortment of Little Brown Birds (LBBs), flit through the forest, and vast flocks of **shore birds** patrol the coasts. If the birding gods smile on you, you may even see a rare **jabiru stork**, a **trogon**, or a **Stygian owl**. Some lodges and tour companies cater specifically to birders.

Tropical River Cruises

One of the very best ways to get close to wildlife (without getting out of breath) is to take a **jungle cruise** on one of the many lagoons, canals and rivers. Monkeys and crocodiles are close enough to touch (but don't). Prime spots are the **New River Lagoon** and **Crooked Tree** in the north, and the **Sittee** and **Monkey** rivers in the south.

Mayan Ruins

Belize has thousands of Mayan sites, many as yet unexcavated. However, several impressive ones are very much ready for visitors. In the north are **Lamanai** and **Altun Ha**; in the west

Belize Facts

Location:	Central America, with the Caribbean Sea to the east, Mexico to the north, and Guatemala to the west and south
Land Area:	22,806 sq km
Highest Point:	Victoria Peak, 1,160 m
Coastline:	386 km
Biodiversity:	153 mammal species, 550 bird species
Population:	301,000
Languages:	English, Spanish, Garifuna, Mayan. Some Mennonite communities speak German.
Life Expectancy:	69 years
Literacy:	77%
Poverty rate:	33%
Government:	Parliamentary democracy
Independence:	1981 (from UK)
Economy:	Agriculture 29%, Industry 17%, Services 54%

Cahal Pech, Xunantunich *(photo on page 11)*, and **Caracol**, which has a pyramid that's still the highest structure in Belize; in the south mysterious **Lubaantun**. Just across the border in Guatemala is **Tikal**, the largest known Mayan site in the world.

Garifuna Villages

The **Garifuna** of the southern coast are a unique people, descended from a mix of Africans and Native American Caribs. Many of their picturesque villages, with thatched-roof huts and wooden fishing boats pulled up on the beach, welcome visitors. Waterfront open-air restaurants serve fresh grilled fish. The Garifuna's distinctive, rhythmic **Punta** music is a staple at the country's lively clubs and discos.

Food & Drink

Belizean cuisine is as varied as her people. Fish, lobster and other

seafood are fresh and delicious. **Mexican** and **Caribbean** cuisine are excellent choices. Ripe **tropical fruits** and locally grown **coffee** are not to be missed. The local beer is tasty and served ice-cold, and a glass of **One Barrel rum** with fresh pineapple juice is the perfect drink to get you in a tropical mood.

Taking the Kids

Belizeans love kids. Kids love the beach and anything to do with monkeys. On Ambergris Caye and around Cayo, you'll find attractions specially aimed at kids, and most tourist areas of the country have organized tours and activities appropriate for the whole family. Many lodging places have larger rooms available for family groups. Burgers, chicken, fried potatoes and other kid-friendly food is not hard to find. **Tropical fruits** are a special treat!

3. WILDLIFE

If you're looking for a place to observe tropical animals and plants in their natural habitat, then Belize is one of the best choices you could make. Like her Central American neighbors, Belize has **an astounding variety of animal and plant life**. Unlike some of her neigh-  bors, Belize has a very low population density, so there are vast wilderness areas where the animals roam free, undisturbed by human contact. And the prosperous Belizeans have so far done an excellent job of preserving their natural treasures. Over 40% of the county has some form of protected status.

Within the borders of this tiny nation are 153 mammal species, 550 bird species, and countless thousands of plant species (and this is just what's been described so far: when it comes to plants and small invertebrates, there are thought to be thousands more that scientists haven't gotten around to classifying yet). Belize has many different habitats, including broadleaf rain forest, tropical pine forest, marshes, mangrove swamps and coral islands. Each has its own unique ecosystem, and its own set of inhabitants.

With **more than 40 national parks, refuges and reserves** of various kinds, the critters have plenty of space to roam around, and you are welcome to pay them a visit. Much of the tourist industry is built around showing off the country's natural wonders. Plenty of lodgings and tour operators are at your disposal to help you get a glimpse of those exotic animals and plants.

Many of Belize's parks are easy to visit on your own, but for a proper trip, I recommend going with a local guide or tour company. With a guide, you'll learn much more about the local ecosystem, and probably see animals you would never have seen on your own. At some parks, going with a guide is your only real option: some areas are accessible only by boat, and the most remote have no trails at all, and require hacking a path with a machete.

Mammals

The **white-nosed coati** (*nasua narica*), which locals call a *quash*, is a cute and gregarious creature with a long tail and a prehensile  nose that it uses to snuffle among the leaf litter on the forest floor for bugs, small lizards and frogs. You're likely to see at least a few, as they are fairly common, diurnal (active during the day), and not particularly shy. In fact, at some of the more frequented parks, where people have been feeding them, you may be accosted by bands of them begging for goodies. Their antics can be amusing, but you really shouldn't feed them or any other wild animals.

Another common forest dweller is the **gibnut** (elsewhere known as the agouti or paca), a rodent that looks something like a large guinea pig. Gibnuts are often seen in the reserves, poking around on the forest floor, but elsewhere they're scarce, because the locals like to eat them. You may see them on the menu in some traditional Belizean eateries.

The **kinkajou** (*potos flavus*) is called a *night walker* in Belize. These cute little guys live in the trees, and have long prehensile tails like monkeys. Kinkajous aren't rare, but are active mainly at night. The **Belizean gray fox** (*urocyon cinereoargenteus*) is a cool little fox that climbs trees! The very patient may catch a glimpse of some of the rarer mammals, including **anteaters** and the **tayra**, a sleek weasel-like carnivore. Herds of **peccaries** (locally called *warries*), like small wild pigs, root around on the forest floor. You may well see the signs of their depredations. **River otters** are especially fascinating to watch. Small forest mammals also include more mundane species such as **porcupines, armadillos, skunks** and dozens of species of rodents. There are eight species of **opossum** and over 75 species of **bats**!

The country's largest animal is **Baird's tapir** (*tapirus bairdii*), which locals call a *mountain cow* (*see photo, page 19*). These pachyderms look something like a rhinoceros without any horns, and can be up to six feet long and up to 500 pounds. They are rare, and mostly nocturnal, so you aren't likely to see one in the wild.

Belize has two species of monkeys. The most famous are the **black howler monkeys** (*alouatta pigra*), which Belizeans call *baboons*. These large vegetarians live in troops of 4-8 individuals, and make a loud noise that sounds less like howling than like the barking of a large dog. Even if you don't see them, you're sure to hear them far off in the forest. The **Community Baboon Sanctuary** protects these primates, and releases animals in other protected areas throughout the country. Another good place to see howlers is the **Cockscomb Basin Wildlife Sanctuary**. Belize's other monkey species is the playful **spider monkey** (*ateles geoffroyi*).

Belize has no less than five wild cats. The kings of the jungle are the magnificent spotted **jaguar** (*panthera onca*) and the **puma** (*puma concolor*), a tawny relative of the North American cougar and Florida panther. Smaller felines are the beautiful little spotted **ocelot** (*leopardus pardalis*) and **margay** (*leopardus wiedii*). The slightly larger **jaguarundi** (*herpailurus yaguarondi*) looks like a strange cross between a bear and a cat.

Belize has one of the healthiest populations of wild cats in Central America, but your chances of seeing one in the wild are almost nil, as they are mostly nocturnal, and very shy of people. At the **Jaguar Reserve** (Cockscomb Basin),

you'll probably see at least a paw print or two. **Chan Chich Lodge** in Northern Belize reports cat sightings from time to time. And of course, you can see most of the native cats at the **Belize Zoo**.

Reptiles & Amphibians

To date, 139 species of reptiles and amphibians have been identified in Belize. But they're slippery little critters, and scientists are finding new ones all the time. Snappy saurians may make you think twice about swimming in the rivers. The lagoons are stiff with **crocodiles** and the smaller **caimans**. You'll see a few on almost any river boat ride.

There's a huge variety of snakes, including the **boa constrictor**, the bright yellow **eyelash palm pit viper** and the **fer-de-lance** (or *tommygoff*), one of the world's deadliest snakes. Watch your step in the forest, but don't worry – snakebites are rare.

There's a variety of brightly-colored frogs, called **poison-arrow frogs** because the local Mayans used to make poison arrows from them. According to legend, if you lick one you'll get high, but take my advice and stick to rum. Notable lizards include enormous green **iguanas** (locally called *wish-willies*), and the **Jesus Christ lizard**, named for its ability to "walk on water" by skipping quickly across the surface.

The Small Stuff

We all want to see something really cool, such as a large mammal or a particularly exotic bird. But this isn't a TV show, and the critters don't always perform on a schedule. Don't obsess about trophy sightings so much that you miss the less glamorous, but fascinating, beauty all around. Trees, flowers, lush tropical greenery, fruits and spices, butterflies and all kinds of interesting bugs (take a night hike to see some really exotic creepy-crawlies) are easy to see, going about their daily business unnoticed by humans who rush by, searching for the elusive quetzal.

Birds

The variety of birds is simply amazing (over 550 species). Birders (or *twitchers*, as the British call them) have plenty of opportunities to add species to their *life lists*. The jungles harbor **parrots, toucans, hummingbirds, chachalacas, trogons, woodpeckers, kiskadees, tanagers** and **oropendolas**. At night, you may see one of the many stately species of **owls**. Coastal regions teem with majestic **herons** (including the **rufescent tiger heron**), **egrets, limpkins, ibises, spoonbills, cormorants, ducks** and other shore birds. **Crooked Tree Wildlife Sanctuary**, in the north, is home to flocks of the rare **jabiru stork**.

Birders will find some action almost anywhere in the country. To maximize your sightings, visit both mountain forests and coastal wetlands. The unique ecosystem of **Mountain Pine Ridge** is home to some species that you won't see elsewhere, and some of the remote cayes have birds that are rare or extinct on the mainland. Yes, your chances of seeing something really rare are better in one of the very remote parks of the interior. However, don't overlook more mundane locations. Mayan archaeological sites can have a surprisingly large number of birds, which may be easier to see at such partially-cleared sites than they are in the deep forest. A boat ride is almost always one of the best ways to spot  birds, whether on a jungle river, a brackish lagoon, or around some of the mangrove islands offshore.

Flora

Plant lovers will likewise be in Heaven. Here are thousands of exotic plant species. The tropical rain forest has many more species of trees than its temperate counterpart. Whereas a typical North American forest is dominated by only a few species of trees, Belizean forests have thousands. Many produce edible fruits or other useful products. The **guanacaste** (also known as tubroos or monkey's ear tree) was sacred to the ancient Maya, and today it's a commercially important tree. The seed pods are

used for cattle feed, and the wood is used to make the dugout canoes that locals call doreys. Flowering trees such as the **jacaranda** and epiphytes (plants that grow on other plants) such as **orchids** and **bromeliads** add splashes of color amid the green.

Many lodges have hiking trails with interesting plants labeled, and some local guides specialize in medicinal plant tours, pointing out species that the Mayans and other local folks use for food and medicine. The **Belize Botanical Garden** (*see Chapter 6*) is a must-visit for any plant lover. The species are all neatly labeled, and you'll learn a lot about fruit trees and other cultivated plants that you aren't likely to see in the rain forest. Hummingbirds and butterflies are frequent visitors.

Dozens of wild and crazy **fruits** are available, both whole and fresh-squeezed. Whether familiar fruits such as mangos, papayas and pineapples (which are much sweeter and juicier here than the mass-shipped varieties you find at the supermarket in Des Moines) or exotic varieties such as mammee apples, I highly recommend trying them whenever offered.

Marine Life

The magnificent menagerie doesn't end at the water's edge. Belize's many aquatic environments are home to a fascinating array of marine mammals, reptiles, fish and invertebrates. Belize is an important breeding ground for the endangered West Indian **manatee**, and you may see them either in brackish lagoons or offshore on the cayes. Gales Point and Caye Caulker are two favorite manatee-watching areas. Eight types of **dolphin** make their homes in Belizean waters, and several species of whales, including **sperm**, **killer** and **pilot whales**, visit from time to time.

There are seven **sea turtle** species in the world, and four of them nest on Belize's beaches. Female sea turtles return year after year to the beaches where they were born, and lay their eggs in the sand. When the babies hatch, they scamper to the sea en masse. In most of Central America, sea turtles have been hunted almost to extinction, both for their meat and for their eggs, which some fools believe to have

aphrodisiac properties. Thanks to Belize's low population density and many protected areas, they are still fairly common here. You're very likely to see some while diving or snorkeling, and if you visit one of the remote cayes at just the right time, you may get to see mama turtle doing her thing on the beach.

Some of the most impressive ocean wildlife is to be seen beneath the surface. Belize is one of the top diving destinations in the world, with the world's second-longest barrier reef (after the Great Barrier Reef in Australia) and three coral atolls. Divers will

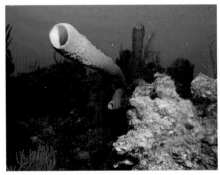

see a rainbow of **coral** and **tropical fish**, including gobies, blennies, sergeant-majors and angelfish, to say nothing of lobsters, octopi and colorful little shrimp. Coral around the world is dying from increased water temperatures, but Belize still has a lot of live coral.

The largest fish in the sea, the **whale shark**, frequents the area around Glover's Reef Atoll from March-June, and divers can swim with these gentle giants. At Shark Ray Alley, just south of Ambergris Caye, you can snorkel with enormous (but harmless) **nurse sharks** and **Southern stingrays**. More sinister sharks, including **blacktips**, **hammerheads** and **tigers**, are often seen, especially around the atolls.

Anglers haul in a vast variety of species. The grass flats offer some of the world's best fly-fishing for **bonefish, permit** and **tarpon**. Rivers and mangrove lagoons hold several species of **snook**, as well as smaller (only 70 pounds or so) **tarpon**. The coral reefs are thick with **snapper** and **grouper**, and trolling offshore produces **sailfish, marlin, tuna, wahoo, jack,** and **sharks**. See *Best Activities* for more information about diving and fishing.

What is Ecotourism, Anyway?

Ecotourism is a term that you'll hear kicked around quite a bit on your travels in Belize. Of course, most visitors to the country are here to enjoy the natural wonders, but does that make us all ecotourists? Does spending a couple of hours strolling through the forest with a herd of other gringos make you an ecotourist? Or must you spend a week helping the students with their research at some remote biological station to earn the title?

In fact, ecotourism is a state of mind, **an ideal of sustainable, minimally invasive tourism** that both visitors and those in the tourism industry should strive for (alas, both groups often fall far short of the ideal). Ecotourists leave no litter, don't feed or interfere with the animals, and consume nothing but products that are harvested in a sustainable manner. A true ecolodge recycles and conserves, releases no waste into the environment, strives to use renewable energy, and generally tries to have as little impact on the natural habitat as possible.

Ecotourism is also about preserving a very important species called local workers. One of the central concepts of ecotourism is the idea that local people can make a better living by helping tourists enjoy the rain forest than they could by chopping it down. Good ecotourists hire local guides, patronize local businesses, and buy local products whenever possible.

The **International Ecotourism Society** defines ecotourism as "responsible travel to natural areas that conserves the environment and improves the well-being of local people." Their web site at www.ecotourism.org includes lists of environmentally friendly lodges and tour operators.

You can learn more about tropical forests at www.nature.org. For those of a scientific disposition, **NatureServe** has a searchable database of every species of bird, mammal, and amphibian found in Belize and neighboring countries. *Info*: www.natureserve.org/infonatura.

4. THE NORTHERN CAYES

Off the coast of Belize lies a sprawling maze of small islands, which the locals call **cayes** (pronounced "keys"). The largest, **Ambergris Caye**, is Belize's most popular tourist destination. A few years ago, it was a laid-back, sleepy little island, but it's rapidly growing into one of the Caribbean's major resort destinations. Smaller **Caye Caulker** remains far quieter.

There are hundreds of smaller cayes, several of them isolated island paradises, home to a single dive lodge. There's little to do on the cayes other than dive, fish and lie around in the sun, but for most of the thousands who visit, that's plenty!

You can get to Ambergris Caye by boat or by plane. Both are quite scenic rides. The plane costs more, but it's quicker, and may be more convenient, especially if you want to avoid Belize City and head straight for the island. *Info*: Both **Maya Island Air** and **Tropic Air** offer numerous flights each day to San Pedro's little dirt airstrip from both the Belize City municipal airstrip ($67 round-trip) and Philip Goldson International Airport ($120 round-trip).

Boat service between downtown San Pedro and Belize City is provided by the (confusingly-named) **Caye Caulker Water Taxi Association**. Open speedboats carry about 30 people and their luggage from Belize City to San Pedro in an hour and a half. *Info*: www.cayecaulkerwatertaxi.com. Tel. 223-5752 or 226-0992. Boats depart from the Water Taxi terminal next to the Swing Bridge in Belize City about seven times per day. The price is $20 round-trip.

ONE GREAT DAY IN AMBERGRIS CAYE

If you can only spare a day for the islands, then **Ambergris** is your best bet. There are flights to and from Belize City all day, and there are a few things to do after the diving is done.

Morning
The first destination on our agenda is Belize's beautiful coral reef. If you've never dove or snorkeled before, don't worry – **Hol Chan Marine Reserve** is a perfect place for beginners to glimpse the glory of the underwater world. It's shallow, it's a short boat ride from Ambergris, and local guides are quite used to taking novices on easy and safe trips. If you can swim, you can snorkel, so let's do it!

For several reasons, early morning is the best time for snorkeling or diving. The seas

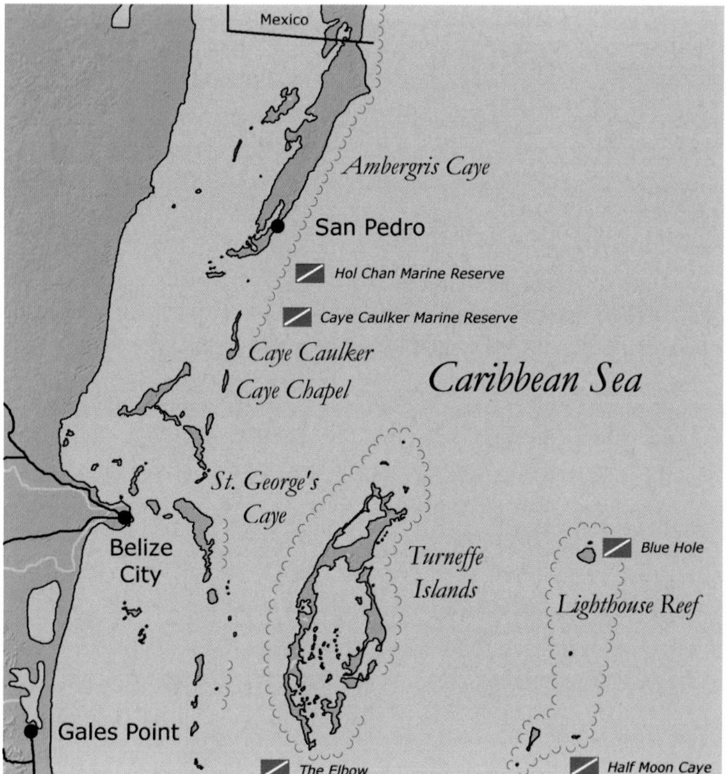
Mexico
Ambergris Caye
San Pedro
Hol Chan Marine Reserve
Caye Caulker Marine Reserve
Caye Caulker
Caye Chapel
Caribbean Sea
St. George's Caye
Belize City
Turneffe Islands
Blue Hole
Lighthouse Reef
Gales Point
The Elbow
Half Moon Caye

are usually calmer in the morning, and the hordes of cruise ship day-trippers begin to arrive towards noon. Also, if you get your diving done first thing, you can start drinking cold beer at lunch! So we're going to take the first plane to Ambergris, and head straight for our dive shop. The large and respected outfit at **Ramon's Village** would be a great choice, as it's right by the airstrip. *Info*: www.ramons.com. Tel. 800/MAGIC 15 (in the US). **Amigos del Mar** is another large operator that caters to beginners. Call the day before and line up a trip, so as soon as you arrive, they'll get you fitted out with snorkel, mask and fins, and you can head out to the reef. *Info*: www.amigosdive.com. Tel. 226-2706.

The **Hol Chan Marine Reserve** protects a large area of coral reef, as well as mangrove and seagrass habitats. Here you can see a luxuriant ecosystem of colorful coral and fishy life just a few minutes' boat ride from town, including snapper, parrotfish, angelfish, barracuda, moray eels, nurse sharks and lots of lobsters. If you're lucky, you may spot a sea turtle, grouper, tarpon or even a manatee.

At the south end of the reserve, **Shark Ray Alley** is a fine place for novice snorkelers, and an unforgettable wildlife encounter even for seasoned divers. Local fishermen use to throw out their fish waste here, attracting nurse sharks and Southern stingrays. You can swim with these enormous fish in water only a few feet deep. Don't worry, they're not dangerous, but friendly, like big dogs eager for a handout (but be safe – don't touch 'em!).

Afternoon

Our first priority after getting out of the salt water is an ice-cold beer and a hearty lunch at one of the island's many beachfront restaurants. The **Blue Water Grill** at the SunBreeze Hotel is a good choice, or stroll into town and try the inexpensive local favorite **Celi's**, or have a Jamaican-style jerk chicken at the **JamBel Jerk Pit**.

After lunch, take a leisurely stroll around the colorful tourist town of **San Pedro**. I'm afraid there's no Louvre or Smithsonian here, but there are some shops well worth visiting. **Ambergris Maya Jade Store and Museum** is a classy shop/museum with many beautiful Mayan jade items on display, as well as exhibits about jade and its significance to Mayan culture. *Info*: Tel. 226-3311. Front Street. **Belizean Arts**, located inside Fido's Courtyard, is an excellent art gallery, with a huge collection of oil paintings by local Belizean artists, several of whose works can be seen in local hotels. *Info*: www.belizeanarts.com. Tel. 226-3019.

ALTERNATE PLAN
Take a boat tour around the island, home to over 260 bird species, and you may also spot crocodiles, manatees or dolphins. **Little Iguana and Rosario Cayes**, two small protected mangrove islands just off Ambergris, are thick with water birds. Bird guru Elbert Greer offers guided bird watching tours. Contact him at Ramon's Village (see *Best Sleeps*), or see www.scubalessonsbelize.com/birds. Or go to the **Caribbean Villas Hotel** (www.caribbeanvillashotel.com), which has a three-story "people perch" with a panoramic view of the entire island.

After we've perused these two cultural highlights, I'm afraid that's about it for touristy activities. Unlike some other Caribbean resorts, Ambergris doesn't (yet) have any "things 2 do" such as ziplines, wildlife parks or waterslides. But you know what? While I've heard a very few visitors complain that there's nothing to do but "stare at the ocean," thousands more come here and are delighted to do just that! If you came to relax and get away from the world of deadlines and stress, you've come to the perfect place. I know it's a cliché, but it really is true – if you can't relax here, you can't relax!

So, let's do some heavy-duty relaxing. First we'll sit down right here at **Fido's**, a fine place for a cold beverage and a chat with some of the local posse. **Estel's** is a shady spot where we can have another cold one, put our toes in the sand and watch the parade of fun-seekers along the beach. The **Cannibal** bar sometimes has a beach strummer playing semi-live music in the afternoons.

Evening

The last planes for Belize City leave at 5pm, so if you're heading back this evening, boo-hoo time comes a bit early. If you're spending the night, then a lobster dinner is on the evening's agenda, perhaps at **Ambergris Delight** or **Caramba**, two good restaurants in San Pedro. If a candlelight dinner for two is your goal, and price is no object, then take a moonlight boat ride to **Capricorn**, one of the finest restaurants in the country. They only have a few tables, so you'll need to make reservations well in advance (see *Best Sleeps and Eats*).

Best Beaches?

Belize's beaches are beautiful, but frankly most are not among the world's top swimming beaches. In most areas, the coastline is shallow, so there are no waves to speak of, and the bottom is mostly seagrass and a little muddy, rather than nice granular sand. Another problem is the trash that washes up. Most island lodgings are on the beach, but some are much better for swimming than others. In the *Best Sleeps* section, we let you know which hotels have nice sandy strands, and which ones keep them clean.

A FANTASTIC AMBERGRIS WEEKEND

A weekend gives you enough time to get a good sample of all the island has to offer: snorkeling, scuba diving, fishing, birding, swimming, eating seafood in funky beach restaurants and sipping umbrella drinks by the pool.

Friday Evening
You can get here by boat from Belize City, or by plane from any of several places in the country. The plane is quicker and cheaper, but either way you come, it will be a scenic trip – speeding through little channels between dozens of tiny mangrove islands or looking down on the islands and shallow grass flats from a low-flying plane.

There's a huge choice of lodging places on Ambergris. Back when we were planning our trip, we picked the perfect spot based not only on our budget, but on the location. Low-budget travelers, or party animals who want to be in the middle of the action, have several good options right in San Pedro town. Those who want to get as far away from civilization as possible will pick one of the upscale resorts to the north of town. Personally, I like to stay south of town, because you get the best of both worlds – it's quiet, with a bit of a secluded atmosphere, but it's easy to walk or bike into town any time you want. For the ultimate in luxury, stay at **Victoria House**. Those of us with more moderate budgets will love **Mata Rocks** (see *Best Sleeps*).

After a short golf cart or boat ride to our hotel, it's time to get into the island lifestyle immediately (the last time we're going to use words like "immediately" all weekend). Take off your shirt and shoes, grab your welcome rum drink from the bar, and stretch out by the pool. As you watch the waves breaking on the coral reef a few hundred feet offshore, you'll feel things like telephones, traffic jams, suburban sprawl and stress begin to fade from your memory. Continue drinking rum until they are completely forgotten. Our only responsibility tonight is to make sure we have a dive trip lined up for tomorrow morning.

Hey! Wake up! The sun's going down, it's time to think about dinner. The ten-minute walk into town is too complicated to

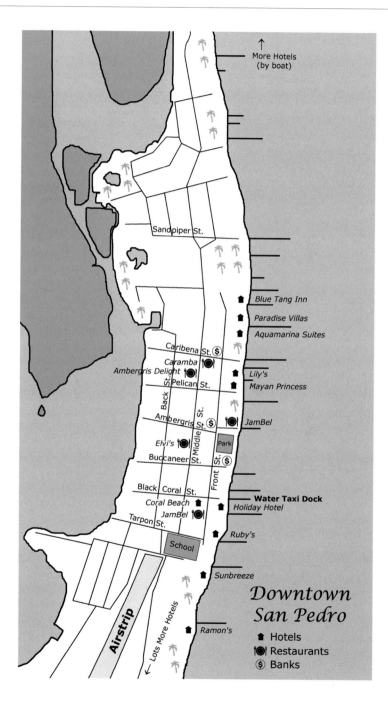

More Hotels
(by boat)

Sandpiper St.

Blue Tang Inn
Paradise Villas
Aquamarina Suites

Caribena St. $
Caramba
Ambergris Delight
Pelican St.
Back St.
Lily's
Mayan Princess

Ambergris St. $
Middle St.
JamBel

Elvi's
Buccaneer St.
Front St. $
Park

Black Coral St.
Coral Beach
JamBel
Tarpon St.
Water Taxi Dock
Holiday Hotel

Ruby's

School

Sunbreeze

Downtown
San Pedro

Airstrip
Lots More Hotels

Ramon's

⬥ Hotels
|O| Restaurants
$ Banks

bother with tonight, but that's no problem. Several of the island's finest restaurants are located at resorts just a short walk away. Walking along the beach is a favorite way to go dining on Ambergris.

Saturday Morning

If you see nothing else in Belize, you simply must see her **beautiful coral reefs**. A living coral reef is the most colorful and fascinating wildlife habitat on the planet, and Belize has some of the finest reefs in the Caribbean, including the world's second-longest barrier reef. We've all seen reefs on nature TV shows, but nothing comes close to experiencing it yourself. Coral reefs worldwide are threatened, and they may not be around forever, so get wet and see this natural wonder while you're here.

The kicker is that seeing the reef in Belize is easy and fun for people of all ages. While scuba diving (diving while breathing compressed air) requires a certification course, anyone can snorkel. All you need is a mask, snorkel and fins, which you can rent anywhere on the island, and a local guide can show you how to do it in five minutes. If you can swim, you can snorkel, and it's especially easy here on Ambergris. Most dive operators pick you up directly from your hotel, and the reef is just a few minutes' boat ride away.

Early morning is the best time for snorkeling or diving. The seas are usually calmer in the morning, and the hordes of cruise ship day-trippers begin to arrive towards noon. And, there's just something special about a good hearty lunch and a cold beer after a morning out in the sun and salt. We lined up a trip yesterday, so all we need to do this morning is slug down some coffee and stumble to the end of the dock. Within minutes, we'll be underwater.

 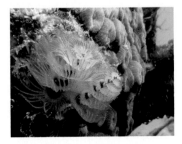

If you have time for just one dive/snorkel trip, make it to **Hol Chan Marine Reserve**, Ambergris Caye's most popular spot for short reef excursions. Just a few miles south of town is the **Hol Chan Channel**, a steep-walled cut through the reef in 30 feet of water that is particularly rich in sea life and that gives the reserve its name (Hol Chan means "little channel" in Mayan).

Hol Chan's protected status means that you can see a wide range of fishy life just a few minutes' boat ride from town. You'll see schools of yellowtail snapper, parrotfish, angelfish, blue tangs, triggerfish, hogfish, barracuda, moray eels, nurse sharks and lots of lobsters. If you're lucky, you may spot a blacktip or hammerhead shark, sea turtles, grouper, snapper, tarpon or perhaps even a manatee. There's also a profusion of colorful coral species, including elkhorn coral, brain coral, starlet coral, staghorn coral, sea fans, lettuce coral and other soft corals.

Just south of the channel, and also part of the reserve, **Shark Ray Alley** is one of the top places in the Caribbean to snorkel with large sea creatures. Lo-cal fishermen have been discarding fish waste here for years, making the area a frequent haunt of nurse sharks and Southern stingrays. You can swim with these enormous fish in water only a few feet deep – it's a fine place for novice snorkelers, and an unforgettable wildlife encounter even for seasoned divers. The nurse sharks (up to six feet long) and rays (up to four foot wingspan) are not dangerous. On the contrary, they seem friendly, like big dogs eager for a handout (but be safe – don't touch them, and let your guide handle the feeding).

All dive shops on Ambergris and Caulker run daily snorkeling trips to Hol Chan and Shark Ray Alley. *Info*: www.holchanbelize.org. There's a park entry fee of $12.50 per person, which is included in the price of your trip. There's a visitors' center in the middle of

San Pedro where you can learn more about the ecosystem of Hol Chan.

Saturday Afternoon

The dive boat drops us off back at our hotel worn out and crusty with salt, but happy. First stop is the pool bar for an ice-cold Belikin, and the next is the pool itself for a quick rinse-off. Then I guess we'll have to put on some pants (but not necessarily any shirt or shoes) if we want to have lunch. We'll borrow a couple of bikes from the hotel and ride into town.

San Pedro is a clapboard and concrete Caribbean town that is slowly evolving from a sleepy village into a major tourist resort area. The visitors are a mix of divers and honeymooners, upscale travelers and backpackers, Americans and Europeans. Golf carts and bicycles outnumber cars, but traffic on the sandy (in rainy weather, muddy) streets can be hectic in high season. The town has a Mexican feel: you'll hear more Spanish spoken than English, and excellent Mexican food is to be had.

Speaking of which, it's high time we were sitting down with a menu. Most San Pedro eateries serve a mix of Mexican dishes, seafood and American favorites. **Elvi's Kitchen** is perhaps the most famous local spot. **Ambergris Delight** and **Caramba** are also good choices, and so are the Jamaican-style **JamBel Jerk Pit** and the inex-

---

ALTERNATE PLAN

If you're a certified diver, do a two-tank dive this morning. If you have non-diving kids or spouses in tow, head for Hol Chan, where they can snorkel and you can dive in peace. Otherwise, choose any of a dozen great sites on the reef just off Ambergris. Shark Ray Alley is strictly a snorkeling spot, so save it for Sunday morning before you leave. A lot of divers go to the famous **Blue Hole** (*photo below*) from San Pedro, but it's a long 12-hour trip, starting at five or six in the morning. If you want to do the Blue Hole and/or **Turneffe**, it's better to stay on Caulker or one of the small cayes, which are much closer.

pensive **Celi's**. We'll start with a little *ceviche* (fish or seafood in a lemon marinade, served with chips), then I'll have a large local fish. The kids can have a burrito or a burger.

After lunch, let's walk down **Front Street** and see the cultural sights of the town, such as they are. San Pedro has just three north-south streets, which the locals very sensibly call Front Street, Middle Street and Back Street. There is a half-hearted effort to replace the first two of these functional names with the more colorful Barrier Reef Drive and Pescador Street, but only tourists seem to take much notice. The beach itself serves as a busy pedestrian street – most of the dive shops and bars are located there, so it's the real center of the action (San Pedro's Broadway or Champs-Élysées, if you will).

The **Ambergris Maya Jade Store and Museum** is a classy shop and mini-museum, with beautiful jade replicas of artifacts from the classical Mayan era, as well as exhibits about Jade and its significance to Mayan culture. **Belizean Arts**, located inside Fido's Courtyard, is an excellent art gallery with a huge collection of oil paintings by local Belizean artists, several of whose works can be seen in local hotels. *Info*: www.belizeanarts.com. Tel. 226-3019. Inside Fido's Courtyard. Other art galleries are **Island Originals Art Gallery** on Front Street and **Isla Bonita Gallery**, just south of the airstrip. And that's about it, folks.

There's not much else to do here that doesn't involve getting yourself wet either outside or inside. I say we do both. There's an outfit right here on the beach, **SailSports Belize** that has all manner of sail-powered craft for rent. How about spending an hour or two making fools of ourselves on a windsurfer or a Hobie Cat? Waverunners and other motorized craft are also available. The beach here stays busy with folks doing every water sport known to man, from water-skiing to parasailing to kitesurfing (one of the reasons why the beach in San Pedro isn't especially good for swimming). *Info*:www.sailsportsbelize.com.

Let's stroll down the beach, stopping in at a few laid-back beach bars such as **Fido's**, sand-floored **Estel's** and the **Cannibal** bar, which sometimes has live music in the afternoons.

Diving gets most of the attention, but there is **excellent fishing** in the area. Bonefish and permit cruise the flats, grouper and snapper haunt the reefs, and tarpon, tuna and billfish swim offshore. Fishing charters from San Pedro are run by freelance boat captains, but you can book a trip through your hotel, or through any of the dive shops.

Saturday Evening
Let's dress up (on Ambergris, that means putting on a shirt) and go out for a really nice gourmet meal tonight. For a delightfully romantic (but expensive) night out, take a moonlight boat ride to one of the gourmet restaurants on the north end of the island. Considered to be one of the best restaurants in Central America,

Capricorn has been featured in any number of fancy food magazines. A table under the stars is yours for the evening, so take your time savoring Belizean goodies such as lobster tails, stone crab or grouper prepared with Continental flair, and a bottle from the nice wine list. In the same area, and also highly recommended, the **Rendezvous Restaurant & Winery** creates seafood and meat dishes with a fusion of Thai and French influences, and proudly serves their own house wines.

South of town, and easily accessible by foot, bike or golf cart, the **Palmilla Restaurant** at the Victoria House is also among the top dining experiences on the island, serving a unique mix of island seafood and Continental cuisine. Their *ceviche* and lobster salad are really special.

See *Best Sleeps & Eats* for more details on these and other restaurants.

After dinner, there's no need to go to bed, as San Pedro has by far the most hopping nightlife scene in Belize. **Fido's**, right in the center of town, is the main hangout, with live music every night. South of town, the **Crazy Canuck** is another stop on the local circuit. If you want to hit the dance floor, make the scene at the **Jaguar**, in the center of town. After midnight, the Red Bull crowd heads to **Big Daddy's**, an after-hours club where the locals get crazy (and I mean very crazy) until dawn. See *Best Activities* for more on island nightlife. Ambergris is a pretty safe place – nothing like Belize City. I don't know if I'd walk back to my hotel all alone, but if you stick with a group and remain reasonably alert, I doubt you'll encounter any problems.

Sunday

No one says you can't snorkel just before flying, so Sunday morning would be a perfect time for a snorkel trip to **Hol Chan** and **Shark Ray Alley** if you didn't go there yesterday (or maybe even if you did). Otherwise, let's take a **boat tour around the island** to see some of the local residents. The sea creatures get most of the press, but Ambergris is also home to **over 260 bird species**, including vireos, fly-catchers, kiskadees, wood-peckers and hummingbirds, to say nothing of the many water birds that hang out in the mangroves.

At the **Caribbean Villas Hotel** (www.caribbeanvillashotel.com), south of San Pedro, aspiring birder Susan Lala has built a three-story "people perch" that offers a panoramic view of the entire island and plenty of interesting bird sightings. It's open to the public daily. Read about her birdy experiences at

Diving & Flying

You don't want to get the bends at 30,000 feet on the flight back to Newark. This means it is a bad idea to scuba dive on the same day as flying. The cabins of modern airliners are usually pressurized at significantly less than sea level pressure. If your body is still slowly expelling nitrogen absorbed while breathing compressed air on a recent dive, flying with a low atmospheric pressure could trigger problems that would not occur at sea level pressures. This doesn't apply to snorkelers, because they don't breathe compressed air. So: Scuba divers shouldn't dive within 24 hours before any flight!

Mangroves

Mangroves are an amazing family of trees that grow on saltwater shorelines, their roots in the tidal water. A mangrove swamp is a unique ecosystem. The underwater forest of their roots makes a perfect habitat for barnacles, oysters, sponges, and sea squirts, which filter their food from the water as the tide goes in and out. Adolescent fish (including snook, snapper, shark, sea trout, tarpon and bonefish), shrimp, lobsters and many other creatures find shelter and food among the mangrove roots. Birds and monkeys live in the trees. Mangrove wetlands have ecological benefits too: preventing coastal erosion, filtering out pollutants, and absorbing some of the wave energy of storm surges caused by hurricanes.

www.caribbeanvillashotel.com/birds/cvbirds.html. Other great places to spot birds are **Little Iguana** and **Rosario Cayes**, two small protected mangrove islands just off Ambergris, and **San Pedro Lagoon**, in the north part of the island. The island's greatest bird guru is **Elbert Greer**, who writes a weekly column about birds for the *San Pedro Sun*, and offers guided bird watching tours by boat around the island. He works as a guide at Ramon's Village (see *Best Sleeps*), so you can contact him there, or see www.scubalessonsbelize.com/birds.

A FANTASTIC CAYE CAULKER WEEKEND

Caye Caulker is smaller and mellower than Ambergris. There are no luxury resorts, nor are there crowds of American spring-breakers (although cruise-shippers are beginning to haunt the island during the day). Things are much cheaper here, and it's closer to the hottest dive sites. Personally, I love Caulker – spend more than a weekend if you can.

Friday Evening
You can get here by boat or by plane. Flying is more expensive, but it's quicker, and it has the added advantage that you can get here directly from the airport, without having to set foot in Belize City. However you get here, you'll need to slow down and adjust to is-land time as soon as you arrive – nothing happens quickly here. When we arrive at our hotel, there may be nobody around. No big deal – we'll go next door and have a cold drink, and somebody will show up before too long.

The two nicest places to stay are **Seaside Cabanas** in the center of town, and the **Iguana Reef Inn**, over on the lagoon side. There are a couple of other fairly upscale condo-style lodgings, but the rest of the island's accommodations are firmly in the rustic-but-colorful category. Low-budget travelers can find clean and pleas-ant waterfront rooms pretty darn cheap (see *Best Sleeps*).

There's nothing on our agenda this evening but having dinner and lining up some activities for tomorrow. After chilling out with a welcome drink at our hotel, we'll take a stroll down the main street. If you're a certified diver, stop in at one of the island's three dive shops and check out their offerings for tomorrow. We'll also drop by Chocolate's gift shop and see if he's running one of his wonderful manatee-watching tours tomorrow (actu-ally, we already called and lined up a trip a few days ago, but we'll stop in and confirm).

At the north end of the village is the **Split**, a little pass that a hurricane carved through the island a few years ago. Here we find the **Lazy Lizard**, a colorful local hangout, and the perfect place to have a drink and watch the sunset.

Getting hungry? I don't know about you, but I've been thinking about lobster tails ever since the ride to the airport this morning. Here on Caye Caulker, my favorite crustacean is abundant and cheap, and we can have it served in a wide variety of ways. At the south end of the village, the **Tropical Paradise Restaurant** serves great lobster specials. The last time I was there, I had a huge portion of lobster in a tasty marinara sauce for about $10. However, the walk all the way from the Split to the Trop is a bit far for a group of lobster-hungry tourists, and we might just get sucked in by one of the streetside barbecue stands that are grilling up lobster, fish and chicken. Some of these are nothing more than a half an oil drum for a grill and a cooler full of drinks. This may be the cheapest way of all to enjoy a grilled lobster tail.

Sated with lobster, cold beer and rum, let's toddle off to our hotel and crash, so we can get an early start on our full day of Caribbean fun tomorrow.

Saturday
A weekend on Caye Caulker is guaranteed to relax even the most stressed-out, high-strung overachiever. The small village has

three dirt north-south streets (Front, Middle and Back), any of which may be adorned with a soundly-sleeping dog right in the middle. The population is only about 1300 people, mostly Mestizos, whose traditional occupations are fishing, lobstering and boat building. The name of the island is believed to derive from *hicaco*, the Spanish name for the cocoplum tree. Caulker has been a stop on the hippy backpacker trail since the 1960s. Nowadays, you'll see more and more groups

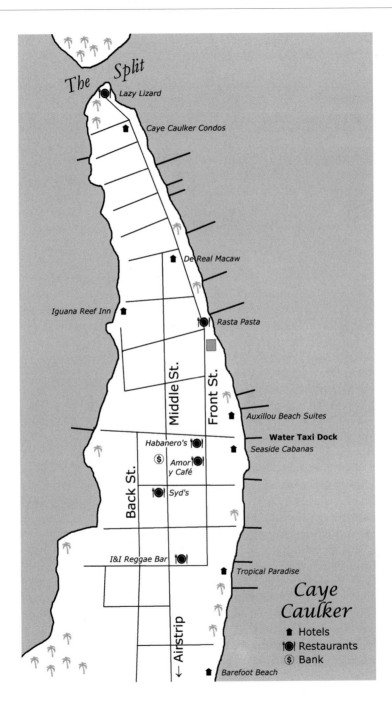

The Split

Lazy Lizard

Caye Caulker Condos

De Real Macaw

Iguana Reef Inn

Rasta Pasta

Middle St.

Front St.

Auxillou Beach Suites

Water Taxi Dock

Habanero's

Seaside Cabanas

Back St.

$ Amor y Café

Syd's

I&I Reggae Bar

Tropical Paradise

Caye Caulker

🛏 Hotels
🍽 Restaurants
$ Bank

Airstrip →

Barefoot Beach

of wide-eyed day-trippers from the colossal cruise ships that anchor in the channel just to the south.

Today we're going to visit with some of Caye Caulker's marine life, both above and below the water's surface. One of the most popular trips on Caulker is to see the manatees off nearby **Swallow Caye**. The West Indian **manatee**, or sea cow, is a docile

and friendly marine mammal that is found in shallow waters throughout the Caribbean and the Gulf of Mexico. Caye Caulker resident Chocolate, also known as Lionel Heredia, has been the local champion of the manatees for many years, and was the prime mover in getting the area around Swallow Caye designated a protected manatee sanctuary. *Info*: www.swallowcayemanatees.org. Several local operators now run manatee-watching tours, but **Chocolate's Manatee Tours** is still the best. The tour lasts all day (9am-4pm) and also includes a stop at Sergeant's Caye, a tiny island right on the barrier reef with a beautiful white sand beach and a splendid snorkeling area. Cost is $60 apiece including snorkel gear. *Info*: Tel. 226-0151. E-mail: chocolateseashore@gmail.com.

We arrive back at Caulker late in the afternoon, and I for one am mighty thirsty. At the south end of town, there's a little stand that sells all kinds of fresh-squeezed tropical juices in plastic milk jugs. I'm getting a jug of mango and one of papaya to take back to the hotel and slug down at leisure. After a couple of tall glasses and a refreshing dip in the pool, it's time to think about dinner. Strolling down Middle Street, we pass a couple of good possibilities. **Habanero's** is a very pleasant spot that's popular with visitors, serving spicy Caribbean-Mexican fare such as fajitas and firecracker prawns (made, of course, with habanero pepper). **Syd's** is a local institution, serving excellent (and cheap) Belizean fare on cheesy chrome dinette tables. Over on the beach, **Rasta Pasta** is a colorful spot even for Caulker. With your toes in the sand, you can sample a mix of Jamaican, Italian, Thai and Mexican dishes. Vegetarians will love it.

After dinner, there are plenty of places to while away the evening. No glitzy discos, but plenty of colorful little bars offering stiff drinks and loose conversation. Several spots have live music from time to time, but we'll have to ask around to find out where it's happening. We'll definitely visit the **I&I Reggae Bar**, where roots reggae will be crankin, and we might catch a whiff of some herbs that aren't on the menu.

Sunday Morning

The place for breakfast on Caye Caulker is **Amor y Café**, on Front Street (formerly Cindy's). Every morning, there's excellent organic coffee from Guatemala, as well as chai, smoothies, homemade muffins, banana bread, fruit plates and other healthy treats. It's a great spot to hang out and swap stories with other travelers.

After a leisurely breakfast, let's head south of the village to visit a small forest reserve, an outpost of the much larger **Caye Caulker Forest Reserve** that covers the northern end of the island. Here we can take a hike to see native trees such as red, white and black mangroves, three varieties of coconut palm, buttonwood, gumbo-limbo, poisonwood, and the colorful ziracote. There are over a hundred species of birds on Caulker, including some that are rare on the mainland.

Also down here near the airstrip is **Cocoplum Gardens Café, Spa and Gallery**. Owned by Dutchman Chris and his Belizean wife, Cocoplum offers healthful

Sand Fleas, Anyone?

Many Belizean beaches are thick with irritating **sand fleas**, almost invisible little buggers that swarm around the beach. Many people have their favorite sauces to drive away the little ankle-biters but, to my knowledge, none of these spreads works for everyone. Many swear by **Avon's Skin-So-Soft**, so it's a good idea to bring some as well as the usual high-DEET mosquito repellant.

cuisine amid lush gardens, and is also a day spa where you can have a massage, a yoga class or even a Mayan spiritual bath. *Info*: www.cocoplum.typepad.com.

FOUR DAYS OF SERIOUS DIVING!

If you're serious about scuba diving, Belize is one of the best places in this hemisphere that you could choose for a dive vacation. The country has the **world's second-longest barrier reef**, with thousands of great dive sites, and (so far) it's far more pristine and laid-back than mass dive destinations such as Cozumel or the Caymans. On this four-day trip, we'll sample the most spectacular of Belize's dive sites with a minimum of distractions.

Friday

Where in Belize should the hard-core diver stay? Well, I recommend somewhere on the water. In fact, almost anywhere you stay on the coast, you'll have access to superb diving, but each region has its own pros and cons for divers. **Ambergris Caye** has a huge variety of dive operators, plenty of nice sites just offshore, a wide choice of resorts in all price ranges, and a fair number of activities for non-diving companions. Ambergris also has crowds of other divers and the highest prices in the country. **Caye Caulker** is smaller, cheaper and closer to advanced dive sites such as the Blue Hole and Turneffe. Down south in **Dangriga** and **Placencia**, you'll also find nice prices, a laid-back vibe and lots of pristine dive sites nearby.

Diving Buddy Selection!

It's a good idea to be sure the people you are diving with over a few days have similar interests and skill levels as yourself, so you won't spend your valuable vacation time diving in areas that hold little interest for you. If you like drift dives best, floating around quietly looking at big fish and coral, you do not want to spend your time poking in and out of caves. So select your dive buddies with care!

On this trip, our goal is to get in as much diving as possible, without having to worry about details such as transport, meals or non-diving wimps, so we'll choose an all-inclusive dive lodge on one of the small cayes. **St. George's Caye Lodge** is a highly-respected dive lodge that's just a short boat ride from Belize City, but close to lots of great sites. The three lodges on **Turneffe Atoll** are just minutes away from some of the country's most spectacular diving (see *Best Sleeps*).

The folks from our lodge will meet us at the airport, and take us by van and boat out to where the fish are. Over a welcome drink, we'll meet with our divemaster and decide where we want to go tomorrow, then give our equipment a quick checkout and load it onto the boat. After dinner and an evening of swapping dive stories with fellow gung-ho guests, it's off to bed.

Saturday
The **Blue Hole** is Belize's Eiffel Tower, the sight that everyone back home will ask you about. This enormous sinkhole (1,000 feet across and 400 feet deep) is almost perfectly round, and its water is bright blue. It formed as a limestone cave millions of years ago, when this region was dry land. When sea levels rose, the weight of the water caused the roof to collapse, and this unique geological feature was formed.

The main attraction for divers is the cavern formations that open up into the sheer walls, beginning at a depth of about 110 feet. You can swim beneath vast overhangs, among massive stalactites. Sizable sharks patrol the limestone cathedrals, adding to the adventure. However, not everyone loves diving the Blue Hole as much as the tourist hype suggests. It's a very deep dive, which means you only get to spend a few minutes at depth, light levels are low, and there's little in the way of fish to be seen. Around the rim of the crater however, you'll see plenty of coral and its attending fish life.

There are several excellent shallow and medium-depth sites around the atoll that make great second dives. Perhaps the most spectacular is **Half Moon Wall**, where you can see a wide variety of underwater habitats in a small area, at moderate depths (30-70 feet). Here are dozens of spur-and-groove coral formations, overhangs and tunnels, as well as sand flats that are home to a colony of thousands of garden eels. Large sharks, eagle rays and manta rays are frequent visitors.

After the diving, most trips make a stop at **Half Moon Caye**  **Natural Monument**, a tiny and remote island that's home to an amazing variety of wildlife. The most famous residents are the red-footed boobies, which nest here in the thousands. From a viewing platform adjacent to their colony, you can watch them feeding their chicks and flying about in their inimitable booby fashion. Magnificent frigate birds hang about waiting for the chance to snatch a booby egg. Over 120 other bird species visit here on their migrations, and three sea turtle species nest here at certain times of the year.

We'll return to the lodge and have a hearty family-style dinner of fresh seafood, then start getting ready for a night dive. Tonight's the night to do it, because tomorrow night might be pushing a little too close to the 24-hour mark before flying home on Monday.

Also, by tomorrow night we are sure to be totally exhausted, in shape for little more than drinking beer and telling dive stories. Diving at night lets you see the reef from another perspective. You'll see fish snoozing away, some of them in cocoons of mucus that they spin for their bed each night (mmm, sounds comfortable). You may also see nocturnal creatures that don't come out during the day. Our divemaster will pick out a great shallow or medium-depth site for our night dive.

Sunday
Rise and shine! Grab a cup of coffee and hurry down to the dock, because today we're going to visit a place that many have called

the most spectacular diving area in Belize: **Turneffe Atoll**. The largest of Belize's three coral atolls, Turneffe is a huge ring of coral reefs, dotted with over 200 tiny mangrove islands. The vast mangrove wetlands nurture a veritable Eden of sea life, and the remote location means that the reefs are in pristine shape and the visibility is usually spectacular. Lots of dive boats visit Turneffe, but the sheer number of great dive sites keeps the diving pressure low.

At the south end of the atoll is the **Elbow**, a steep coral wall that drops off into a deep channel swept by strong ocean currents. This is one of the few drift dives in Belize, and perhaps the best place to see really big fish. As we drift with the current along the

wall, we'll swim amid vast schools of snapper, grouper, mackerel, jack, permit and tuna, and maybe glimpse pelagic creatures such as lemon, blacktip and hammerhead sharks, manta and spotted eagle rays, green and hawksbill turtles, and bottlenose and spotted dolphins.

For our second dive, we can choose among some of the finest wall dives in the Caribbean. **Myrtle's Turtles** is an awesome wall that starts at 60 feet and drops off to infinity. Here you'll see schools of jacks, snappers and permits, and a huge resident turtle. **Lefty's Ledge**, another wall dive starting around 50 feet, offers consistent sightings of large pelagics, including jacks, mackerel, eagle rays, and occasional hammerhead, blacktip and bull sharks. If you'd rather dive a wreck, let's check out the **Sayonara**, an old passenger boat that was intentionally sunk in 1985 at a depth of 50 feet.

Monday Morning
Monday morning – time for one last visit to the beautiful coral reefs. We won't dive this morning, because we'll be flying back home this evening, but we should have time to squeeze in a snorkel.

The western edge of Turneffe Atoll has lots of shallow reefs, perfect for beginning divers and snorkelers. The most popular is **Rendezvous Cut**, an area of large coral heads in 40-50 feet of water. Other easy dive sites include the **Aquarium**, a shallow (12 foot) spot with a lot of nice coral and a wealth of little reef fish; Hollywood, a sheltered site with depths of 20-45 feet and lush forests of soft corals and sponges; and **Susie's Shallows**, an area of colorful reef with a maximum depth of 15 feet.

Once we're all packed up and ready to go, the resort's boat will take us back to Belize City, where we'll transfer to a van to the airport and (sniff!) home.

A WONDERFUL WEEK IN THE CAYES

The cayes of Belize have plenty to keep you busy for a week (or a lifetime), at least if you're into water sports. Diving, snorkeling, fishing and sailing present endless possibilities. Above the waterline, birders, manatee-watchers and lobster-eaters will be more than content. And it's amazing how many people are delighted to lie around on the sand and do absolutely nothing!

RECOMMENDED PLAN: In a week, you could easily visit several of the cayes, but all offer similar activities and access to many of the same dive sites, so it makes more sense to choose the island that best fits your idea of a perfect vacation, and spend your week there. That's what most visitors choose to do, so many lodgings specialize in **weeklong all-inclusive packages**. If you want a luxury resort, or you want to be a part of the tourist scene and the nightlife, opt for Ambergris. If you want a mellower scene and lower prices, head for Caulker. If you want a week of hard-core diving or fishing with no distractions, choose one of the lodges on the small islands.

San Pedro

The largest, nicest, and only town on Ambergris Caye is **San Pedro**, a clapboard and concrete Caribbean town that is slowly evolving from a sleepy village into a major tourist resort area. The visitors are a mix of divers and honeymooners, upscale travelers and backpackers, Americans and Europeans. Cars are outnumbered by golf carts (both gas and electric), all-terrain-vehicles, and bicycles. Taxi vans ferry visitors to and from the various resorts, most of which are located just outside of town. Traffic on the sandy (in rainy weather, muddy) streets can be hectic in high season. The town has a Mexican feel – you'll hear more Spanish spoken than English, and excellent Mexican food is to be had.

There are only three north-south streets in San Pedro. The one nearest the beach is called either Front Street or Barrier Reef Drive, the next one is called either Middle Street or Pescador

Street, and the third one back is called Back Street. The alternate names are interchangeable, but for clarity, this book will refer to them as Front, Middle and Back Streets. The beach serves as a pedestrian street, and is where you will find most dive shops and restaurants.

Don't Miss ...

Hol Chan & Shark Ray Alley – Safely snorkel with huge nurse sharks and stingrays.
The Blue Hole – This enormous sinkhole is Belize's most popular advanced dive site.
Fishing on the Flats – World-class fly fishing for bonefish, tarpon and permit.
Lazing on the Beach – Doing nothing is a fine art here.

There are a number of hotels right in San Pedro, mostly along or just off Front Street. A string of larger resorts spreads out to the south of town. To the north, there are several (mostly higher-end) resorts that are accessible only by boat. Most dive shops and other tour operators will pick you up from your hotel, so staying outside of town needn't be a problem.

The **Ambergris Maya Jade Store and Museum**, on Front Street, is a classy shop and mini-museum, with beautiful jade replicas of artifacts from the classical Mayan era, as well as exhibits about Jade and its significance to Mayan culture. *Info*: Tel. 226-3311. **Belizean Arts**, located inside Fido's Courtyard, is an excellent art gallery with a huge collection of oil paintings by local Belizean artists, several of whose works can be seen in local hotels. *Info*: www.belizeanarts.com. Tel. 226-3019. Other art galleries are **Island Originals Art Gallery** on Front Street and **Isla Bonita Gallery**, just south of the airstrip.

If you're on Ambergris for a week, and run out of things to do, don't forget that it's easy to take a day trip to the mainland to visit the Lamanai ruins, Caves Branch, the Baboon Sanctuary or any of various other attractions. Check with any of the island tour operators to see what's offered. *Info*: www.ambergriscaye.com.

If you want to get around by bike, they can be had (free or paid) at almost every hotel. If you're really lazy, you can rent a golf cart from **Carts Belize** (www.cartsbelize.com) or **Castle Cars** (www.ambergriscaye.com/castle). Golf cart rentals cost about $65 per day. A driver's license is required to rent or drive a cart.

Hol Chan Marine Reserve
This protected marine reserve a few miles south of San Pedro is

by far the most popular spot for short snorkel and dive trips. The reserve includes sections of mangrove and seagrass habitat that, together with the coral reef, form an interconnected ecosystem where fish and other sea life grow up, feed and breed. The dive action is in the area around the **Hol Chan Channel**, a steep-walled cut through the reef in 30 feet of water that is particularly rich in sea life and that gives the reserve its name (Hol Chan means "little channel" in Mayan).

As elsewhere in the Caribbean, coral reefs near human settlements tend to be devoid of large fish, for the simple reason that the locals caught and cooked them long ago. Hol Chan's protected status means that you can see a wide range of fishy life just a few minutes' boat ride from town. You'll see schools of yellowtail snapper, parrotfish, angelfish, blue tangs, triggerfish, hogfish, barracuda, moray eels, nurse sharks and lots of lobsters. If you're lucky, you may spot a blacktip or hammerhead shark, sea turtles, grouper, snapper, tarpon or perhaps even a manatee. There's also a profusion of colorful coral species, including elkhorn coral, brain coral, starlet coral, staghorn coral, sea fans, lettuce coral and other soft corals.

Just south of the channel, and also part of the reserve, **Shark Ray Alley** is one of the top places in the Caribbean to snorkel with

Ambergris History

When the first Europeans arrived on the island in 1508, they found several thriving Mayan villages. It is believed that the Mayans dug the channel that turned the southern end of a peninsula into an island. There are several small **Mayan ruins** scattered about the island. In the 1600s the island was a haven for **British pirates** who preyed on Spanish shipping in the region, and it was they who named the island for ambergris, an oily substance produced by sperm whales that was very valuable back in those days for making perfumes. In the 19th century, **refugees from the Caste War** in the Yucatan came to Ambergris and mingled with the British settlers, forming the ancestry of today's mostly bilingual islanders. Traditional economic activities are logging, fishing, chicle, coconuts, lobster, and now tourism.

 large sea creatures. Local fishermen have been discarding fish waste here for years, which has made the area a frequent haunt of nurse sharks and Southern stingrays. You can swim with these enormous fish in water only a few feet deep – it's a fine place for novice snorkelers, and an unforgettable wildlife encounter even for seasoned divers. The nurse sharks (up to six feet long) and rays (up to four foot wingspan) are not dangerous. On the contrary, they seem friendly, like big dogs eager for a handout (but be safe – don't touch them, and let your guide handle the feeding).

All dive shops on Ambergris and Caulker run daily snorkeling trips to Hol Chan and Shark Ray Alley. There's a park entry fee of $12.50 per person, which is included in the price of your trip. There's a visitors' center in the center of San Pedro where you can learn more about the ecosystem of Hol Chan. *Info*: www.holchanbelize.org.

Ambergris Caye Birding

The marine creatures get most of the press, but Ambergris is also home to over 260 bird species, including vireos, flycatchers, kiskadees, woodpeckers and hummingbirds, to say nothing of the many water birds that hang out in the mangroves.

At the **Caribbean Villas Hotel**, south of San Pedro, aspiring birder Susan Lala has built a three-story "people perch" that offers a panoramic view of the entire island and plenty of interesting bird sightings. It's open to the public daily. Read about her birdy experiences at her website. *Info*: www.caribbeanvillashotel.com/birds/cvbirds.html. Tel. 226-2715.

Other great places to spot birds are **Little Iguana and Rosario Cayes**, two small protected mangrove islands just off Ambergris, and **San Pedro Lagoon**, in the north part of the island.

The island's greatest bird guru is **Elbert Greer**, who writes a weekly column about birds for the San Pedro Sun, and offers guided bird watching tours by boat around the island. He works as a guide at Ramon's Village (see

Best Sleeps). Contact him there or go to his very informative website at www.scubalessonsbelize.com/birds.

Ambergris Caye Diving
The majority of visitors to Ambergris are there for the diving. Even if you've never dove before, when in San Pedro you must at least take a snorkeling trip. The abundance and beauty of the world beneath the sea will amaze you.

Ambergris has a passel of dive operators to choose from. A few of the resorts have their own dive shops, and there are a dozen more on the beach in downtown San Pedro. Many of the hotels have arrangements with certain dive operators, but most dive outfits will pick you up from any hotel dock. All the shops offer equipment rental and PADI instruction, and all offer similar prices, but be sure to inquire as to what's included, as some may nickel-and-dime you on equipment rentals and such. See *Best Activities* for information on Ambergris dive operators.

You'll pay around $70-80 for a two-tank local dive. Most of the dive sites are very close to shore, so boat rides are short, and trips leave at a civilized hour, usually 9am or so. Many operators also offer afternoon and night dives. Most of the dive shops also arrange snorkeling and fishing trips.

Belize's most famous dive spot, the Blue Hole, is accessible from San Pedro, but it's a rather long boat ride. Most Blue Hole trips leave at 5 or 6 in the morning, and return about 12 hours later. You'll pay about $250 for a three-tank dive trip, including lunch (snorkelers pay around $150).

Ambergris Caye Water Sports

Fishing plays second fiddle to diving on Ambergris. Not because the fishing isn't great (it is!), but because San Pedro isn't known as a fishing resort (hard-core fishermen tend to stay out on Turneffe, or down south). Fishing charters from San Pedro are run by freelance boat captains. You can book a trip either through your hotel, or through any of the dive operators.

There are all kinds of other water sports going on, so many that the beach in San Pedro often resembles a busy train station more than a peaceful vacation spot, as people tear around on all manner of watercraft. **SailSports Belize**, located in  the Caribbean Villas Hotel rents all things with sails, from windsurfers to Hobie Cats to Lasers. They also do kiteboarding, the latest extreme sport. With a board strapped to your feet and a huge kite up in the air, it's a bit like a cross between windsurfing and parasailing. *Info*: www.sailsportsbelize.com; Tel. 226-4488.

Lighthouse Reef & The Blue Hole

The **Blue Hole** is Belize's Eiffel Tower. Every tourist brochure features a picture of it, every dive shop runs trips to it, and when you get back home, everyone will ask you if you saw it. Completing the Parisian metaphor, the reality falls far short of the hype. Like the Eiffel, the Blue Hole is grand and impressive, but there are far more interesting dive sites in Belize.

Located at the center of **Lighthouse Reef**, a coral atoll about 60 miles southeast of Belize City, the Blue Hole is an enormous round sinkhole, over 1,000 feet across and 400 feet deep. Its almost perfect circular shape and the bright blue color of its water make it a unique sight from the air. It formed as a limestone cave millions of years ago, when this region was dry land. When sea levels rose, the weight of the water caused the roof to collapse, and this unique geological feature was formed.

The main attraction for divers is the **cavern formations** that open up into the sheer walls, beginning at a depth of about 110 feet. You can swim beneath vast overhangs, among massive stalactites. Sizable sharks patrol the limestone cathedrals, adding to the adventure. Because of the depth, the caverns and the long boat ride to get here, this dive should be made by advanced divers only. However, the coral-lined rim of the crater is a good spot for shallow diving and snorkeling.

There's no question that the Blue Hole is a truly unique place, but many divers find the dive itself disappointing. It's a very deep dive, so you only get to spend a few minutes admiring the sights. As with all deep dives, light levels will be low, and you'll see little in the way of fish and other sea life. At the end of your dive however, as you poke around in the shallows, you'll see plenty.

There are several excellent shallow and medium-depth sites around the atoll that make great second dives. Out here in the open ocean the visibility is usually superb, and you may catch a glimpse of some large pelagic fish. The most spectacular site of all is **Half Moon Wall**, where you can see a wide variety of under-water habitats in a small area, at moderate depths (30-70 feet). Here are dozens of spur-and-groove coral formations, overhangs and tunnels, as well as sand flats that are home to thousands of garden eels. Large sharks, eagle rays and manta rays are frequent visitors.

After the diving, most trips make a stop at **Half Moon Caye Natural Monument**. This tiny island so far from the mainland is home to an amazing variety of wildlife. The most famous residents are the **red-footed boobies**, which nest here in the thousands.

 From a viewing platform adjacent to their colony, you can watch them feeding their chicks and flying about in their inimitable booby fashion. Magnificent frigate birds hang about waiting for the chance to snatch a booby egg. The best time to see the boobies is March-July, when the young are in the nests. Over 120 other bird species visit here on their migrations, and three sea turtle species nest here at certain times of the year. There are also scads of iguanas, geckos and anole lizards, as well as pretty orange flowers called ziricotes.

Lighthouse Reef is within day-trip range of just about everywhere in Belize. Dive boats come here from Ambergris Caye (2.5 hours), Caulker, Belize City and even down south in Dangriga. Live-aboard dive boats also frequent the area. If you want to be right here, stay at one of the small island lodges. There is no lodging right on the atoll, but the lodges on Turneffe are a short boat ride away.

Turneffe Islands
The largest of Belize's three coral atolls is 25 miles east of Belize City. This huge ring of coral reefs is dotted with **over 200 tiny mangrove islands**. There's nothing out here but mangroves, palm trees, birds, fish and the humans who stalk them. Here you'll find what may just be the best diving and fishing in all of Belize. The vast mangrove wetlands nurture a veritable Eden of sea life, and the fairly remote location means that the reefs are in pristine shape and the visibility is usually spectacular. The sheer number of great dive sites keeps the diving pressure down.

Turneffe is no secret – it's visited by several dive boats every day – but with over 160 miles of reefs and walls, there's plenty of room to spread out. There's a huge range of different kinds of diving, and plenty of sites suitable for all skill levels.

The western edge of the atoll has lots of shallow reefs, perfect for beginning divers and snorkelers. The most popular is **Rendez-vous Cut**, an area of large coral heads in 40-50 feet of water. Other easy dive sites include the **Aquarium**, a shallow (12 feet) spot with a lot of nice coral and a wealth of little reef fish; **Hollywood**, a sheltered site with depths of 20-45 feet and lush forests of soft corals and sponges; and **Susie's Shallows**, an area of colorful reef with a maximum depth of 15 feet. **Triple Anchors** is a 40-60 foot site where three anchors and some other remnants of an old sailing ship lie encrusted with corals and sponges. **Permit Paradise** is a 60-foot dive where you'll see schools of the eponymous (and delicious) game fish.

There are several wrecks around Turneffe. The most popular, and an excellent choice for a beginning wreck diver, is the **Sayonara**, an old passenger boat that was intentionally sunk in 1985 at a depth of 50 feet.

Intermediate divers enjoy some of the finest wall dives in the Caribbean. **Myrtle's Turtles** is an awesome wall that starts at 60 feet and drops off to infinity. Here you'll see schools of jacks, snappers and permits, and a huge resident turtle. **Lefty's Ledge**, another wall dive starting around 50 feet, offers consistent sightings of large pelagics, including jacks, mackerels, eagle rays, and occasional hammerhead, blacktip and bull sharks. **Gail's Point** is yet another awesome wall frequented by large open-ocean fish and turtles. When diving these walls, you're likely to be enthralled by the huge fish you'll see swimming in the water

column. But don't forget to turn your gaze back to the wall from time to time, as the variety of hard and soft corals, sponges, gorgonians, starfish, shrimp and flamboyant little reef fish is amazing.

At the south end of the atoll is the **Elbow**, one of the most impressive dive sites in the country. A steep coral wall drops off into a deep channel where strong ocean currents sweep around the south end of the atoll. This is an excellent drift dive, and perhaps the most likely place in the area to see really big fish. Advanced divers can drift with the current along the wall, swimming with vast schools of snapper, grouper, mackerel, jack, permit and tuna, and perhaps getting a glimpse of pelagic creatures such as lemon, blacktip and hammerhead sharks, manta and spotted eagle rays, green and hawksbill turtles, and bottlenose and spotted dolphin. A few divers have even spotted marlin and sailfish! Because of the strong current and rough seas, the Elbow is for advanced divers only.

The miles of shallow **seagrass flats** inside the atoll are one of the world's finest places for flats fishing. Anglers come from all over the world to try to catch a wily bonefish or a tackle-busting tarpon on a fly. Fishing on the reefs for grouper and snapper, and offshore for billfish, are similarly spectacular.

There are three diving/fishing lodges on the atoll: **Turneffe Island Resort** (www.turnefferesort.com); **Blackbird Caye Resort** (www.cayeresorts.com) and **Turneffe Flats** (www.tflats.com; see *Best Activities*). **The Oceanic Society**, a non-profit conservation group (www.oceanic-society.org), operates a research station here that also welcomes visitors on weeklong packages to dive and participate in their studies.

Not all the wonderful wildlife lives below the surface. Turneffe is the most biologically diverse coral atoll in the Western Hemisphere. **More than 60 bird species** have been spotted here, some of them rare or extinct on the mainland. Obviously there's a huge variety of water birds (magnificent frigatebirds, kingfishers, double-crested cormorants and several species of herons) and raptors (ospreys, peregrine falcons). You may also see mangrove warblers, golden-fronted woodpeckers, mockingbirds, humming-birds, vireos, swallows, tanagers and brown boobies.

The vast atoll is home to many rare creatures, including the endangered **American crocodile** and **West Indian manatee**. Several species of dolphins are frequently seen. Turneffe Flats offers wildlife tours of the islands for those who prefer to enjoy the natural world without getting wet.

Caye Caulker

Caulker has a very different vibe than Ambergris. Most visitors find Ambergris to be pretty laid-back (although it is steadily becoming less so), but Caulker makes Ambergris seem like downtown Paris. There's *nothing* going on here but water sports, lying around on the beach and perhaps languidly gazing at a bird from time to time. Even the dogs seem lazier. With its **two nature reserves** and lack of large resorts, Caulker has a green feel. You'll see more Rastas and more European visitors on Caulker than on Ambergris. You'll also find slightly lower prices, particularly for the lovely local lobster. When you arrive at your hotel, there may be no one in the office (which may be located in a nearby shop, or someone's house). Go relax on the beach, or have a drink next door – they'll be back soon.

As Belize rapidly evolves from a sleepy backwater to a major tourist destination, the character of the island is changing. Caye Caulker is a short boat ride away from the main channel where the gargantuan cruise ships anchor, and groups of t-shirt-buying, ice-cream-cone-gobbling day-trippers are now mingling uneasily with the hairy backpackers that have traditionally been Caulker's main visitors.

There are three main north-south streets, called Front, Middle and Back streets. Most of the best accommodations are located on

Front Street, right across from the sea. There is nothing on Caulker that could really be called a luxury resort, but there are a couple of very nice midrange lodgings, and lots of lower-budget options (see *Best Sleeps*).

The airstrip on Caye Caulker has direct air service from Goldson International Airport, Belize City Municipal Airstrip, and San Pedro. Contact **Tropic Air** (www.tropicair.com) or **Maya Island Air** (www.mayaislandair.com) for current schedules. Boats leave several times per day from the **Water Taxi Terminal** in Belize City, and stop at Caye Caulker on the way to Ambergris. The fare to Caulker is $7.50 one-way, $15 return.

The main activities on Caulker involve watching wildlife, both above and below the water's surface. The **Caye Caulker Marine Reserve** includes all of the barrier reef that runs parallel to the shore, as well as the turtle grass lagoon on the west side of the island. There are plenty of excellent dive sites along the barrier reef just a short boat ride offshore. Caye Caulker dive operators also run trips to Hol Chan, as well as the Blue Hole and the Turneffe Islands, both of which are closer from here than they are from Ambergris. See *Best Activities* for information on Caulker dive and snorkeling operators.

One of the most popular trips on Caulker is to see the manatees on nearby Swallow Caye. The West Indian manatee, or sea cow, is a docile and friendly marine mammal that is found in shallow waters throughout the Caribbean and the Gulf of Mexico. Caye Caulker resident Chocolate, also known as Lionel Heredia, has been the local champion of the manatees for many years, and was the prime mover in getting the 9,000-acre **Swallow Caye Wildlife Sanctuary** set up to protect the manatees.

Chocolate, who earned his nickname not for his complexion, but for his weakness for a certain sweet goodie, can be found at his gift shop on Front Street, where he also has a guest room for rent. Several local operators now run manatee-watching tours, but **Chocolate's Manatee Tours** is still the best. The tour lasts all day (9am-4pm) and costs $60 apiece including snorkel gear. It's a beautiful day of cruising around the grass flats and mangrove islands around Caulker, keeping our eyes peeled for wildlife all the way. We'll spend an hour or two observing the manatees, and we may also spot some dolphins and even the endangered American saltwater crocodile. We're sure to see flocks of seabirds. *Info*: Tel. 226-0151. E-mail: chocolateseashore@gmail.com.

The next stop is **Sergeant's Caye**, a tiny island right on the barrier reef south of Caulker. It has a beautiful swimming beach and excellent snorkeling on the coral reef. Novice snorkelers can paddle around in the shallow protected waters on the lagoon side of the island, while more adventurous types can check out the deeper and more spectacular reefs on the ocean side. You'll see a wealth of colorful coral species, including elkhorn coral, brain coral, starlet coral, staghorn coral and sea fans, with swarms of brightly-colored tropical fish such as blue tangs, sergeant majors, parrotfish and angelfish. You may also encounter barracuda, moray eels, nurse sharks and lobsters. *Info*: www.swallowcayemanatees.org.

Caye Caulker is also the home of a less cuddly sea creature, the American saltwater crocodile. These endangered reptiles are now protected in Belize, and they are common in the lagoons around the island. If you take a boat trip around the island, you can probably spot crocs, manatees, dolphins and a wealth of birds. It's also exciting to go crocodile hunting at night (in the safety of a boat, of course).

The northern 100 acres of Caye Caulker are part of the **Caye Caulker Forest and Marine Reserve**, which is managed by a consortium of local tourist and conservation groups. The Forest Reserve has a small visitors' center and picnic area, and is a common stop on boat tours. There's also a two-acre mini-reserve just south of town, where you can take a hike to see native trees such

as red, white and black mangroves, three varieties of coconut palm, buttonwood, gumbo-limbo, poisonwood, and the colorful ziracote. There are over a hundred species of birds on Caulker, including some that are rare on the mainland. There's a huge profusion of water birds from egrets to cormorants, raptors such as hawks and ospreys, and rarities like the black catbird and rufus-necked rail. *Info*: www.gocayecaulker.com; www.cayecaulkerchronicles.com.

Cruising for Disaster?

Belize's evolution from sleepy backwater into major tourist destination is in high gear. Cruise ship arrivals have risen from 14,000 people in 1998 to well over a million this year. Many Belizeans fear that the remote cayes and jungle lodges may lose their natural, unspoiled flavor under the onslaught of thousands of day-trippers. Locals also complain that too little of the cruise passengers' money ends up in the pockets of ordinary Belizeans, and that too much of the ships' trash ends up on Belizean beaches. Many cruise passengers are first-time travelers with little interest in the country beyond the beach, the bar and the t-shirt shop, very different from the backpackers, birders and divers that Belize is used to. Only time will tell if Belize can balance the various interests wisely.

Other Northern Cayes

Caye Chapel, a small caye a short way offshore from Belize City, is completely occupied by a luxury golf resort that features the only championship-level golf course in Belize (see *Best Sleeps*). Water taxis between Belize City and Ambergris Caye will stop here on request. But if you can afford to stay here, you can probably afford to charter a plane to the private landing strip.

St. George's Caye is one of the closest cayes to Belize City, but it surely feels isolated. There is nothing here but two resorts and a couple dozen private homes (see *Best Sleeps*). A couple of rusty cannon recall the 1798 Battle of St. George's Caye, in which the Spanish were defeated and ceded control of the region to Britain. Water taxis between Belize City and Ambergris Caye will stop here on request.

There are lots and lots of tiny islands (over 200 at last count) strung out along the coast. A few, including **Gallows Point Caye** and **Spanish Lookout**

Caye, have a single diving/fishing lodge (see *Best Sleeps*). A few others are visited by tourists on day-trips or overnight camping trips. Others are visited only by birds and drug smugglers.

5. BELIZE CITY & NORTHERN BELIZE

Much of Northern Belize is uninhabited jungle and forest, with a few small settlements here and there. Large tracts of the wilderness are protected as nature reserves. Here you'll find two of Belize's most-visited Mayan sites: Altun Ha and Lamanai. Belize City, the country's largest, is frankly a place that most tourists don't find very attractive.

You'll fly into the International Airport just outside of town, but whether you want to use the city as a hub for visits to the islands and the jungle, or blow right by it, as many visitors do, is entirely up to you.

ONE GREAT DAY IN BELIZE CITY

Belize's largest city is no bustling metropolis, nor is it a quaint seaside village. Rather, it's a somewhat sleepy third-world town, drab and a little mildewy under the oppressive heat and humidity. But I happen to have a soft spot for such places, so let's have a look around!

Morning

We'll start our walking tour in the Fort George neighborhood, the locale of the two best hotels: the popular Radisson and the elegant Great House. Nearby is the **National Handicraft Center**, the best shopping experience in town. Belize has some wonderful artists, and you'll find some of their charming paintings here, as well as carvings in coral, slate and wood, bottled Belizean herbs and sauces, and of course postcards and t-shirts. *Info*: 2 South Park Street. Tel. 223-3636.

For a look at how the cruise tourists are spending their vacations, let's pay a quick visit to the **Fort Street Tourism Village**, a walled compound built around the dock where the tender boats from the cruise ships come in. This plastic paradise has several restaurants, bars and shops selling tourist supplies and expensive luxury goods (many of which have nothing to do with Belize). You may scoff at the square megaship passengers, most of them on their first venture out of the States, but I'm happy to see them getting a glimpse of another culture, even if it's a brief, prepackaged glimpse. And, whatever they think of the mass tourism that has recently descended on Belize, locals all concede that the Tourism Village has raised standards of cleanliness and safety in the neighborhood.

Next we'll walk up North Front Street, running the gauntlet of locals aggressively hawking their wood carvings, to the **Swing Bridge**. This bridge across the river serves as a local landmark, dividing the city in two. Crossing over to the south side, we'll pass the **City Market**, a multi-story building full of stalls selling

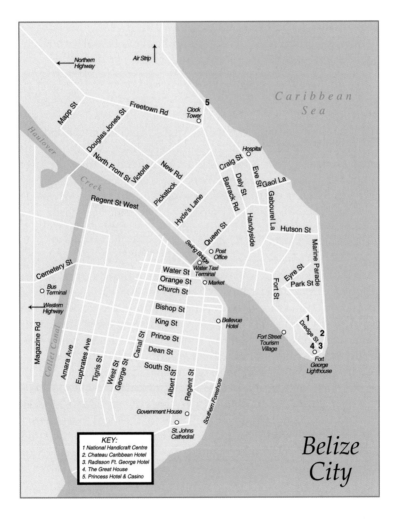

fruits, vegetables and every little thing. Take a look around, but keep your hand on your wallet! On the top floor of the market is **Big Daddy's**, where we can have a cheap and filling Belizean lunch with a view of the bay. Or we can cross back over to the north side of town and walk up Queen Street to **Nerie's**, which most folks agree has the best traditional Belizean food in town.

Afternoon

Belize City has its interesting aspects, but Paris it ain't. Our morning walk has already covered most of the tourist highlights, so this afternoon let's head a little way out of town and check out the **Belize Zoo**. We could take a guided tour of the zoo, but it isn't really necessary. Let's just grab one of the taxis that congregate around the Swing Bridge (budget travelers can even take the bus).

Watch Your Step!

Wherever you go in Belize City, or in any city in Belize, watch your step! Covered drains run along the edges of each street, and the covers are very often missing. If you gawk at the sights and don't watch where you put your feet, you risk plunging knee-deep into foul liquid, or worse. All manner of yucky stuff lurks everywhere, just waiting for an unwary tourist's shoe.

Just an hour's ride out of town on the Western Highway, this unique zoo has 125 species of native Belizean animals, all of them rescued as orphans or bred in captivity. They aren't kept in cages, but in large fenced enclosures that duplicate their natural habitats. You'll see jaguars, margays, ocelots, coatis, gibnuts, howler monkeys and tree-climbing foxes, as well as colorful birds such as toucans and scarlet macaws, and scaly reptiles such as croco-

diles, iguanas and boa constrictors. The zoo is an absolute must if you're traveling with kids. The mosquitoes here are brutal, so wear long-sleeved clothing and bring your bug spray.

Just past the zoo on the highway heading west is **JB's**

Watering Hole, a Belizean institution frequented by a colorful crew of locals, tourists and expats (see *Best Sleeps & Eats*). Let's stop there for a cold beer and a snack before heading back into town. *Info*: www.belizezoo.org; Tel. 220-8004. The Belize Zoo is at mile 29 on the Western Highway. Open 8am-5pm daily. Entry $8 adults; $4 kids.

Evening
Most parts of town are dodgy to walk around after dark, so our best bet for dinner might be to stick around the relatively safe Fort George area. Fortunately, two of the most atmospheric restaurants in town are right here. The **Harborview Restaurant**, next to the Tourism Village, has nice harbor views and vaguely Continental cuisine. The **Smoky Mermaid**, at the Great House, has grilled meats, seafood dishes and a special lobster menu with such delights as lobster quesadillas and lobster burgers! The plant-filled courtyard is a peaceful place for a leisurely dinner.

If you want to get out and sample some nightlife, head for the area around the Princess Hotel. The hotel's **Calypso Club** is usually hopping, and there are a couple of other local discos in the area (the action starts after 10pm). Do not walk there or anywhere else after dark. Take a taxi!

A FANTASTIC BELIZE CITY WEEKEND

This wild region has lots of interesting things to see. There's no way we can see it all, but a weekend gives us enough time for a taste of the city, the ruins and the jungle.

Friday
We'll fly into Belize City in the afternoon and take a taxi straight to our hotel. My favorite is the elegant **Great House** in the pleasant Fort George neighbor-

hood, but if you want a pool and all the other amenities, choose the **Radisson** across the street (don't tell anyone I said this, but if you buy a couple of drinks at the Radisson's pool bar, you can probably get away with having a dip there, even if you're staying across the street). If you have a lower budget, head for the clean and friendly **Hotel Mopan**, facing the water south of the Swing Bridge.

We need a few hours to decompress from the US express lane and get used to the slow dirt road of the tropics, so take off your shirt and shoes, order a panty ripper (rum and pineapple juice) or a cold Belikin beer, and forget about any further activities for the moment.

When dinnertime rolls around, we have two excellent choices right here in the Fort George area. The **Harborview Restaurant** has nice harbor views, good Continental cuisine, a lobster menu and a decent wine list. The **Smoky Mermaid**, a pleasant plant-filled courtyard at the Great House, has grilled meats, creative seafood dishes and their own lobster menu and pretty good wine list. Eat, drink and bask in your good fortune – you're in Belize!

Saturday Morning

If you're staying at one of the Fort George hotels, our walking tour starts right outside the door. If you're south of the Swing Bridge, then do this tour in reverse. A couple of blocks from the Radisson is the **National Handicraft Center**, the best shopping experience in town. Everything here is Belizean: charming paintings, coral, slate and wood carvings, baskets, jewelry, bottled Belizean herbs and sauces, Belizean music, postcards and t-shirts. It's a one-stop shopping center for Belizean souvenirs. *Info*: Tel. 223-3636. 2 South Park Street.

For a look at how those "other" tourists are spending their vacation, let's pay a quick visit to the **Fort Street Tourism Village**, a McDonaldsesque walled compound where the tender boats from the cruise ships dock. Within this artificial paradise are several restaurants and bars, a bandstand with live music, and lots of shops and stalls selling t-shirts, handicrafts (by no means all local), sunscreen and other tourist supplies. The only really interesting shop is an art gallery that has some nice local paintings on display.

The sophisticated travelers who read this book may be tempted to scoff at the portly cruise ship tourists, with their braided hair and fanny packs. However, the cruise lines provide a safe travel alternative to first-time travelers who might otherwise never encounter even this prepackaged glimpse of another culture. And few would dispute that the Tourism Village has raised standards of cleanliness and safety in the neighborhood.

Next let's have a look at the real Belize City. We'll walk up North Front Street, running the gauntlet of locals aggressively hawking their wood carvings, to local landmark the **Swing Bridge**. This bridge across the river divides the city in two. Crossing over to the south side, we'll pass the **City Market**, a multi-story building full of stalls selling fruits, vegetables and every little thing. On the top floor of the market is **Big Daddy's**, where we can have a cheap and filling Belizean lunch with a view of the bay. Or we can cross back over to the north side of town and walk up Queen Street to **Nerie's**, which most folks agree has the best traditional Belizean food in town.

Saturday Afternoon

Well folks, that's about it for tourist attractions right in the city. After lunch, let's head a little way out of town and check out the **Belize Zoo**. We could take a guided tour of the zoo, but it isn't really necessary. Let's just take a taxi out there (budget travelers can even take the bus). Taxis congregate around the Radisson hotel and the water taxi terminal just north of the Swing Bridge.

The zoo is very convenient from Belize City, just an hour's ride out of town on the Western Highway. It's an absolute must if you're traveling with kids. This unique little zoo has 125 species of native Belizean animals, all of whom were orphaned, injured, and rescued from the illegal pet trade, bred in captivity, or donated by other zoos. They aren't kept in cages, but in large fenced enclosures full of trees and plants, as close as possible to their natural habitats. The Belize Zoo isn't just for tourists. Its most important mission is educating Belizeans about their native wildlife, and the importance of protecting it.

You'll see jaguars, margays, ocelots, coatis, gibnuts, howler monkeys, kinkajous, tapirs and the tree-climbing Belizean gray fox, as well as colorful birds such as toucans and scarlet macaws, and scaly reptiles such as crocodiles, iguanas and boa constrictors. Perhaps because of the undisturbed natural state of the vegetation, the mosquitoes here are brutal. Wear long-sleeved clothing and bring your bug spray.

Adjacent to the zoo is the **Tropical Education Centre**, 84 acres of pine savannah. You can take a hike along their nature trail and climb up on several platforms in the forest canopy to see a vast number of resident and migratory birds. There's a small gift shop and snack bar at the zoo.

Just past the zoo on the highway heading west are a couple of restaurants that tend to be mobbed with tour groups. A little farther, at mile 32, is **JB's Watering Hole**, a piece of Belizean history where you can find excellent Belizean food and great conversation with a colorful crew of locals, tourists and expats (see *Best Sleeps & Eats*). *Info*: www.belizezoo.org; Tel.  220-8004. The Belize Zoo is at mile 29 on the Western Highway. Open 8am-5pm daily. Entry $8 adults; $4 kids.

Saturday Evening
We're going to have dinner at **Chef Bob**, just down the road from the faded Princess Hotel. This local favorite serves Belizean and international fare in a somewhat upscale atmosphere. The seafood is exquisite. *Info*: Tel. 223-6908.

After dinner, we're in position to sample some of the local nightlife, much of which goes on in the area around the Princess. We'll have a couple of drinks at the hotel's **Calypso Club**, and ask the bartender which of the local discos is the current place to be (they come and go). Tempted to walk back to the hotel to clear your head? Not in this town! We're calling a taxi.

Stay Safe - Take a Taxi!

At the risk of being redundant, I have to tell you that **it is not safe to wander around Belize City at night** (and some areas are dodgy even during the day). After dark, a taxi is the only safe way to travel. Fortunately, **taxis are cheap,** and they're easy to spot with their green license plates.

Sunday
Even if you're leaving Sunday evening, there's plenty of time for a trip to the **Community Baboon Sanctuary,** an hour's drive west of Belize City, near the village of Burrell Boom. No, these aren't what the rest of the world calls baboons. *Baboon* is the Belizean name for the black howler monkey, a vegetarian monkey that's actually a lot cuter than the fierce and ill-mannered baboons of Africa. This community-based ecotourism project provides protected habitat for over 2,000 howlers.

The endangered black howlers live in troops of 4-12 individuals, and spend most of their time in the trees eating fruits and leaves. Their distinctive call, which sounds more like a big dog barking than like howling, can be heard through the forest for a mile or more. The sanctuary is also home to many other animals, including wild cats and over 200 bird species. We'll take an hour-long tour with a local guide, who can tell us all sorts of fascinating things about the Belizean rain forest. *Info*: Entry and tour $7 per person. www.howlermonkeys.org; Tel. 220-2181.

If we have time, we can visit a couple of other popular attractions nearby: the Mayan ruins of **Altun Ha**, and the **Maruba Resort Jungle Spa**, which welcomes visitors for lunch, a swim and a quick spa treatment. Personally, I'm a little wary of both these places because they are sometimes mobbed with day-trippers from the cruise ships (although, as of this writing, few ships are calling in Belize on Sundays). You may want to call Maruba beforehand (see *Best Sleeps*), or check www.cruisecal.com to see if any of the fanny-pack crowd are expected today.

ALTERNATE PLAN
You can't come to Belize without seeing the coral reef. The reefs aren't far offshore, and you can take a dive or snorkeling trip right from Belize City. If you are not going to the Cayes, take a trip with **Hugh Parkey's Dive Connection** (www.belizediving.com; Tel. 223-5086 or 888/223-5403 US), on the dock at the Radisson Fort George hotel, or with **Sea Sports Belize** (www.seasportsbelize.com; Tel. 223-5505).

A FANTASTIC LAMANAI WEEKEND

Staying in Belize City and driving around on day trips may be a little too hectic if you only have a weekend. This trip to the **Lamanai ruins** is more relaxed, a getaway to the jungle. But don't worry, you'll have plenty to do – in fact, the most common complaint heard in Belize is that people wish they could stay longer!

Friday
There are several isolated jungle lodges tucked away in the barely inhabited forests of northern Belize. These resorts are a long ride from civilization, so you don't come for the nightlife or the shopping, but rather to immerse yourself in the natural world for a weekend of hiking, horseback riding, canoeing, birding or relaxing with umbrella drinks.

The **Lamanai Outpost Lodge** offers a chance to enjoy the Mayan ruins, the jungle and the bird-filled **New River Lagoon**. There are

ALTERNATE PLAN
Chan Chich would be another excellent choice for a weekend jungle getaway. It's also located at a Mayan site on a nice little river in the middle of the jungle. Like Lamanai, it's a first-class lodge that consistently gets great reviews. Birding, hiking, horseback riding and canoeing are on the menu. Travelers with lower budgets may enjoy the **Bird's Eye View Lodge**, on the water adjacent to the Crooked Tree Wildlife Sanctuary, with its 250 bird species.

several nice trips you can take right from the lodge, with no need to drive anywhere, so it's a perfect place for a short visit (or a long one). The accommodations and service are first-class (see *Best Sleeps*). A three-night all-inclusive package costs about 800 bucks per person.

Someone from the lodge will meet us at the airport in Belize City and drive us to the little village of Tower Hill, where we'll board a boat for a beautiful ride up the river to the lodge. The whole trip takes about 2.5 hours from the airport. Get your camera out, because we'll be seeing crocodiles, turtles, herons, cormorants and all sorts of water birds as we motor along through the steaming jungle.

The cares and problems of the modern world fade farther away with every mile we travel into the jungle. Traffic jams? Deadlines? What are they? We'll be met at the lodge with a nice cold drink. Take your shoes off. Shirt too. Order another drink, plop down in a hammock and enjoy doing nothing for a while. There'll be plenty of time at dinner to plan our activities for tomorrow.

Saturday Morning
One wonderful thing about staying right here at the **Lamanai Ruins** is that we can dodge the cruise ship day-trippers. The t-shirted ones show up at the north end of the ruins, whereas the Out-

post is located to the south. We'll get to the site first thing in the morning, and have a couple of hours alone with the howler monkeys and the spirits of the ancient Mayans. By the time the cattle arrive, we'll be thinking about heading back to the lodge for lunch.

For centuries, Lamanai was a wealthy trading center with a population of over 35,000. It had a longer history than most other Mayan cities, and was still inhabited when the Spaniards arrived. The ruins of a Spanish church bear witness to their vain attempts to convert the natives to Catholicism.

The name Lamanai means "Crocodile," obviously a reference to the many crocs in the surrounding waterways, and the many representations of crocodiles at the site. Only about five percent of the 700 structures have been excavated. Some notable ones are the **Mask Temple** with its 13-foot stone carvings of Mayan gods, and the **High Temple**, one of the largest structures in the Mayan world. We can climb to the top for a spectacular view of the forest and lagoon. Finally we'll stop at the museum for a look at some fascinating carvings and other artifacts that have been found at the site.

Saturday Afternoon

Yet another wonderful thing about Lamanai Outpost (there are many) is that there are so many activities right here on-site. Because we don't have to get in a van and ride anywhere, we can get in two nice tours per day, with plenty of time for lying around with umbrella drinks. After lunch, we can hike some of the trails around the lodge. A guide can point out some of the local plants that the ancient Maya used for medicines, some of the resident  howler monkeys, or perhaps a few of the **over 400 bird species** that live in the area. A dozen different herons and egrets, a dozen types of hawks, parrots, hummingbirds, trogons, toucans, motmots…and literally hundreds of LBBs (a technical birder term meaning Little Brown Birds).

Saturday Evening

After dinner, let's take a cruise around the lagoon on a pontoon boat. With a cooler full of drinks and our own personal bartender on board, we'll watch the sunset and spot even more animals and birds. Later on we can venture out at night with spotlights in search of some of the nocturnal residents. This is our best chance to spot an elusive ocelot or jaguar, to say nothing of owls and nightjars.

Sunday

Every nature lover knows that early morning is the best time to spot animals and birds. We can easily be in the woods or on the water in time for the dawn flighting. We can take a hike with one of the resort's resident guides, or paddle around the lagoon in a canoe in search of manatees, otters and crocs.

A WONDERFUL WEEK IN NORTHERN BELIZE

In a week you can see the colorful chaos of **Belize City**, several majestic **Mayan sites**, vast areas of **undisturbed wilderness**, and the pastoral lands of the **Mennonites**.

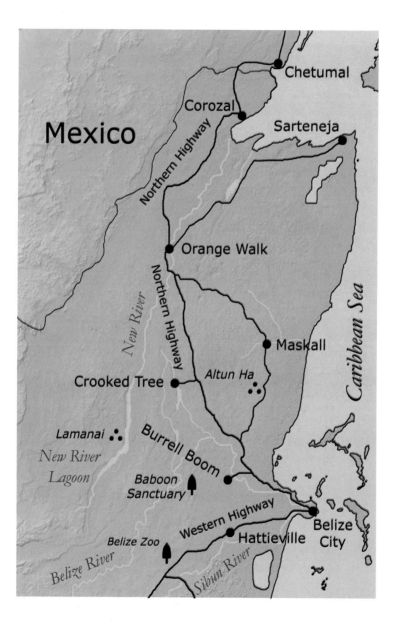

RECOMMENDED PLAN: Stay at one of the upscale jungle lodges in the area. My favorites are **Chan Chich** and **Lamanai Outpost** (see *Best Sleeps*). Both are pretty remote, but both have plenty of activities to keep you busy for a week. Observe birds and animals on jungle hikes, horseback rides and river cruises, take your time visiting the Mayan ruins, and spend a couple of days relaxing by the pool. It's no problem to visit the **Belize Zoo** and/or the **Baboon Sanctuary** on the way in or out.

Belize City

Belize City was founded in the 17th century by the **Baymen**, British buccaneers-turned-loggers who used the river to bring lumber from the forests to the coast. The town is said to have been built on wood chips and rum bottles. For much of its history it was a rough-and-tumble boom-and-bust frontier town.

Today Belize City is the country's largest, though that isn't saying much (population is about 70,000). The capital was moved to Belmopan in 1970, but Belize City remains the center of business and finance, and a place where people come from more remote regions to stock up on supplies. One thing it isn't is a major center of tourism, although you can certainly take diving trips and all sorts of other tours from here.

The city is divided in half by **Haulover Creek**, where herds of beef cattle were once "hauled over" by means of a rope. Today it's easier to cross – just walk over the **Swing Bridge**, a swinging drawbridge that opens twice a day to let boats pass.

North of the Swing Bridge is

Don't Miss ...

Lamanai – One of the country's most interesting Mayan sites is deep in the jungle, a spectacular spot for birding. The river trip to get there is an adventure in itself.

The Belize Zoo – See Belize's forest denizens in large natural-looking enclosures.

The Baboon Sanctuary – Everyone loves the black howler monkeys.

the **Fort George neighborhood**, the nicest (or at least the safest) part of town, the locale of the popular Radisson and the elegant Great House. A couple of blocks from these hotels is the **National Handicraft Center**, the best shopping experience in town. Everything here is Belizean: charming paintings, coral, slate and wood carvings, baskets, jewelry, bottled Belizean herbs and sauces, Belizean music, postcards and t-shirts. It's a one-stop shopping center for Belizean souvenirs. Among the benefits: it's air-conditioned, they take credit cards, and you can buy coral items without worrying about whether they're legal. *Info*: Tel. 223-3636. 2 South Park Street.

For a fascinating sociological study, and a look at how those "other" tourists are spending their vacation, pay a quick visit to the **Fort Street Tourism Village**, a McDonaldsesque walled compound where the tender boats from the cruise ships dock. Within this artificial island paradise are several restaurants and bars, an internet café, a bandstand with live music, and lots of shops and stalls selling t-shirts, handicrafts (by no means all local), sunscreen and other tourist supplies. The busiest shop of all is the one selling expensive diamond jewelry (no, diamonds have nothing to do with Belize). There's also a nice **art gallery** here, where you can see some of the charming paintings done by some of Belize's many excellent artists.

The Tourism Village has the feel of a gated community. Cruise passengers exit the compound through a couple of exits, each with a posted guard, and must show ID cards from their ships to re-enter. Passengers are funneled into vans that take them on day tours all over the country. Non-passengers may enter after obtaining a visitor's pass from the guard station.

The sophisticated travelers who read this book may be tempted to scoff at the portly cruise-ship tourists, with their braided hair and fanny packs. However, the cruise lines provide a safe travel alternative to first-time travelers who might otherwise never encounter even this prepackaged glimpse of another culture. And few would dispute that the Tourism Village has raised standards of cleanliness and safety in the neighborhood.

Fearing (perhaps correctly) that they would be ripped off six ways from Sunday, were they to wander alone through the streets of Belize City, many cruisers won't bother to leave the safe and sanitary confines of the Fort Street Tourism Village. And that's just fine with the cruise lines, who are skillful at ensuring that most of their passengers' money stays on their ships, or at least in the hands of their chosen local partners. Outside the Wall, taxi drivers, tour operators and touts gather to offer their services to those who venture outside (and claim to offer lower prices than the cruise line-approved vendors within).

North Front Street, lined with vendors aggressively hawking wood carvings (and other less respectable products), runs from the Fort George area to the Swing Bridge. Stop in at the **Image Factory**, a local art cooperative that has rotating exhibitions of Belizean visual art, as well as a shop selling fine crafts and books. *Info*: www.imagefactory.bz. Open Mon-Fri 9am-5pm;

At the next corner is the **Caye Caulker Water Taxi Association**, where you can catch a boat to Ambergris Caye or Caye Caulker. Boats depart every hour or two starting around 8am (see *Practical Matters*).

Now we're into the real Belize City, where the locals shop. Turn right (north) to head up **Queen Street**, lined with stores and cheap eateries. Turn left and cross the Swing Bridge to get to the **City Market**, a multi-story building full of stalls selling fruits, vegetables and every little thing (it's a great place to see a little local color, but keep an eye out for pickpockets). Heading south from here is **Albert Street**, another shopping street. Here are several record stores where you can buy CDs and tapes of Belizean musicians.

The Belize Zoo

This unique little zoo has 125 species of native Belizean animals. All the animals here were orphaned, injured, rescued from the illegal pet trade, bred in captivity, or donated by other zoos. They aren't kept in cages, but in large fenced enclosures full of trees and plants, as close as possible to their natural habitats. Founded in 1983, the Belize Zoo is not just for tourists. Its most important mission is educating Belizeans about their native wildlife, and the importance of protecting it.

You'll see jaguars, margays, ocelots, coatis, gibnuts, howler monkeys, kinkajous and tapirs, colorful birds such as toucans and scarlet macaws, and scaly reptiles such as crocodiles, iguanas and boa constrictors. My favorite critter is the Belizean gray fox, a cute little fox that actually climbs trees.

The zoo is very convenient from Belize City, just an hour's ride out of town on the Western Highway. It's an absolute must if you're traveling with kids. Perhaps because of the undisturbed natural state of the vegetation, the mosquitoes here are brutal. Wear long-sleeved clothing and bring your bug spray.

Adjacent to the zoo is the **Tropical Education Centre**, 84 acres of pine savannah. You can take a hike along their nature trail and climb up on several platforms in the forest canopy to see a vast number of resident and migratory birds. They also offer (by advance reservation) half-day guided canoe trips down the Sibun River, and behind-the-scenes tours of the zoo, including a nocturnal tour.

There's a small gift shop and snack bar at the zoo. Just past the zoo on the highway heading west are a couple of restaurants, beloved of tour groups. *Info*: www.belizezoo.org; Tel. 220-8004. The Belize Zoo is at mile 29 on the Western Highway. Open 8am-5pm daily. Entry $8 adults, $4 kids.

A little farther, at mile 32, is **JB's Watering Hole**, a piece of Belizean history where you can find excellent Belizean food and great conversation with a colorful crew of locals, tourists and expats (see *Best Sleeps & Eats*).

The Community Baboon Sanctuary

Baboon is the local name for the **black howler monkey**. The baboon sanctuary is a perfect example of the type of community-based ecotourism project that offers the best hope of saving Central America's rain forests and their inhabitants. Two hundred private landowners have voluntarily agreed to conserve their land to protect the habitat of the endangered monkeys. Since the sanctuary was founded in 1985, the population has grown to over 2,000 monkeys.

There are six species of howler monkey in Central and South America. The endangered black howler lives only in Belize, Mexico and Guatemala, and is one of two monkeys found in Belize (the other is the spider monkey). These vegetarian monkeys live in troops of 4-12 individuals, and spend most of their time in the trees eating fruits and leaves. Their distinctive call, which sounds more like a big dog barking than like howling, can be heard through the forest for a mile or more. The sanctuary is also home to many other animals, including wild cats and over 200 bird species.

There's a small museum and visitors' center at the site, as well as a traditional restaurant. Entrance, including a guided tour, is $7 per person. Various other tours are available, including night-time walks through the sanctuary and canoe trips on the river. There is some basic lodging available at the site, as well as bed and breakfast options in nearby villages. *Info*: www.howlermonkeys.org; Tel. 220-2181. An hour's drive west of Belize City, near the village of Burrell Boom.

Lamanai Ruins

One of the largest Mayan sites in Belize, the ruins of **Lamanai** include over 700 structures, only about five percent of which have been excavated. Located 35 miles from the town of Orange Walk, it has a spectacular setting, on the banks of the vast New River Lagoon, with trackless jungle for miles around. The name Lamanai means "Crocodile," obviously a reference to the many crocs in the surrounding waterways. You'll see many representations of crocodiles here.

Lamanai was inhabited much longer than most other Maya sites, from 1500 BC until around 1650 AD. In its prime it was a wealthy trading center with a population of over 35,000. Lamanai survived the end of the  Maya's Classic Period in the ninth and tenth centuries, when many other Mayan city-states collapsed. When the Spaniards arrived in the sixteenth century, they worked hard to convert the natives to Catholicism, but were never able to completely suppress the Mayan traditions. You can see the ruins of a Spanish church, which the locals burned in 1640.

Highlights of Lamanai include the **Mask Temple**, faced with 13-foot-high stone carvings of Mayan gods; and the **High Temple**, which is one of the largest structures in the Mayan world, over 100 feet high. The view of the forest and lagoon from the top is magnificent. At the **Ball Court**, the Mayans played a game that involved putting a hard rubber ball through a small hoop. They took the game as seriously as today's Belizeans do their soccer – the losers were sacrificed to the gods! There's a small museum that houses an impressive collection of carvings and other artifacts found at the site, with a basic visitors' center.

Lamanai is also a wildlife reserve, and the area is teeming with birds and other wildlife. You're likely to see some of the resident howler monkeys as you tour the site. Labels identify the various types of trees, many of which were (and are) used by the Maya for food and medicine.

Although it's possible to get to Lamanai by road, it's easier and much more fun to take the 26-mile boat ride up the **New River** from Orange Walk Town. Along the way, you'll see crocodiles, turtles, and maybe even the Jesus Christ lizard, named for its ability to walk on water. Colorful orchids and bromeliads as well as an unbelievable variety of birds round out the show. If you have time, be sure to take a boat ride around the lagoon, where you'll see even more water birds and other wildlife.

Lamanai is remote, so just about the only way to visit is on a guided tour, and that's fine – you'll learn much more about the ruins, and see more wildlife, than you would on your own. The oldest and best-known operator is **Jungle River Tours** (Tel. 302-2293 or 615-1712). *Info*: The park is open daily 8am-5pm.

Cruising Buddies

Tour groups from cruise ships are venturing ever farther into the interior of Belize on day trips. For better or worse, every place in this chapter is within easy reach of the ice-cream-cone-and-water-bottle posse. You'll encounter the thundering herds not only at the wildlife attractions and the Mayan ruins, but also at jungle lodges such as Maruba. To avoid them, make your visits early in the morning or late in the afternoon. A handy web site is www.cruisecal.com, which has complete schedules for all the major cruise lines. Check it to see when the ships are in Belize, and plan accordingly.

Mennonite Country
Mennonites are members of an Anabaptist sect that originated in Europe in the 16th century. They believe in pacifism and a strict separation of church and state. Their resistance to serving in the military and paying taxes tends to set them at odds with worldly governments, so over the years, many have wandered the world looking for a paradise where they can live as they please. Belize's Mennonites began to arrive in 1958, and today they are very successful farmers, producing much of the country's dairy products, as well as sturdy wooden furniture.

Most of the Mennonites live around **Orange Walk** in Northern Belize, and around Spanish Lookout in the Cayo district. Their country looks rather incongruous, with green pastures and farmhouses that wouldn't look out of place in Pennsylvania.

Traditional Mennonite sects speak a dialect of German, and shun modern technology, getting around in horse-drawn buggies. More progressive types speak English and prefer pickup trucks. You'll see them in town, the men in overalls and cowboy hats, the women in sober long skirts. Some Mennonites are friendly and happy to talk, but others want no contact with our sinful society, so please respect them and don't treat them like a tourist attraction. If you'd like to visit the Mennonite country, try **Hillside Bed & Breakfast** in Blue Creek Village (between Orange Walk and Lamanai), which is run by a local Mennonite family. *Info*: Tel. 323-0155. Basic rooms for $21-40.

Altun Ha

Altun Ha is the best-known Mayan site in Belize – you'll see its **Sun God Temple** every time you hoist a bottle of beer – but it is neither the largest nor the most interesting. Its easy accessibility from Belize City is its blessing and its curse. Most days of the week it's mobbed with day-trippers from cruise ships. Nearby Lamanai is more interesting, and it has the bonus of the wonderful river trip to get there.

The name Altun Ha means "Rockstone Pond" in the Mayan language, and refers to a rock-lined reservoir that the ancient Mayans built, an impressive feat of engineering for those times. Altun Ha's heyday was during the Mayan Classic era, from around 200 to 900 AD, when the city had a population of about 10,000.

Other Mayan Sites

If you're a true Maya buff, you may want to visit some of the other Mayan sites in the region. **Nohmul**, a large but mostly unexcavated site out in the middle of the sugar cane fields a few miles north of Orange Walk, has one of the highest pyramids around. **Cuello**, also near Orange Walk on the site of a rum distillery, is one of the oldest Mayan sites, and has a large plaza with three temples. Near Corozal are the sites of **Santa Rita** and **Cerros**. For more information about the ancient Mayans and their works, see Chapter 6.

Crooked Tree Wildlife Sanctuary

About 30 miles northwest of Belize City is an area of intersecting rivers, lagoons and swamps, of which 3,000 acres is a protected sanctuary run by the **Belize Audubon Society**. This is one of the finest bird-watching areas in Belize, home to vast flocks of water birds and a favorite stopover for migrating birds on their way north.

Residents include many species of herons, egrets and kingfishers, both of Belize's native duck species, ospreys, hawks, and the star of the show: the **jabiru stork**, the largest flying bird in the Western Hemisphere. These majestic birds, which have a wingspan of up to 12 feet, assemble here in vast numbers during April and May, then again in November. The waterways are also home to scads of crocodiles and turtles, and black howler monkeys hang around in the trees.

The peaceful and charming little village of **Crooked Tree** is on an island surrounded by rivers and lagoons. Until recently, when a causeway was built from the Northern Highway, the village was accessible only by boat. The villagers welcome tourists, especially during the yearly **Cashew Festival**. There are several rustic B&B-style lodgings as well as several forest lodges, of which perhaps the nicest is **Bird's Eye View Lodge** (see *Best Sleeps*). *Info*: www.belizeaudubon.org.

6. WESTERN BELIZE & TIKAL

After the cayes, **Western Belize** is the country's most visited region. It's easy to see why, as there's a huge variety of interesting places to see. Here you'll find several major Mayan sites, including **Cahal Pech, Xunantunich, Caracol** and **Tikal** just across the Guatemalan border; vast areas of pristine forest, including distinct broadleaf and pine-forest ecosystems; lazy tropical rivers that invite you to paddle or swim; and a spelunker's paradise of caves. Facilities for the visitor are first-rate, with a selection of excellent lodges in budget, midrange and luxury categories.

ONE GREAT DAY IN THE CAYO DISTRICT

Western Belize offers more ways to spend a day than almost anywhere in the world. In **San Ignacio**, an army of tour operators entices you with jungle hikes, river trips, horseback riding, caving...it's tough to choose! We can't do it all, but a trip to **Caracol** will let us check out the **tropical pine forest**, commune with the spirits of the ancient Maya, and cool off in a verdant waterfall pool, all in one day!

Morning
Get up at the crack of dawn and have a Belizean breakfast (beans and fry bread) with some fresh fruit and rich Belizean coffee. Our tour guide will pick us up at our lodge in a nice air-conditioned van, and take us up into the Central American forest. Caracol is about a two-hour drive from San Ignacio, south over the Mountain Pine Ridge.

Caracol ("Snail") is the largest Mayan site in Belize. Back in the seventh century AD, it was a planned city with a radial street plan and over 140,000 people – twice the size of modern Belize City! The residents were prosperous, and fond of beautiful artworks in jade and obsidian. They were also doughty warriors, and even defeated nearby Tikal in a famous battle.

The site is spectacular, at about 1,500 feet above sea level, with stunning views of the surrounding Maya Mountains. The high point of the city is a complex of structures called Caana. Here is an elaborate

ALTERNATE PLAN
You could also do any of the itineraries in this chapter via **rented car**, though you'd miss the history lessons and local color that you get with a good guide. There is a rental agency or two in San Ignacio (see *Practical Matters*), but the most convenient deal is to pick up a car from one of the half-dozen agencies at the International Airport and head out west (or north, or south).

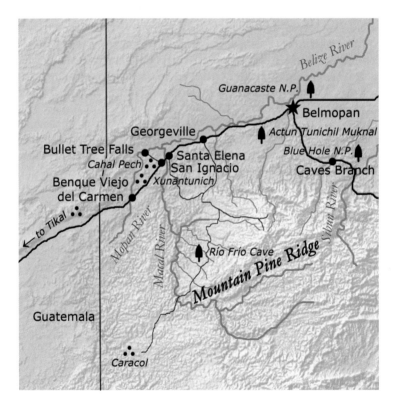

tomb, the resting place of the wife of one of the city's most powerful kings, which is still the tallest structure in Belize. The small museum displays artifacts from the site, as well as exhibits on the ancient Mayan world and the history of the excavation of the site. *Info*: www.caracol.org.

Afternoon
After a few hours at Caracol, we'll head back through the **Mountain Pine Ridge Forest Reserve**, the country's largest protected area. The forests of this highland region are mostly pine trees, rather than the broadleaf species that you see elsewhere in Belize. The area is chock-full of wonderful waterfalls and caves. The pine forest ecosystem is home to rare birds such as orange-breasted falcons, not to mention toucans, parrots, hummingbirds and animals such as coatis.

On our way back to San Ignacio, we'll take a leisurely ride through the Pine Ridge, stopping off to see a waterfall or two and a cave. There are several very nice jungle lodges in the area, including two of Belize's finest, **Hidden Valley Inn** and **Blancaneaux Lodge** (see *Best Sleeps*). Either of these might be a great place to stop for a nice lunch.

Hidden Valley (or Thousand Foot) Falls, up past the Hidden Valley Inn, is the highest of the many waterfalls in the area, the highest in Central America, in fact. They're worth a quick look. We may also visit **Big Rock Falls** near Blancaneaux Lodge, or **Five Sisters Falls**, by the lodge of the same name; both are beautiful places for a swim, with clear pools amid the verdant jungle.

The most popular stops of all, visited by every day tour group, are

the **Río On Pools** and the nearby **Río Frío Cave**. Check out the lovely waterfalls and swim in the warm pools, then explore the large cave. The river running through the cave keeps things cool, and nurtures ferns and mosses.

Evening

No visit to western Belize would be complete without a stop in **San Ignacio** (also known as **Cayo**), the largest town in the region, and a lively little hub of adventure travel and ecotourism. Wide-eyed backpackers roam the streets, courted by tour guides promising days of fun at the ruins, on the rivers or in the caves. **Eva's Restaurant**, on Burns Street in the center of town, is *the* local gathering spot. We'll stop in there for a cold beer and a chat with Bob about what's going on in the region. Alas, I fear it will only get us worked up for the next trip, when we can spend more time here! *Info*: www.evasonline.com; Tel. 804-2267.

A FANTASTIC TIKAL WEEKEND

Tikal National Park, just across the border in **Guatemala**, is the world's largest excavated Mayan site. It's possible to visit Tikal on a day trip from San Ignacio, but it really deserves at least an overnight stay. It's very large and spread-out, so you're going to do a lot of walking if you want to see even half of it. Also, it would be a shame not to be there early in the morning, when the site is shrouded in that mysterious jungle mist, and you're more likely to see some of the birds and other wildlife that abound around the site.

Friday Evening

You can fly to the Guatemalan town of Flores from Belize City, or take a bus or rental car from San Ignacio directly to Tikal National Park. There are three inexpensive hotels adjacent to the park, but none of them have much going for them except proximity to the ruins. The **Tikal Inn**, with its refreshing pool, is the best of the mediocre lot. There are some nicer hotel options along Lake Petén Itzá, a bit less than an hour's drive from the ruins (see *Best Sleeps*).

If we get here early enough, we'll drop by the visitors' center and **line up a guide** for tomorrow morning. It's well worth paying a few bucks to learn about the history of the site, and it's always a good thing to support the local economy. We'll take a guided tour tomorrow morning, then wander about on our own the rest of the day.

Speaking of that pool, it may just be time for a dip and a cold beer, then dinner at our hotel restaurant. There's no big nightlife scene around here, but the hotel bars often harbor some lively conversation among the visitors from all over the world.

Saturday Morning

The name Tikal means "Place of Voices." The voices of the

The Ancient Maya

During their Golden Age (300-900 AD), the Mayans built a highly advanced empire that extended from Mexico through Guatemala and Belize to Honduras. Their calendar and knowledge of astronomy were unequalled until modern times. Their monumental ceremonial sites were the scenes of elaborate rituals, including human sacrifice. Although Mayans continue to live in the area today, their advanced civilization collapsed before the Spanish arrived. The exact reasons for their demise are a mystery, but most scientists agree that climate change and droughts did them in. Some believe that poor stewardship of the environment played a role (sound familiar?). With its wealth of Mayan sites, Belize is an excellent place to explore the history of this fascinating people. To learn more, see:
- www.mayaruins.com
- www.mayan-world.com
- www.mayaweb.nl
- www.lost-civilizations.net
- www.mesoweb.com
- www.gomaya.com

ancient Mayans speak most clearly early in the morning, so we'll be there right at 6am when the gates open. Early morning mist rises from the jungle, revealing the huge stone heads of long-dead kings. Ceiba roots entwine the stones, flocks of colorful parrots flit about, and deer graze irreverently among the ancient palaces.

By late morning, the hot tropical sun has burned off the mist, and the deer are replaced by herds of irreverent gringos, each clad in ball cap and t-shirt, with an ice cream cone in one hand and a water bottle firmly clutched in the other. It's not possible to evade them altogether, but if you time your visit just right, you can avoid the midday rush.

During the Maya's **Classic Period** (around 300-900 AD), Tikal was one of the largest and most powerful city-states in the Mayan world, a metropolis of over 100,000 residents that traded with cultures as far away as Teotihuacan in Mexico, and made war with neighbors such as Caracol and Naranjo. Rulers such as Dark Sun, Stormy Sky and Jaguar Paw built grand palaces, temples and monuments, and recorded their deeds in the Mayan glyphs on **stelae** (stone columns).

Archaeological work at the site began in 1882, but only a fraction of the city of Tikal has yet been excavated. Don't worry though, even that fraction will be enough to keep us stomping about all day: over 3,000 structures, including six large pyramids, 250 stelae, several royal palaces, no less than seven ball courts and hundreds of small residential buildings. The centerpiece is the **Grand Plaza**, where two pyramids, the Temple of the Great Jaguar and the Temple of the Masks, face each other with a large plaza in between, surrounded by dozens of stelae and altars. Around the corner is the complex called the **Lost World**, with a huge pyramid and other structures from several different historical periods.

Visiting Tikal is a good workout, as it is an enormous site. It's no place to visit with small children, or anyone who minds walking. The walk from the entrance to the Grand Plaza is almost a mile. Raised causeways connect other sections of the city. It's another long walk to the **Temple of the Two-headed Serpent**, at 230 feet the tallest Mayan structure in the world. We'll really get a workout as we scramble to the top of the partially excavated pyramid, to be rewarded with a spectacular panorama of the surrounding jungle. The trails that connect the various parts of the site make for a pleasant hike through the jungle. Parrots, toucans, spider and howler monkeys are common, and the partially cleared landscape makes spotting them easier than in the dense jungle.

ALTERNATE PLAN

Lakefront **Santa Elena** is a typically chaotic and colorful little Guatemalan town, and adjacent **Flores** is quite pleasant, on a little island in the lake. If you're traveling by bus or air, you'll probably pass through here anyway, so why not linger a while for lunch and a look at the loud and lively street market?

Saturday Afternoon

When the midday heat starts becoming oppressive, we'll amble back to the hotel and cool off with a quick dip in the pool, then try one of the small *comedores* across from the visitors' center for an authentic Guatemalan lunch. After lunch, we'll visit the two small museums at the site. The Morley Museum, named for a colorful character who was one of the early explorers, displays beautiful ceramic and jade artifacts from the site. At the visitors' center, the most interesting of Tikal's stelae are protected.

In this climate, it makes sense to get up early, as we did, and do our walking around before it gets really hot. We might even indulge in that civilized Spanish/Latin American custom called a *siesta*, and nap for a couple of hours. In the evening, we'll go back into the park for another hour or so, perhaps seeing the **Palace of the Inscriptions**. *Info*: www.tikalpark.com. Tikal National Park is open daily 6am-6pm. Entry is $20 which includes the Morley Museum.

Saturday Evening
The park normally closes at 6pm, but we have heard that on full-moon nights, you can get a special ticket to go in at night – surely a spiritual and spooky experience! Otherwise, it's another night of drinking beer and swapping travel stories at the hotel bar.

Sunday
If we get going fairly early, we'll have time for a little side trip on the way back to San Ignacio (or, if you haven't had your fill of the Mayans, we could certainly spend another morning at Tikal). The stretch of the Western Highway between San Ignacio and the Guatemalan border is sprouting tourist attractions and lodges at a steady pace. The **Belize Botanic Gardens**, next to Du Plooy's lodge, are worth a visit. You could also do a float down the river here. The Lodge at Chaa Creek, with its butterfly breeding center, is also a nice place for a quick stop.

A FANTASTIC CAYO DISTRICT WEEKEND

The sights in this region are endless – and so are the local tour operators eager to show them to you. On this itinerary, we'll try to see a little of everything – rivers, caves, monkeys and Mayans.

Friday
There are lots of nice places to stay in the region. Most are jungle lodges, and they run the scale from budget-priced rustic cabanas to luxurious all-inclusive resorts. If you want an upscale place in the Mountain Pine Ridge area, you'll love the rooms and the personal service at the **Hidden Valley Inn**. If a place on the river

sounds better, try the eco-friendly **Du Plooy's**. If your budget is a little smaller, and you'd like to stay right in town, head for the **San Ignacio Resort Hotel** or **Cahal Pech Village Resort**. One of the best of the really inexpensive lodges is **Midas Tropical Resort**, just outside of town in a pleasant setting on the Macal River (see *Best Sleeps*). Wherever you're staying, I always recommend making a reservation well in advance.

Intercity buses leave Belize City for Cayo about every hour. The local bus takes about four hours, so it may be worth paying a bit more for the more comfortable and faster express bus. Various tour operators operate air-conditioned vans from Belize City to Cayo. Once you get to San Ignacio you can take a van or taxi to your lodge. If you have a rental car, you can drive straight to your lodge, but you should still stop in San Ignacio for a look around.

San Ignacio, also known as **Cayo**, is the largest town in western Belize, and a major center of ecotourism. Cayo serves as a transport hub, a place to stock up on supplies, and headquarters for the area's multitude of tour operators. **Eva's Restaurant**, on Burns Street in the center of town (www.evasonline.com; Tel. 804-2267), is *the* tourist gathering spot. There you'll find all the latest info on hotels, transportation and tours, so you may want to make Eva's your first stop.

Located on the **Macal River** with the sister town of Santa Elena on the other bank, San Ignacio has a more salubrious feel than Belize City, though some neighborhoods are dodgy after dark. You'll meet a broad mixture of people here – locals in town to do some

shopping, travelers en route to and from nearby Guatemala, and of course scads of American and European visitors. There's a good variety of restaurants and bars, and an endless supply of stories to be swapped with hip travelers from all over the world.

San Ignacio is home to a host of tour operators, who can arrange any of an endless list of activities in the nearby wilderness. Canoe trips on the Macal River, birding and hiking trips, horseback riding, mountain biking, caving, visits to the Mayan ruins…the list goes on and on. Contact one of the operators listed in the *Practical Matters* chapter, or simply stop in at Eva's Restaurant and check out the bulletin board.

Saturday
Caracol ("Snail") is the largest Mayan site in Belize. In its heyday, around the seventh century AD, it was one of the largest Mayan cities, with a population of over 140,000 people – twice the size of modern Belize City! Unlike other Lowland Maya cities, Caracol was planned on a large scale, with a radial street plan that covered some 65 square miles. Luxurious objects

of jade and obsidian have been found throughout the city, indicating that the residents of Caracol were especially prosperous. They were also doughty warriors, defeating the mighty city-state of Tikal in a famous battle in 562 AD.

Caracol was occupied as early as 1200 BC, but most of the major monuments were built during the Mayan Classic Period, between about 500-900 AD. The site was "discovered" in 1937. Excavation began in the 1950s and continues today. The site is spectacular, at about 1,500 feet above sea level, with stunning views of the surrounding Maya Mountains. Caracol is about 50 miles south of San Ignacio, through the Mountain Pine Ridge area. The road has recently been improved, so it takes about two hours to get there from San Ignacio.

The excavated area of the site is pretty large, with several tombs and temples, and a ball court. The high point of the city, both literally and figuratively, is a complex of structures called **Caana**. Here is a very elaborate tomb, believed to be the resting place of the wife of one of the city's most powerful kings. The magnificent pyramid of Caana remains the highest man-made structure in Belize. You can climb to the top to enjoy a spectacular view – nothing but uninhabited forest for miles and miles.

There's a small museum with lots of artifacts from the site, as well as exhibits on the ancient Mayan world and the history of the excavation of the site. You can arrange a tour through any of the local tour operators or lodges. Most visitors opt for an all-day tour: you'll spend the morning at Caracol, then visit a couple of other points of interest on the way back, perhaps the **Río On Pools** for a cooling swim. *Info*: www.caracol.org.

The **Mountain Pine Ridge Forest Reserve** is the country's largest protected area, 300 square miles of wilderness that forms a distinct ecosystem. The Caribbean pine trees contrast with the broadleaf species that dominate the forests in most of Belize. The backbone of the landscape is mostly solid granite, which explains the large number of waterfalls and caves in the area. The wildlife, and especially the birds, are a little different than you'll see elsewhere. Rare orange-breasted falcons, Stygian owls and ocellated turkeys join more commonly seen birdies such as toucans, parrots, hummingbirds and woodpeckers. Baird's tapir, pumas, jaguars and ocelots prowl at night.

This vast uninhabited area is traversed by a few graded dirt roads that are kept in pretty good repair and should be passable in an ordinary car, except during periods of heavy rain. There are several very nice jungle lodges in the area, including two of Belize's finest, **Hidden Valley Inn** and **Blancaneaux Lodge** (see *Best Sleeps*). Many day tours stop off at one or more of Mountain Pine Ridge's attractions on the way back from a visit to the Caracol archaeological site.

Hidden Valley (or Thousand Foot) Falls, up past the Hidden Valley Inn, is the highest of the many waterfalls in the area, the highest in Central America, in fact. They're worth a quick look. There's an overlook with a picnic area that's easy to reach by road. Near Blancaneaux Lodge, **Big Rock Falls** are shorter, wider and more interesting, and there are nice pools where you can swim. On the grounds of **Five Sisters Lodge**, the falls of the same name are another beautiful place for a swim.

The most popular stops of all, visited by every day-tour group, are the **Río On Pools** and the nearby **Río Frío Cave**. Check out the lovely waterfalls and swim in the warm pools, then explore the large cave. The river running through the cave keeps things cool, and nurtures ferns and mosses.

Sunday
This region has all kinds of wonderful eco-adventures for us to get into for a half or full day. Look for some of the 300 species of birds that hang around the **Belize Botanic Gardens**. Learn about the life cycle of butterflies at the **Green Hills Butterfly Farm**. Ride horses through the jungle from the **Windy Hill Resort** equestrian center. Take a rafting trip on the **Macal River**, or a canoe trip through **Barton Creek Cave**.

There are a couple of interesting attractions right around San Ignacio. The **Green Iguana Project** at the San Ignacio Resort Hotel is a must if you are traveling with kids. The resort also has some very easy jungle trails. The small Mayan site of **Cahal Pech** is well worth a visit, and offers a panoramic view.

There are also several worthwhile sights along the Western Highway, so if you're driving back to Belize City, you could easily stop off at **Guanacaste National Park**, **Caves Branch** or the **Belize Zoo**.

A WONDERFUL WEEK IN WESTERN BELIZE

A week would give you time to see the best of the **Mayan sites**, hike through the **Mountain Pine Ridge**, visit a **cave** or two, and do some **rafting** on the river. But that would still only be a taste of all there is to see in this region.

RECOMMENDED PLAN: Most of the sights covered in this chapter are in pretty easy day-trip range, whether you stay around **Cayo** or at one of the nearby lodges, so choose the option that fits your personality. If you thrive on the touristy bustle, stay in Cayo. If you'd rather have trackless jungle all around, stay at a remote lodge. Spend at least two nights at **Tikal**.

Belmopan

The Belizean government moved the capital to the newly-built city of **Belmopan** in 1970, a few years after Hurricane Hattie wiped out a big chunk of Belize City. Everything about the new city was planned. The name is a combination of "Belize" and "Mopan," one of the rivers in the area. The government buildings were designed to resemble stylized versions of Mayan temples, and they are set in parklike grounds studded with beautiful poinciana trees, and connected by pedestrian walkways.

Despite (or because of) the careful planning, the city has grown very slowly. The US embassy was relocated here from Belize City only in 2006. Many government workers still commute from Belize City. Belize's **National Museum** is apparently still in limbo. Formerly located in Belize City, it was supposed to reopen in Belmopan in 2005, but as of this writing, this hasn't happened. So, unless you're interested in the dos

Don't Miss ...

Tikal – This is the ultimate Mayan site, just over the border in Guatemala.
Caracol – Once a major rival of Tikal, this large Mayan site makes a wonderful day trip.
Mountain Pine Ridge – The largest protected area in Belize, this fascinating pine forest hides many beautiful waterfalls and caves.
Caves Branch – Tubing through the caves is one of the country's top tourist draws, and spelunkers will find plenty of other caves to explore.
Cayo Jungle Lodges – Explore the jungles on foot or horseback, and the rivers in a canoe or an inner tube.

and don'ts of city planning, there's nothing in particular for a tourist to see here. However, if you take a bus to any place in Western Belize, you will be stopping here to change buses, whether you want to or not. There is a selection of good restaurants, and a couple of decent places to stay (see *Best Sleeps*). *Info*: www.belmopancityonline.com.

Guanacaste National Park

This tiny (50 acre) park, run by the Belize Audubon Society, is located at the intersection of the Western Highway and the Hummingbird Highway. It makes a very convenient place for a quick walk or a picnic on your way to the Cayo district.

The park is named for a huge **guanacaste tree** overlooking the river near the entrance. The guanacaste (also known as tubroos or monkey's ear tree) can grow to heights of over 130 feet, and is a commercially important tree in Belize. The seed pods are used for cattle feed, and the wood is used to make the dugout canoes that locals call *doreys*. This particular tree escaped being made into a boat because its trunk divided into three at an early age. Today it's a huge spreading old gentleman, covered with epiphytic bromeliads.

Two miles of walking trails feature labels for many other native plants, including mammee apple and mahogany trees, and Belize's national flower, the black orchid. You may also spot a trogon, motmot, kingfisher, magnolia warbler, red-lored parrot or one of over 120 bird species. Deer, kinkajous, pacas, agoutis and enormous iguanas are common. The river is a nice place for a cooling swim. *Info*: There's a small visitors' center and gift shop, where you'll pay the entry fee of $2.50. Opening hours are 8am-4:30pm. www.belizeaudubon.org/parks/guanacaste.htm.

Blue Hole National Park

This park, on the Hummingbird Highway a few miles southeast of Belmopan, covers 575 acres, some of which is primary forest (never logged).

The sinkhole for which the park is named is not to be confused with the more famous Blue Hole offshore (see Chapter 4), but it does resemble it a bit – 25 feet deep and filled with bright sapphire-blue water, it's a capital place for a swim.

The other main attraction here is **Saint Herman's Cave**. This remarkable karst cavern is probably the easiest cave to visit in the country. You can take a peek inside on your own, but to take the grand tour, you'll need a local guide (easily arranged at the visitors' center). You can also take a guided tour of **Crystalline Cave**, where you'll see 2,000-year-old Mayan artifacts and human skeletons calcified in the limestone.

There are five miles of well-marked hiking trails, several picnic areas and a campsite. Over 200 species of birds have been sighted, including trogons, motmots, honeycreepers and cotingas. Other residents include deer, agoutis, tapirs, peccaries and anteaters. A few very fortunate souls have sighted jaguars, ocelots and jaguarundis. *Info*: Entry $4. Open daily 8am-4:30pm. www.belizeaudubon.org/parks/bhnp.htm.

Caves Branch

Western Belize is a spelunker's dream. The limestone landscape

is riddled with caves, sinkholes and underground rivers. Caves were sacred spots to the ancient Maya, who called the underworld **Xibalba**, and all sorts of artifacts, skeletons and such have been found in caves in the area, some of them entombed forever in limestone.

The big daddy of caving in Belize is Ian Anderson, a Canadian who began exploring the caves and caverns of the region in the early 1990s, and now presides over an empire of adventure travel that includes a jungle lodge just south of Belmopan and a wide variety of tours in the area. The nearby **Jaguar Paw Resort** is a worthy competitor. *Info*: www.jaguarpaw.com; Tel. 820-2023 or

877/624-3770 in the US. Lots of operators run cave tours (and especially cave tubing trips) in this area, but if you're a serious spelunker, **Ian Anderson's Caves Branch Adventure Company** is the place to go. *Info*: www.cavesbranch.com.

River tubing is an extremely popular activity all over western Belize. Here on the Caves Branch River, you can combine tubing (or kayaking) and caving, as the river runs through several underground caverns. It's quite an adventure to float through the darkness, stalagmites sticking up from the river and stalactites hanging from the roof. Underground waterfalls thunder, and openings let in rays of light from the jungle above. Shorter tubing trips are suitable for everyone, but longer trips involve some hiking, both above and below ground. Ian's flagship full-day trip includes over seven miles underground.

Cave tubing is perhaps the single most popular activity on mainland Belize, attracting day-trippers from the many lodges in the area, as well as huge hordes from the cruise ships. During the high tourist season, the masses of tubes jostling down the river seem more like a water ride at Disney World than the wilds of Central America.

Another popular spot is **Crystal Cave**, one of the largest caves in Belize. Here are spectacular crystal stalactites, stalagmites and fanciful formations. Two millennia ago, this was a major ceremonial center for the Maya. Paintings and carvings adorn the walls, and all kinds of artifacts and skeletons have been found here.

Local resorts offer all kinds of activities in addition to caving. Jungle hikes, mountain biking, rappelling, rock climbing and ziplines are on the menu. Horseback riding trips from nearby **Banana Bank** are highly recommended (see *Best Sleeps*). *Info*: www.bananabank.com.

San Ignacio (Cayo)

San Ignacio, also known as **Cayo**, or **El Cayo de San Ignacio**, is the largest town in western Belize (about 14,000 people), and a major center of ecotourism. Although San Ignacio has a good selection of budget lodgings, most visitors to the region don't stay right in town, but rather in one of the jungle lodges in the surrounding countryside. Cayo serves as a transport hub, a place to stock up on supplies, and headquarters for the area's multitude of tour operators. **Eva's Restaurant**, on Burns Street in the center of town, is *the* gathering spot for visitors. There you'll find all the latest info on hotels, transportation and tours, so you may want to make Eva's your first stop. *Info*: www.evasonline.com; Tel. 804-2267.

Intercity buses leave Belize City for Cayo about every hour. *Info*: Tel. 227-7372. The local bus takes about four hours, so it may be worth paying a bit more for the more comfortable and faster express bus. Various tour operators operate air-conditioned vans from Belize City to Cayo. Ask at your hotel or at Eva's for details.

Located on the Macal River with the sister town of Santa Elena on the other bank, San Ignacio has a more salubrious feel than Belize City, though some neighborhoods are dodgy after dark. You'll meet a broad mixture of people here – locals in town to do some shopping, travelers en route to and from nearby Guatemala, and of course scads of American and European visitors. There's a good variety of restaurants and bars, and an endless supply of stories to be swapped with hip travelers from all over the world.

The **San Ignacio Resort Hotel** operates the **Green Iguana Project**,

which is well worth a visit, especially if you are traveling with kids. Green iguanas – very cute when they're small, dinosaurish and scary-looking (but harmless) when they get big – are a vital part of the jungle ecosystem. In many parts of Central America, they're endangered, mainly because locals like to eat them. The resort runs a captive breeding program, incubating and hatching the eggs and releasing juvenile iguanas into the wild.

The exhibit is well-organized and informative, and takes about an hour to see. Also here is a **Medicinal Jungle Trail**, where you can learn about the many native plants that are used as medicine in traditional Mayan and African cultures. This is part of a network of trails that traverse the resort's 14-acre jungle preserve, the home of animals such as gibnuts, agoutis, armadillos, and over 150 species of birds. Some of the trails are very easy, and would be an excellent choice for older (or younger) travelers who may not be up for a strenuous jungle hike.

San Ignacio is home to a host of tour operators who can arrange any of an endless list of activities in the nearby wilderness. Look for some of the 300 species of birds that hang around the **Belize Botanic Gardens**. Learn about the life cycle of butterflies at the **Green Hills Butterfly Farm**. Ride horses through the jungle from the **Windy Hill Resort** equestrian center. Take a rafting trip on the **Macal River**, or a canoe trip through **Barton Creek Cave**. Contact one of the operators listed in the *Practical Matters* chapter, or simply stop in at Eva's Restaurant and check out the bulletin board.

Cahal Pech

This Mayan site in the hills above San Ignacio is well worth a visit. Although it's much smaller than Caracol, Xunantunich or Tikal, the site is beautiful, amid bird-infested jungle with an awesome view of the Maya Mountains and the Belize River valley, and it's easily accessible from San Ignacio. Don't let the name, which means "place of ticks," put you off.

Cahal Pech was occupied as early as 1200 BC, making it one of the earliest Maya settlements in Belize. It is believed to have been a major trading center that had contact with other Mayan city-states in Guatemala and the Olmec to the north. The site consists of 34 structures on a two-acre site, including pyramid temples (the tallest is 77 feet high), palaces, two ball courts, and one of the earliest carved stelae in the region. Cahal Pech was abandoned around 800 AD, during the Maya Collapse.

Caracol

Caracol ("Snail") is the largest Mayan site in Belize. In its heyday,

around the seventh century AD, it was one of the largest Mayan cities, with a population of over 140,000 people – twice the size of modern Belize City! Unlike other Lowland Maya cities, Caracol was planned on a large scale, with a radial street plan that covered some 65 square miles. Luxurious objects of jade and obsidian have been found throughout the city, indicating that the residents of Caracol were especially prosperous. They were also doughty warriors, defeating the mighty city-state of Tikal in a famous battle in 562 AD.

Caracol was occupied as early as 1200 BC, but most of the major monuments were built during the Mayan Classic Period, between about 500-900 AD. The site was "discovered" in 1937. Excavation began in the 1950s and continues today. The setting is spectacular, at 1,500 feet above sea level, with stunning views of the surrounding Maya Mountains. Caracol is about a 50-mile ride south of San Ignacio, through the Mountain Pine Ridge area. The road has recently been improved, so it takes around two hours to get there from San Ignacio.

The excavated area of the site is pretty large, with several tombs and temples, and a ball court. The high point of the city, both literally and figuratively, is a complex of structures called **Caana**. Here is a very elaborate tomb, believed to be the resting place of the wife of one of the city's most powerful kings. The magnificent pyramid of Caana remains the highest man-made structure in Belize. You can climb to the top to enjoy a spectacular view – nothing but uninhabited forest for miles and miles.

There's a small museum on-site with lots of artifacts from the site, as well as exhibits on the ancient Mayan world and the history of the excavation. You can arrange a tour through any of the local tour operators or lodges. Most visitors opt for an all-day tour:

you'll spend the morning at Caracol, then visit a couple of other points of interest on the way back, perhaps the **Río On Pools** for a cooling swim. *Info*: www.caracol.org.

Xunantunich

This Mayan site is about eight miles west of San Ignacio, on a hill above the Mopan River. The name means "Stone Woman," a reference to a ghost that several people claim to have seen climbing the steps of El Castillo, and then walking through a stone wall. Getting here includes taking a quaint hand-cranked ferry across the river from the little village of San José Succotz.

Xunantunich was an important ceremonial center, with six plazas and over 25 temples and palaces. Historians believe that the city was an up-and-coming power, but was abandoned after an earthquake destroyed part of the city. The largest structure is the pyramid called El Castillo, which rises 130 feet above the jungle, Belize's second-highest structure after Caana at Caracol. The view from the top is an awesome panorama of Belizean and Guatemalan jungle. A finely-detailed frieze depicting the sun god, attended by the moon and the planets once encircled the entire pyramid, but only about half of it is still intact (actually, as at many Mayan sites, what you see here is a plaster reproduction – the original has been covered up to protect it from the elements).

Xunantunich was "discovered" by a British medical officer named Thomas Gann in the 1890s. Gann is suspected of removing several art treasures from the site. Anyway, various important artifacts disappeared, and no one knows exactly where they are today.

There's a nice visitors' center with a museum featuring a scale model of the site, three stelae from the site and exhibits on the history of the city. *Info*: Open daily 8am-4pm. Entry $10.

Actun Tunichil Muknal

This cave, called ATM for short, was an important ceremonial

center for the Maya. Here they sacrificed young virgins to the rain god Chac. During the Terminal Classic era, the Maya performed these ceremonies ever more often and ever deeper into the cave, as they strove to appease the gods and end the terrible droughts that finally did them in.

The cave was only discovered in 1989 and opened to the public in 1998, and all the artifacts have been left exactly where they were found. You can visit only as part of an organized tour, which you can arrange through your lodge or any of the tour operators in San Ignacio. It's a fairly strenuous trip. To get here, you ride 45 minutes from San Ignacio, and then hike 45 minutes through the **Tapir Mountain Nature Reserve**, crossing three streams on the way. Once you get to the cave, you actually have to swim a short way, and there are several more spots inside where you'll have to wade. And that water is cold! I recommend bringing a large Ziploc bag or two for your camera and a change of clothes. The site can be a bit of a circus during tourist season – there'll be lots of groups visiting and, unlike at large sites like Tikal, you don't have much room to spread out in a cave.

The wonders of ATM are many. There are beautiful stalagmites and stalactites, some of them carved by the Maya so that a light placed in the right spot casts the shadow of a human figure on the wall. There are chambers strewn with ceramic pots and stoneware. There are altars where the Mayan elite performed bloodletting ceremonies, piercing themselves with stingray spines in order to talk to the gods. And of course, there are the macabre skeletal remains of 14 humans, which lie encrusted with calcium that leached from the limestone over the centuries. The most famous of these is the **Crystal Maiden**, the skeleton of a young girl that has become encased in sparkling calcite.

In the immediate area are a couple of other caves, which serious spelunkers or Maya buffs may arrange to visit. **Actun Nak Beh** contains a few human burials and shards of pottery. **Actun Uayazba Kab**, the "Cave of the Handprints" has a very unusually shaped mouth, and extensive carvings, including a large turtle that is believed to have figured in coming-of-age ceremonies, as well as four painted handprints on the walls. In the center of a triangle formed by the three caves is **Cahal Uitz Na**, the "Place of the Mountain House," a ceremonial center consisting of a plaza with six stelae, surrounded by several temples and a ball court.

Cayo Jungle Lodges

Wherever you stay in the Cayo District, you can visit any of the forests, rivers and caves of the region by taking day trips with any of the hordes of local tour operators (or, if you have a car, by driving around on your own). This can get a little hectic however, and some tour operators will charge you extra if they have to pick you up from a remote lodge. To get the most for your time and money, it makes sense to choose a lodge that offers activities that interest you right on-site.

If you're into birding, you'll love **Du Plooy's**, a very ecologically-oriented lodge right on the Macal River, with the Belize Botanic Gardens next door. Expert bird guides on staff can show you some of the 300 species that hang out in the area. If horseback riding interests you, check out **Windy Hill Resort**, which has an equestrian center and a central location that's convenient for day trips. **Black Rock Lodge** is another eco-friendly establishment directly on the Macal River, surrounded by rain forest, mountains and waterfalls. See *Best Sleeps* for details on these and other area lodges.

Mountain Pine Ridge

The **Mountain Pine Ridge Forest Reserve** is the country's largest protected area, 300 square miles of wilderness that forms a distinct ecosystem. The Caribbean pine trees contrast with the broadleaf species that dominate the forests in most of Belize. The backbone of the landscape is mostly solid granite, which explains the large number of waterfalls and caves in the area. Looking at the pine trees, red clay soil and granite outcroppings, you might almost think you're in Georgia.

The wildlife, and especially the birds, are a little different here than you'll see elsewhere. Rare orange-breasted falcons, Stygian owls and ocellated turkeys join more commonly-seen birdies such as toucans, parrots, hummingbirds and woodpeckers. Baird's tapir, pumas, jaguars and ocelots prowl at night.

Bark Beetle Infestation

Nasty little bugs called **bark beetles** went crazy in 2001, and infested some 20% of all the pine trees in Belize. Mountain Pine Ridge was especially hard-hit, with 80% of the trees killed! The forest service has been pretty successful at combating the little buggers, and the pines are now almost fully recovered. A silver lining is that the country is now a little bit more open than it was before, making it easier to see the huge variety of birds, who are just as abundant as ever.

This vast uninhabited area is traversed by a few graded dirt roads that are kept in pretty good repair, and should be passable in an ordinary car, except during periods of heavy rain. There are several very nice jungle lodges in the area, including two of Belize's finest, **Hidden Valley Inn** and **Blancaneaux Lodge** (see *Best Sleeps*). Many day tours stop off at one or more of Mountain Pine Ridge's attractions on the way back from a visit to the Caracol archaeological site.

Hidden Valley (or Thousand Foot) Falls, up past the Hidden Valley Inn, is the highest of the many waterfalls in the area, the highest in Central America, in fact. They're worth a quick look. There's an overlook with a picnic area that's easy to reach by road. Near Blancaneaux Lodge,

Big Rock Falls are shorter, wider and more interesting, and there are nice pools where you can swim. On the grounds of **Five Sisters Lodge**, the falls of the same name are another beautiful place for a swim.

The most popular stops of all, visited by every day tour group, are the **Río On Pools** and the nearby **Río Frío Cave**. Check out the lovely waterfalls and swim in the warm pools, then explore the large cave. The river running through the cave keeps things cool, and nurtures ferns and mosses.

Tikal Ruins, Guatemala
One of Belize's most popular tourist destinations isn't in Belize at all, but rather just across the border in Guatemala. **Tikal** is the world's largest excavated Mayan site. Today it's a UNESCO World Heritage Site, and Guatemala's most popular national park.

Some of Tikal's monuments have been dated as far back as the fourth century BC. During the Maya's Classic Period (around 300-900 AD), Tikal was one of the largest and most powerful city-states in the Mayan world, a metropolis of over 100,000 residents that traded with cultures as far away as Teotihuacan in Mexico, and a military power that made war with neighbors such as Caracol and Naranjo.

During the Maya's **Early Classic period**, Tikal was the dominant power in the region, led by such rulers as Dark Sun, Stormy Sky and Jaguar Paw, who built a fine palace that survives today. Around 562 AD however, Tikal lost a lengthy war with nearby Caracol. This was followed by a century or so when no large monuments were built at Tikal, a period researchers call the "Tikal hiatus," and which divides Mayan history into the Early and Late Classic periods. In 682 AD, the ruler Jasaw Chan K'awiil I (or Ah Cacau) and his queen Lady Twelve Macaw began to restore Tikal's former glory, defeating Calakmul in a bloody battle in 711. Later rulers built the city's most impressive temples and tombs, but as the Maya declined, Tikal was abandoned by the end of the 10th century.

Tikal was mentioned in John Lloyd Stephens's 1841 book *Incidents of Travel in Central America, Chiapas and Yucatan*, and the first scientific expedition arrived in 1848. In 1882, Sir Arthur Percival Maudslay began clearing the forest, and made the first drawings and photos of the site. Other important early researchers were Teobert Mahler and Sylvanus Morley (a fascinating character whose archaeological travels provided cover for his WWI espionage activities). The raised causeways that connect sections of the city have been named for some of the important researchers.

Even after many years of work, only a fraction of the city of Tikal has yet been excavated. That fraction however, is so large that a long day is barely enough time to see it all. Archaeologists have found over 3,000 structures, including six large pyramids, 250 stelae, several royal palaces, no less than seven ball courts, hundreds of small residential homes and even a building that seems to have been a jail.

The centerpiece of the city is the **Grand Plaza**. Here two pyramids face each other with

Traveling to Tikal

Many visitors take a guided tour from Belize, but you can get to Tikal by car or public transport and hire a guide at the site. Some buses from Belize City go to Melchor de Mencos on the Guatemalan side, where you can catch a bus for Flores or for Tikal. Both Maya Island Air and Tropic Air offer two flights per day from Goldson International to Flores, which is about a 45-minute ride from Tikal. Border formalities are no major hassle. Visa requirements are similar to those for Belize. You will have to pay your $40 (!) departure tax, even if you're just going for the day. If you're driving, expect your car's papers to be closely scrutinized. Guatemala has a far higher crime rate than does Belize, and tourists have been robbed on some of the isolated trails at Tikal. Recently-deployed Tourist Police have made things much better, but be more cautious on this side of the border.

a large plaza in between, one of several sets of twin pyramids here at Tikal. The Temple of the Great Jaguar was built by the king Ah Cacau around 700 AD, and contains his tomb. The Temple of the Masks, named for the carved faces on its lintel, was built for his queen

(naturally it's a little smaller). The Grand Plaza is an enormous and very complex site in itself, with a huge palace and dozens of stelae and altars.

Around the corner from the Grand Plaza is an area called El Mundo Perdido, or the **Lost World**, a large complex centered on an enormous pyramid. Here are all kinds of sinister structures, including the Temple of the Skulls, and a mysterious tunnel with an entrance shaped like the mouth of a snake. The interesting thing about this complex is that you can see structures from several different historical periods, which is unusual, as the Mayans usually built new temples on top of older ones.

A good walk along the Tozzer Causeway brings you to the **Temple of the Two-headed Serpent**, at 230 feet the tallest existing Mayan structure. It was built by the ruler Yik'in Chan Kawil in 741 AD. The pyramid is only partially excavated, so it's a hardscrabble climb to the top, but the physically fit will be rewarded with a spectacular panorama of the surrounding jungle. In fact, you'd better be pretty fit to visit Tikal, as it is an enormous site. The walk from the entrance to the Grand Plaza is almost a mile, and you'll walk many miles by the time you've seen most of it. Walking the trails that connect the various parts of the site is quite pleasant (but hot), as the jungle grows all around and within the park. You'll see huge ceiba (*kapok*) trees, which were sacred to the Maya, as well as mahogany and sapodilla (*chicle*). Spider and howler monkeys are common, and coatis and other small mammals are not rare. Don't stand below monkeys in trees!

Birding here is wonderful – parrots, toucans and other rarer species abound, the partially cleared landscape makes spotting them easy, and the pyramids make splendid viewing platforms. There are two small museums at the site. The **Morley Museum** displays beautiful ceramic and jade artifacts from the site. At the visitors' center, the most interesting of Tikal's stelae are protected. Adjacent to the park are three hotels, a campground and a few small eateries (see *Best Sleeps*). *Info*: www.tikalpark.com. Tikal National Park is open daily 6am-6pm. Entry is $20 which includes the Morley Museum.

7. SOUTHERN BELIZE

The southern **Stann Creek** and **Toledo** districts are far less known to outsiders than are the Cayes and the Cayo district. This is starting to change, as **Placencia** is evolving into one of the country's top beach resorts, but much of the region is still off the beaten path.

Down south you'll find **some of Belize's best beaches**, isolated islands offering delightful diving and fantastic fishing, jungle reserves teeming with birds and wildlife, and more mysterious Mayan ruins.

ONE GREAT DAY AT COCKSCOMB BASIN

If you have only a day, your best bet is to head for Cockscomb Basin Wildlife Sanctuary, also known as the Jaguar Reserve. This is one of the largest and nicest wildlife reserves in Belize, and it's easy to visit, even on a short trip. The 128,000-acre park is the world's only official jaguar sanctuary, and 60-80 of Belize's largest pussycats roam the mountains and river valleys.

Morning

The gateway to the park is **Maya Center**, home to a couple dozen local families who were relocated here when Cockscomb was declared a wildlife sanctuary. The villagers support themselves by providing guided tours, lodging and other services to park visitors. Although many tour operators can take you to the Reserve, the local guides from Maya Center are the best. These guys know the forest better than you and I know the way to our local post office, and if we call ahead, they're happy to pick us up from our lodge in Hopkins (or wherever) and take us straight to jaguar country. *Info*: www.mayacenter.com; Tel. 520-3044.

Cockscomb features an excellent network of **well-maintained trails** of various levels of difficulty. We'll hike along the river

through some of the lushest rain forest in Belize, admiring the orchids and bromeliads, and checking off a few of the over 300 species of birds. All five of Belize's cat species live here, as does the rare Baird's tapir (see photo on page 123). Even here in the heart of **jaguar country**, we're not likely to see one of these shy nocturnal predators. We may very well see their tracks, however, and we're almost certain to

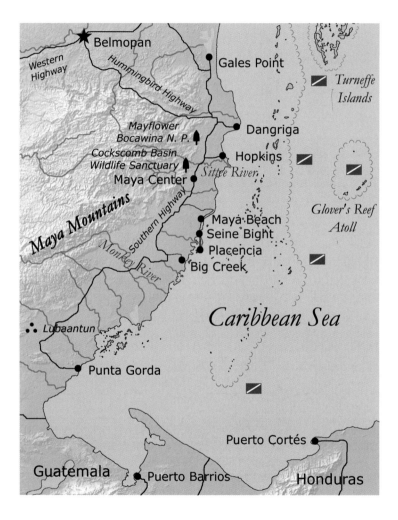

hear one of the troops of black howler monkeys that live in the area. After a couple of hours of hiking, we'll stop at one of the lovely waterfall pools and cool down with a swim.

Afternoon
On our way back, we'll make a short stop at the **Maya Center Women's Group Gift Shop**, where you'll find nice wood and stone carvings, woven apparel and jewelry, most with the obligatory jaguar and/or ancient Mayan imagery. This is what the local women do while the men are leading tours in the jungle, and it provides another way for the locals to make some money and preserve their beautiful forest.

If we still have some time, we might pay a brief visit to Dangriga, the largest town in Southern Belize and the country's center of **Garifuna** culture. This colorful and funky town is the home of the **Punta Rock** style of music, and some of Belize's best folk musicians. The sound of drums pulsates through the city night and day.

The **Gulisi Garifuna Museum** has exhibits on the history and customs of this fascinating people, including dancing, drum-making and traditional medicine. *Info*: Open Mon-Fri 10am-5pm, Sat 8am-noon. Entry $2.50. www.ngcbelize.org.

There are several local artists and craftsmen who welcome visits to their studios. **Austin Rodriquez** makes traditional Garifuna drums, and **Benjamin Nicholas** paints charming paintings depicting events in Garifuna history.

A FANTASTIC HOPKINS AREA WEEKEND

The sleepy Garifuna fishing village of **Hopkins** is conveniently located for trips to the forests of **Cockscomb** and **Mayflower**, as well as for the **excellent reefs** just offshore. With careful planning, we can get in visits to the rain forest and the mangroves, with some time left over for enjoying one of the finest beaches in Belize.

Friday Evening
This pleasant little town has a long sandy beach, and a wide selection of waterfront lodgings in all price ranges. **Hamanasi** and **Jaguar Reef** are both excellent luxury lodges. Travelers with moderate budgets will be delighted with the friendly **Hopkins Inn**. Even if you have a backpacker budget, you can stay right on the beach, at **Tipple Tree Beya** or the **Seagull's Nest** (see *Best Sleeps*).

Despite the increasing number of tourists, Hopkins remains a fairly low-key village where the locals slowly go about their age-old business of fishing, drumming and carving dugout canoes. After we've lined up a tour for tomorrow morning, let's stroll around and soak up some of the thick Garifuna culture. We can have dinner at **King Kasava's**, the main hangout in town, featuring cheap meals, stout drinks and colorful characters. We'll also pay a visit to **Lebeha**, a center for the local music scene. By day, it's a school where local youngsters take lessons in traditional Garifuna drumming. By night, it's a bar with a kicking drum jam where local musicians slap the skins until the wee hours. We'll head back to our hotel fairly early though, because we plan to be up at dawn to visit the rain forest.

Saturday
Cockscomb Basin Wildlife Sanctuary, also known as the Jaguar Reserve, is one of the largest and nicest wildlife reserves in Belize. It was established in 1990 to protect one of Central America's largest remaining populations of jaguars. The reserve includes some of the lushest rain forest in Belize, thick with orchids and bromeliads, and over 300 species of birds. It's home to all five of Belize's cat species – jaguar, puma, margay, ocelot and jaguarundi – as well as the rare Baird's tapir (see photo), gibnuts, kinkajous, armadillos, boa constrictors and deadly fer-de-lance vipers. Even here in the heart of jaguar country, your chances of seeing

one of these shy nocturnal predators are almost nil. You may very well see their tracks, however, and you are likely to see (and will certainly hear) black howler monkeys.

Various local tour operators offer guided tours to the reserve, but the best deal is to hire a local guide directly from **Maya Center**, a village near the entrance to the sanctuary. Before the establishment of the park, the area was home to a few dozen Maya families, who were relocated to Maya Center and trained to support themselves by guiding visitors to the rain forest (instead of cutting it down to grow crops). This is a classic ecotourism success story that we want to support with a few of our dollars. If we contact the Maya Center guides ahead of time, they'll pick us up from Hopkins. *Info*: www.mayacenter.com; Tel. 520-3044.

ALTERNATE PLAN
Cockscomb Basin is the most popular park in the area, largely because it's so easily accessible, but it's far from the only one. In fact, over half the interior of this district is protected as some sort of park or reserve. If you'd like to get off the beaten tourist trail a little, visit **Mayflower Bocawina National Park** with its three small Mayan sites and the 100-foot-high **Antelope Falls**.

Cockscomb features an excellent network of well-maintained trails of various levels of difficulty. We'll spend a few hours hiking along the river, or perhaps up to Ben's Bluff, an overlook with a panoramic view of the undisturbed forest. Later on we'll cool down with a swim near one of the many lovely waterfalls.

Sunday
Just south of Hopkins is the estuary of the **Sittee River**, a beautiful area of mangroves, marshes and lagoons that offers a nice contrast to mountainous Cockscomb. A river cruise with local guide **Horace Andrews** is one of the very best ways to see wildlife (and also a good way to rest our feet after all that hiking yesterday). We'll see turtles, crocodiles and iguanas, and some of the 200 species of birds that hang out around the river, from water birds such as tiger herons and snowy egrets to jungle birds such as oropendolas, chachalacas, trogons and parrots. If you prefer fish,

Horace can put us on to them too. Anglers bag snook up to 26 pounds and tarpon from 10-70 pounds in the nearby Anderson and Boom Creek lagoons. *Info*: www.belizebyhorace.com; Tel. 603-8358.

A FANTASTIC PLACENCIA AREA WEEKEND

The pleasant peninsula of **Placencia** might just be the perfect spot for a "surf and turf" vacation – let's find out! We'll spend a day out in the Caribbean on a tiny caye, and a day cruising up a jungle river, getting glimpses of the two most biologically diverse habitats on Earth in a single weekend.

Friday Evening

Placencia is easy to get to. Both Maya Island Air and Tropic Air offer several daily flights from Belize City. We can fly to Belize City from the States, change planes, and be at Placencia's little airstrip in the afternoon. Our hotel will send a van to pick us up, and we'll be on island time in no time.

There's a huge selection of lodging in all price ranges, both on the peninsula and in the surrounding area. We plan a day of diving tomorrow, so we may choose one of the resorts that run their own dive operations: the **Inn at Robert's Grove**; **Rum Point Inn** or the super-luxurious **Blancaneaux's Turtle Inn**. Those with more moderate budgets will like the **Sea Spray** or **One World**. See *Best Sleeps* for more information on these.

Wherever we stay, the first order of business on arrival is to remove shirt, shoes and wristwatch, grab an ice-cold beverage, and mosey on over to the beach or the pool.

Once we're properly refreshed from our travels, we'll take a stroll down Placencia's sidewalk, famous as the narrowest main street in the world, line up a dive trip for tomorrow morning, and see about a lobster dinner. Placencia is slowly but surely evolving into a major resort, but it still has a low-key, island-time vibe, more like Caye Caulker than like Ambergris Caye. It's one of the oldest communities in Belize. The ancient Mayans came here for fish and salt. British buccaneers founded the village in the 1600s, and it changed hands between the Spanish and the English a time or two. Today's residents are a broad mix of Creoles, Garifuna, Mestizos and plenty of Anglo expats.

Let's stop in at one (or both) of the two main local hangouts: the **Pickled Parrot** and the **Tipsy Tuna**. Either is a good place to have a cold beer (or the more adventurous may try a glass of "parrot piss") and a chat with some of the locals, expats and tourists propping up the bar at happy hour. When we get hungry, we can grab an inexpensive burger or plate of shrimp here, or we can head back to our hotel for a sit-down dinner. In either case, we'll hit the hay early tonight, so we can hit the reefs early tomorrow. *Info*: www.placencia.com.

Saturday

In the morning, we'll slug down a cup of fresh Belizean coffee, and stumble down to the end of the dock to meet our boat for a trip to the reefs. The barrier reef is quite close to shore in this area, and there's an endless selection of sites for diving and snorkeling. If you leave yourself in the hands of your divemaster, you're almost certain to be delighted with the sites he selects. Today however, we're going to visit some of the most pristine dive sites in the country, off the most remote of Belize's three coral atolls, **Glover's Reef Atoll**. An atoll is a ring of coral reefs surrounding a shallow lagoon. An atoll is formed when coral reefs grow around the shoreline of an island, then the island itself erodes away as the reefs continue to grow.

Glover's Reef, a protected Marine Reserve and a UNESCO World Heritage Site, offers a vast variety of dive sites for all skill levels, from snorkelers to expert divers. **Emerald Forest Reef** is an excellent site for snorkelers and novice divers, with depths of 15-

70 feet, no current, and an amazing abundance of coral providing food and shelter to crabs, sea urchins, starfish and sponges, who are eaten in their turn by large jacks, snapper and grouper. Speaking of which, **Grouper Flats**, a large area of reefs ranging from 30-80 feet, is home to several species of our favorite fish: Nassau, tiger, black, spotted and marble groupers. If you're an advanced diver, we might visit **Shark Point**, a remote site frequented by nurse, blacktip, hammerhead and tiger sharks. Enormous (but harmless) **whale sharks** can be seen around Glover's from March-June. Getting to see the largest fish in the sea is the dive experience of a lifetime.

After the diving, let's pay a visit to one of the tiny coral islands that dot the ring of the atoll. We'll see huge flocks of seabirds, some of them seldom seen on the mainland, as well as wishwillies (iguanas), and possibly a saltwater crocodile or two. Sea turtles nest on the beaches from June-August. By the way, another animal that thrives here is the irritating sand flea, so bring a variety of bug repellents! On the way back to Placencia, we may see huge pods of spotted, bottlenose and spinner dolphins.

ALTERNATE PLAN
Glover's Atoll is also an excellent place for **fishing**. The lagoon inside the atoll has miles of shallow grass flats that are perfect territory for fly-fishing for bonefish, permit and tarpon, as well as over 700 patch reefs thick with yellowtail snapper. Offshore trolling produces billfish, wahoo and shark. Inquire at any of the dive shops about half- and full-day fishing charters.

Sunday
The **Monkey River**, one of Belize's major rivers with its headwaters high in the Maya Mountains, meets the Caribbean Sea about a half hour's boat ride south of the Placencia peninsula. A boat trip up the river is an excellent way to spend a day. A jungle river cruise is my

favorite way to observe wildlife. You sit in (relative) comfort, instead of trudging through the mud, and your chances of seeing birds and animals are better than on a hike, because the river provides an opening in the thick forest.

South of the river is the large protected area of **Payne's Creek National Park.** Most of the park is impenetrable jungle, and there  are no facilities for visitors, although there are a few hiking trails right around Monkey River Town. There are many troops of black howler monkeys in the area, as well as deer, armadillos, tapirs, ocelots and jaguars. The river is slap-full of crocodiles and manatees (to say nothing of tarpon and snook). Huge colonies of tiger heron and ibis live and breed in the area, and hawksbill sea turtles nest on the beaches.

At the mouth of the river is **Monkey River Town,** a very funky little village of about 200 people. There's no proper road to the village, so almost all access is by boat. Back in the bad old days of the banana industry, Monkey River was a sizable town, but as the banana industry declined, so did the town, and today the few villagers make their living from fishing and guiding ecotourists on trips to the river and the jungle. There are several local families with boats who run day trips, and you can contact them through any of the lodges in the area.

A few of the villagers offer rooms and meals, but the only thing that approximates a hotel is Clive's Place, also known as the **Sunset Inn.** Clive Garbutt is the best-known of the local guides. He and his family run wildlife and fishing trips. The inn has eight rooms with private bath, hot water and 24-hour electricity (a real luxury around here) as well as a restaurant and bar. *Info*: www.monkeyriverbelize.com; Tel. 709-2028 or 720-2025.

A WONDERFUL WEEK IN SOUTHERN BELIZE

If you can spare a week for your Belize trip, the south is the best place to spend it. Here you can easily enjoy both the offshore world of the cayes and the jungles of the interior without any rushing around.

RECOMMENDED PLAN: Southern Belize is the ideal locale for a surf and turf itinerary. Spend three days in the jungle at the **Cotton Tree Lodge**, then four days on the beach, around Hopkins or Placencia, or on one of the small cayes offshore. **The Inn at Roberts Grove** is an excellent choice in the luxury price range, while **Laru Beya** has some nice mid-price rooms, and the **Hopkins Inn** in the peaceful village of the same name is a sleeper budget value.

Gales Point

A short way south of Belize City, this tiny fishing village sits on a narrow strip of land between the ocean and the Southern Lagoon, a mangrove-lined estuary that's home to the largest community of West Indian manatees in the Caribbean (see the section on Caye Caulker in Chapter 4 for more about these gentle marine mammals). Much of the lagoon is a protected area, the **Gales Point Wildlife Sanctuary**. Inquire at the **Manatee Lodge** (see *Best Sleeps*) for a local guide to take you on a manatee-watching boat tour.

There's also excellent fishing for tarpon and snook in the lagoon and adjoining waterways. Between May and October, hawksbill and loggerhead sea turtles lay their eggs on the beaches around here.

Dangriga

Dangriga, formerly called Stann Creek, is the largest town in Southern Belize (population around 10,000) and the country's center of **Garifuna** culture. Locals claim that **Punta Rock**, the

Don't Miss ...

Cockscomb Basin Wildlife Sanctuary – The Jaguar Reserve is one of the finest wildlife reserves in Belize, and it's easy to visit.
Mayflower Bocawina National Park – This smaller park has most of the same attractions as Cockscomb, but fewer tourists.
Placencia – This laid-back beach village has nice beaches and a full range of accommodations from budget to luxury.
Coral Reefs – The famous barrier reef and a huge coral atoll are just a short boat ride offshore.

music that rules the Caribbean coast of Central America, originated here. Some of Belize's best folk musicians make their home here, and the sound of drums pulsates through the city night and day. The region is also famous for Garifuna cuisine, which features cassava bread, grilled fish and *hudut*, a savory dish made of mashed plantains.

As you ride into town, you are greeted by a large sign that reads *Mabuiga!* (Garifuna for Welcome!) and the **Drums of Our Fathers Monument**, a bronze sculpture of traditional Garifuna drums. Dangriga centers on a bridge over the North Stann Creek River. The south bank bustles with boats taking travelers to the various nearby cayes. On the north bank is the wild and wooly street market where fruit, vegetables and fresh fish are on sale.

Dangriga isn't for everyone. It's more of a regional commercial center than a tourist resort. It's a typical Central American town of decaying wooden shacks on stilts, and the poverty you'll see here may be a little shocking. Though the town is on the water, the beaches right in town are grungy.

There are a couple of very minor tourist attractions in town, and most day tours of the region stop in at one or more of them for a little culture and a chat with some of the locals. The **Gulisi Garifuna Museum** is named for a Garifuna heroine named Gulisi, who came to Belize from Roatan with her 13 children and founded the settlement of Punta Negra. It's worth a short visit on the way out of town. *Info*: Open Mon-Fri 10am-5pm, Sat 8am-noon. Entry $2.50. www.ngcbelize.org; Tel. 502-0639.

There are several local artists and craftsmen who welcome visits to their studios. **Mr. Austin Rodriquez** and his daughters make traditional Garifuna drums, curing deer and cow hides with lime and salt and stretching them over carved wood bodies. **Benjamin Nicholas's** charming paintings are in the Caribbean Primitive tradition, and depict events in Garifuna history. Dangriga's most famous son, **Pen Cayetano**, considered the founder of Punta Rock, is also an accomplished painter. His gallery is usually open only in November. Another popular shop is Marie Sharp's famous hot sauce factory. *Info*: www.mariesharps-bz.com)

The biggest party of the year takes place around November 19, **Garifuna Settlement Day**. The anniversary of the Garinagu's 1832 arrival in Belize is a national holiday, and in Dangriga it's the occasion for a whole week of revelry (see photo on next page), including parades, all-night drumming, and a reenactment of the arrival of the first Garinagu in a *dorey* (dugout canoe).

The Garifuna

The ancestors of the **Garifuna** (or Garinagu) were indigenous Caribs on the Caribbean island of St Vincent, and blacks from West Africa who arrived on the island in the 1600s. During the Napoleonic wars, the Garinagu allied themselves with French settlers. As punishment, the British deported them to the island of Roatan, off Honduras. Soon the Garinagu began to migrate to the mainland, and today they live all along the Caribbean coast from southern Belize to northern Nicaragua. They have their own Garifuna language (most also speak Spanish or English) and several styles of folk music. Visitors also love Garifuna cuisine, served at thatched beach restaurants: cassava, conch soup and grilled fish. To learn more, see www.garinet.com or www.ngcbelize.org.

There's a handful of very funky nightclubs and bars that sometimes have live music. You have a better chance here than anywhere else of seeing a good Punta Rock band inducing dancers to shake their hips at unbelievable speeds. You'll have to ask around to find out where the latest happening spot is, however.

The bus ride takes about three hours from Belize City, changing in Belmopan. By car, you should make it in less than two hours on the scenic Hummingbird Highway. Maya Island Air and Tropic Air both offer hourly flights from Belize City. *Info*: There's some good info on the city's web site at www.dangrigalive.bz and the regional site www.stanncreek.com.

Hopkins & Sittee River

The sleepy Garifuna fishing village of **Hopkins** is conveniently located for trips to the forests of Cockscomb and Mayflower, as well as for the excellent reefs just offshore. The long and sandy beach is a fine one, and you'll find a nice selection of beachfront accommodations and plenty of beachy activity. A couple of places in town rent windsurfers, kayaks and other watercraft, and two dive resorts just south of town run daily trips to the barrier reef and Glover's Atoll (see *Best Activities*).

Despite the fair number of tourists milling about, Hopkins has less bustle than San Pedro or Cayo. The hairy backpackers and tanned jet-setters tend to rush from the rain forest to the reefs, while the locals slowly go about their age-old business of fishing, drumming and carving their dugout canoes. The Garifuna culture is thick here. Be sure to pay a visit to **Lebeha**, a drum school offering lessons by day, a bar with a happening drum jam by night. *Info*: The town runs a decent little web site with the unwieldy address of www.telcomplus.net/gbrandt/Web_Dev/hopkins/hopkinshome.html.

Just south of Hopkins is the estuary of the **Sittee River**. One of Belize's largest rivers, the Sittee has its source high in the jungles, and ends up here in a vast area of mangroves, marshes and lagoons. Whether you like birds or fish, you'll find them here. Local guide **Horace Andrews** can put you on to either or both.

Anglers bag snook up to 26 pounds in the nearby Anderson and Boom Creek lagoons. River cruises are one of the very best ways to see wildlife. You're sure to see turtles, crocodiles and iguanas, and you may see any of the 200 species of birds that hang out around the

river. Tiger herons, snowy egret, kingfishers, flycatcher, oropendola, seedeater, kiskadee, chachalaca, honeycreeper, tanager, trogon, parrots hawks, kite, falcons etc etc...It's also easy to rent canoes or kayaks and poke about on your own. *Info*: www.belizebyhorace.com; Tel. 603-8358.

Cockscomb Basin Wildlife Sanctuary

Also known as the **Jaguar Reserve**, this is one of the largest and nicest wildlife reserves in Belize. It's quite easy to visit, whether you're coming for a short hike or a multi-day backcountry trek. The 128,000-acre reserve was established in 1990, largely thanks to the efforts of naturalist Alan Rabinowitz, who came here to study the jaguar, Belize's largest cat (as told in his fascinating book, *Jaguar*). Today the park is run by the **Belize Audubon Society**, and 60-80 jaguars are believed to roam the jungle-clad mountains in peace. *Info*: www.belizeaudubon.org.

The reserve includes some of the lushest rain forest in Belize, and is home to all five of Belize's cat species – jaguar, puma, margay, ocelot and jaguarundi – as well as the rare Baird's tapir, howler monkeys, boa constrictors, and deadly *tommigoffs*.

This is such a great place to see wildlife! On my last visit, we saw a kinkajou, a paca, a tayra and a beautiful margay, as well as jaguar footprints and scat! Comments in the visitors' book detailed recent sightings of pumas, jaguars and jaguarundis. I highly recommend a night hike (guided, of course).

The park features a network of wide, well-maintained trails. You can hike along the river for an hour or two, swim in one of the many lovely waterfalls, or float down the river on an inner tube. One of the most popular medium-difficulty hikes takes you to Ben's Bluff, an overlook with a panoramic view of the undisturbed forest. Serious adventurers can tackle the four-to-five day expedition to **Victoria Peak**, the highest point in Belize at 3,828 feet.

The area was formerly home to a few dozen Maya families, who were relocated to a place called **Maya Center** near the entrance to the sanctuary. Today, the villagers support themselves by working as guides, providing lodging for visitors and selling their crafts (instead of by clear-cutting the rain forest to grow corn). This is a classic eco-tourism success story, but it will only work if the locals do make some money, so be sure to hire a local guide, and stop in at Maya Center and drop a few dollars!

Maya Center is about 20 miles south of Dangriga on the Southern Highway. Here you pay the park entrance fee of $5, then take a dirt road another six miles to the sanctuary entrance. Buses to Punta Gorda will stop here on request.

Tutzil Nah Cottages, run by the Chun family, offers rudimentary rooms with private bath and 24-hour electricity (luxury!) for under $30 double. The ladies cook basic meals on request. Staying here is an unbeatable cultural experience, like staying at the home of a Mayan family. Contact them ahead of time, and they'll pick you up from your lodge. Maya Center has a couple of other families that offer cottages. There are also some very basic cabins and a campground, right at the sanctuary entrance.

Any of the local Maya Center guides will give you a great tour, but if they're available, go with one of the Chun brothers, who lived here before the sanctuary was founded, and know the jungle better than you and I know the way to our local post office.

Julian Chun was one of Alan Rabinowitz's main assistants during his work here, as detailed in *Jaguar*. A walk with him is the wildlife experience of a lifetime. Tours cost about $50 per person. *Info*: www.mayacenter.com; Tel. 520-3044.

Mayflower Bocawina National Park

Just south of Dangriga, Mayflower is a newer (2001) and smaller (7,000 acres) park than Cockscomb Basin. Mayflower sees fewer tourists, but it has equally beautiful rain forest and a couple of nice waterfalls. It's also teeming with wildlife, and it has a well-maintained network of hiking trails. To date, 238 species of birds have been observed here, including several rare varieties of motmots, trogons, macaws, parrots and toucans. Black howler monkeys are often seen, and you might also spot a coati (a *quash*), a tree-climbing Belizean gray fox, a paca, agouti, kinkajou, peccary, giant anteater or the paw print of a jaguar.

There are three **Mayan sites** in the park, all of them small sites belonging to the Post-Classic Period. The Mayflower Site is right across from the visitors' center. A short hike away are the Maintzunun ("hummingbird") and T'au Witz sites. All are only partially excavated, and not terribly interesting.

The most popular hiking trail is a nice easy walk to the Bocawina and Three Sisters waterfalls, beautiful falls with large pools at the bottom that are perfect for a cooling swim. A more strenuous hike (2-3 hours) leads to **Antelope Falls**, a 100-foot-high cascade that also has nice pools for swimming, as well as an awesome view of the jungle and the Caribbean Sea below.

There are several camping places in the park for those who want to make a multi-day trek. You can hire licensed tour guides in the nearby village of Silk Grass, but the best way to experience this park is to stay a couple of nights at the eco-friendly **Mama Noots Backabush Lodge**, which is located within the park boundaries.

They have basic but comfortable cabins at a moderate price (see *Best Sleeps*). *Info*: The visitors' center is about four miles up a well-maintained dirt road that takes off at mile six of the Southern Highway. Entry $5.

Glover's Reef Marine Reserve

Glover's Reef Atoll, named for pirate John Glover, is the most remote of Belize's three coral atolls (about 35 miles southeast of Dangriga), and it has some of the most pristine dive sites in the country. An atoll is a ring of coral reefs surrounding a shallow lagoon. An atoll is formed when coral reefs grow around the shoreline of an island, then the island itself erodes away as the reefs continue to grow. There are only four atolls in the Western Hemisphere, and three of them are in Belize. This unique ecosystem is a protected Marine Reserve and a UNESCO World Heritage Site.

The eastern side of the atoll is dotted with a few tiny coral islands, a few of which have small dive lodges. **Glover's Atoll Resort** (www.glovers.com.bz) has camping, dorm beds and thatched cabins. **Slickrock Adventures** (www.slickrock.com) has some basic cabanas on Long Caye. These places are pretty rustic, but are perfect for those want to be right in the middle of the best diving and fishing, and don't require luxury (in case you do, try **Thatch Caye** (see below), or one of the upscale resorts near Dangriga.

The nicest (and priciest) of the resorts right on Glover's Atoll is **Isla Marisol Resort** (www.islamarisolresort.com), which has cabanas with private bath, hot water and AC (see *Best Sleeps*).

Glover's offers a vast variety of dive sites for all skill levels, from snorkelers to advanced divers. The outside of the ring has some excellent walls, and within the lagoon are over 700 patch reefs.

Emerald Forest Reef, on the northeast end of the atoll, is an excellent site for snorkelers and novice divers, with depths of 15-70 feet and no current. The site is named for its amazing abundance of coral. Every variety of coral known to live in this area has been

seen here, including boulder, finger, brain, pencil and 10-foot-high stands of elkhorn. Hiding in this underwater rain forest are all kinds of crabs, sea urchins, starfish and sponges. Farther up the food chain, jacks, snapper and grouper prowl.

Long Caye Wall is a great site for both beginners and advanced divers, and it's possible to dive from shore. Depths range from less than 20 feet to infinity. A shallow reef leads to a sloping region of sand inhabited by a forest of garden eels. Beyond is the wall, dropping straight down thousands of feet to the ocean bottom. All kinds of coral, including black coral, cover the wall, while off in the water column you may see pelagic creatures such as sharks, sea turtles, eagle and manta rays.

Grouper Flats is a name to get any diver's heart pumping. This large area of reefs ranges in depth from 30-80 feet, and is home to several species of our favorite fish: Nassau, tiger, black, spotted and marble groupers.

Shark Point might just kick your blood pressure up yet another notch. It's a remote site requiring a bit of a long boat ride, with typically rough seas and depths down to 90 feet, so it's recommended for advanced divers only. Nurse, blacktip, hammerhead and tiger sharks consistently hang around this large area of reef.

The area is also famous for **whale sharks**. These enormous (but harmless) fish can be seen around here from March-June around full moon nights. Snapper spawn here in vast numbers around that time, and the whale sharks come to feed on the eggs. The sight of thousands of snappers spawning in a huge ball while giant whale sharks swim overhead slurping up the eggs is the dive experience of a lifetime.

There are a few other things to do out here other than dive. There's **excellent fishing** in the lagoon – snapper on the patch reefs, bonefish and permit on the flats. The lagoon is also a splendid place for cruising around in a kayak. Spotted, bottle-nose and spinner dolphins hang around in huge schools. Sea turtles nest on the beaches from June-August. On land, you'll see huge flocks of seabirds, as well as wish-willies (iguanas), and possibly a saltwater crocodile or two. By the way, another animal that thrives here is the irritating sand flea, so bring a variety of bug repellents!

Southwater Caye

This little island sits right on top of the barrier reef, about 14 miles off of Hopkins. Splendid wall diving is right offshore, protected by the new Southwater Caye Marine Park. There are three basic dive lodges on the island: **Pelican Beach Resort** (www.pelicanbeachbelize.com), the **Blue Marlin Lodge** (www.bluemarlinlodge.com) and **International Zoological Expeditions** (www.ize2belize.com), which mainly caters to student groups (see *Best Sleeps*).

Thatch Caye

My favorite Belizean island lodge is on its own tiny island just north of Southwater Caye. **Thatch Cay Resort** (www.thatchcaye.com) is new eco-friendly resort offers first-class accommodations (camping is also available), a small but excellent dive operation, guided fly-fishing and other water sports (see *Best Sleeps*).

Tobacco Caye

Just north of Southwater Caye, this tiny dot of sand is also smack-dab on top of the barrier reef. There's fantastic snorkeling and diving right from the shore – a spectacular wall is just a few hundred feet out. Tobacco Caye has a little more action going on than the other cayes in the area. There's regular boat service from Dangriga, and half a dozen rustic lodges. In fact, things can get a little crowded here during high season, as it's quite a popular destination, and only a small island. See *Best Sleeps* for my take on area accommodations.

Placencia

Once an off-the-beaten-path spot known only to a few divers and backpackers, the **Placencia** area is slowly but surely evolving into a major resort (the same is true of Belize as a whole). However, it still has a low-key, island-time sort of vibe. Beachfront resorts, including luxury complexes and backpacker shacks, are strung out along a long, narrow peninsula. The villages of **Maya Beach** and **Seine Bight** are towards the north, and **Placencia Town** itself is at the southern end.

The **beaches** here are beautiful but, typical for Belize, there's lots of seagrass and few waves. Between the peninsula and the mainland, Placencia Lagoon is a peaceful waterway where nature-lovers take canoe trips to see manatees and a wealth of birds, and anglers tangle with huge snook. Just offshore are world-class diving and snorkeling on the barrier reef and Glover's Reef Atoll (see above), and the rain forest preserves of Cockscomb Basin and Mayflower Bocawina are a short ride inland. From the tourist's standpoint, Placencia has everything Ambergris has, and then some.

Placencia town itself is quite small (about 600 residents), and far from urban – a few clusters of buildings among the palms. There's one dreadful dirt road and a long pedestrian sidewalk ("the narrowest main street in the world") that passes by most of the hotels, restaurants and other points of interest. The airstrip, just north of town, is served by several daily flights from Belize City on both Maya Island Air and Tropic Air. At the southern tip of the peninsula are the docks, where you can catch a boat out to one of the Cayes, or south to Honduras.

Placencia is one of the oldest communities in Belize. The ancient Mayans came here for fish and salt. British buccaneers founded the village in the 1600s, and it changed hands between the Spanish and the English a time or two. Today's residents are a broad mix of Creoles, Garifuna, Mestizos and plenty of Anglo expats.

There are a few resorts in the area that have their own dive shops, including the **Inn at Robert's Grove** (www.diverobertsgrove.com) and **Blancaneaux's Turtle Inn** (www.blancaneaux.com). See *Best Sleeps* for more information on these. There are also a couple of independent dive shops in Placencia Town: the **Seahorse Dive Shop** (www.belizescuba.com) and **Splash Dive Shop** (www.splashbelize.com). See *Best Activities* for more information on Placencia diving. *Info*: www.placencia.com.

Monkey River

The **Monkey River**, one of Belize's major rivers with its headwaters high in the Maya Mountains, meets the Caribbean Sea about a half hour's boat ride south of the Placencia peninsula. A boat trip up the river is an excellent way to spend a day. A jungle river cruise is my favorite way to observe wildlife. You sit in (relative) comfort, instead of trudging through the mud, and your chances of seeing birds and animals are better than on a hike, because the river provides an opening in the thick forest.

To & From Honduras

The **D-Express boat** makes weekly trips to Puerto Cortés in Honduras, stopping at Big Creek and Placencia. The boat leaves from Placencia every Friday at 9:30am, and from Puerto Cortés every Monday at 11:30am. Cost is $55. *Info*: Tel. 663-5971 or 523-4045.

South of the river is the large protected area of **Payne's Creek National Park**. Most of the park is impenetrable jungle, and there are no facilities for visitors, although there are a few hiking trails right around Monkey River Village. There are many troops of black howler monkeys in the area, as well as deer, armadillos, tapirs, ocelots and jaguars. The river is slap-full of crocodiles and manatees (to say nothing of tarpon and snook). Huge colonies of tiger heron and ibis live and breed in the area, and hawksbill sea turtles nest on the beaches.

At the mouth of the river is **Monkey River Town**, a very funky little village of about 200 people. There's no proper road to the village, so almost all access is by boat. Back in the bad old days of  the banana industry, Monkey River was a sizable town, but as the banana industry declined, so did the town, and today the few villagers make their living from fishing and guiding ecotourists on trips to the river and the jungle. There are several local families with boats who run day trips, and you can contact them through any of the lodges in the area.

If you really want to experience the jungle, spend the night in Monkey River Town, so that you can be on the river at dawn. This will give you your best chance of seeing birds and wildlife, and your only realistic chance of a trophy sighting such as a cat or a tapir. A few of the villagers offer rooms and meals, but the only thing that approximates a hotel is Clive's Place, also known as the **Sunset Inn**. Clive Garbutt is the best-known of the local guides. He and his family run wildlife and fishing trips. The inn has eight rooms with private bath, hot water and 24-hour electricity (a real luxury around here) as well as a restaurant and bar. *Info*: www.monkeyriverbelize.com; Tel. 709-2028 or 720-2025.

Punta Gorda & The Toledo District

Punta Gorda ("PG" for short) is the southernmost town of any size in Belize and the capital of the Toledo district, about four hours by car (closer to six on the bus) from Belize City. The 6,000 residents are a mixture of Maya, Garifuna and Creoles.

PG has a pleasant waterfront promenade (though the beach is not very nice for swimming), an active morning street market four days a week, and some lively drumming and other local music going on in the bars. Sleepy, hot, humid and not terribly clean, the town has a friendly, relaxed vibe – some love it, some hate it. Its main attraction is as a gateway to the various sights in the region,

To & From Guatemala

Requena's Charters offers daily boat service from Punta Gorda to Puerto Barrios, Guatemala. The boat leaves PG at 9am, and returns from Puerto Barrios at 2pm. The crossing takes about an hour. *Info*: www.belizenet.com/ requena; Tel. 722-2070.

including the Mayan site of **Lubaantun**, the nearby Maya villages, wildlife reserves and boat trips to Guatemala.

There are several tour operators in town. I highly recommend **Tide Tours**, which is associated with TIDE, a conservation group that manages several local national parks and reserves. They offer a wide range of tours from half a day to a week or more. Hiking, horseback riding and canoeing are all fine ways to see the jungle, the Mayan villages, and the many waterfalls and caves. Fishing, diving, snorkeling, kayaking and river cruises are also on the menu. *Info*: www.tidetours.org; Tel. 722-2129.

The Toledo District has several easily-accessible attractions for day trips, including the Agua Caliente hot springs at Big Falls, the Hokeb Ha Cave at Blue Creek and the small but fascinating Mayan site of **Nim Li Punit**, which has over 25 elaborately-carved stelae.

There are also several large nature reserves, including some of the country's most remote and pristine rain forest areas: the **Columbia River Forest Reserve**, **Río Blanco National Park** with its splendid waterfalls, and **Payne's Creek National Park**, 39,000 acres of broadleaf forest, pine savannah and mangrove lagoons, a major breeding area for the West Indian manatee and home to over 300 species of birds.

Offshore are the 500-square-mile **Port Honduras Marine Reserve** and the **Sapodilla Cayes Marine Reserve**, which protects the southernmost set of islands in Belize. These parks have few or no facilities for visitors, but can be explored in the company of a local guide.

If you'd like to venture off the usual tourist trail for a real cultural experience, visit one of the small Mayan villages in the region. The **Toledo Ecotourism Association** has developed a program to bring visitors to ten local villages, with a focus on cultural exchange and environmental conservation. The TEA guesthouses are clean but very basic: bunk beds with mosquito netting, and a bucket outdoors for showering. *Info*: www.southernbelize.com/tea.html; Tel. 722-2096.

Residents live in simple thatched huts, and live on beans and tortillas made from the corn they grow in their *milpas*. Electricity and running water are newfangled innovations. Most of the people are friendly but a bit shy. As usual, you'll find the children the best cultural ambassadors. This would be an excellent trip to take with your kids, if they can handle roughing it a bit.

Each of the villages has various points of interest nearby that you can hike to, including caves, waterfalls, Mayan ruins and nature reserves. Local guides will show you the medicinal plants that the villagers harvest from the jungle, and demonstrate traditional crafts. Getting to the villages by public transport is not so easy, as buses generally run from Punta Gorda only once per week, on market days. *Info*: www.southernbelize.com/puntagorda.html.

Lubaantun

The largest Mayan site in Southern Belize is about 26 miles northwest of Punta Gorda, near the village of San Pedro Columbia. **Lubaantun** dates from the Mayan Classic era, and was a prosperous commercial center from around 700-900 AD. The five plazas are surrounded by 14 major structures, including three ball courts, on a lovely site between two small rivers.

Lubaantun has some architectural features that are unique among Belizean Mayan sites. Most of the structures were built of large stones laid without mortar (perhaps inspiring the modern name, which means "Place of Fallen Stones"), and some of the pyramids have unusual rounded corners.

The modern history of the site is quite colorful. One early explorer is believed to have dynamited a couple of the temples, and

144 OPEN ROAD'S BEST OF BELIZE

another apparently planted a fabulous (but fake) crystal skull at the site in 1926, causing a controversy that went on for years.

Lubaantun is easy to get to by car, or on a guided tour from Punta Gorda. You can also hire a local guide at the small visitors' center, which has a small display of ceramic figurines and pottery found at the site. *Info*: www.southernbelize.com/lubaantun.html. Open daily 8am-5pm. Entry $5.

8. BELIZE IN TWO WEEKS

This country has an awful lot to see and do – coral reefs, beaches, rain forests, rivers and lagoons, Mayan ruins, spooky caves. In two weeks, we'll just have time for a taste of each, while leaving a little time for relaxing in the sun.

RECOMMENDED PLAN: Most folks opt for a **"surf and turf"** itinerary, including both the beaches and coral reefs of the cayes and the forests and Mayan ruins of the interior. Belize is small enough to visit all four of the main tourist regions in two weeks, so let's do it!

Don't Miss ...

Mayan Ruins of Lamanai – The most interesting Mayan site in Northern Belize is also a great place to see wildlife.
Mountain Pine Ridge – This tropical pine forest is a distinct ecosystem from the broadleaf jungle, and the area is full of waterfalls and caves.
Mayan Ruins of Tikal – This is the grandest Mayan site of them all, just over the border in Guatemala.
Cockscomb Basin Wildlife Sanctuary – This large and beautiful park, the home of the jaguar, is easy to visit.
Diving/Snorkeling on the Barrier Reef and Atolls – Some of the finest diving in this hemisphere is easily accessible from your choice of locations.

Day One – Lamanai
We'll begin our grand tour of Belize in the north, a region of vast uninhabited forests, rivers and lagoons, and mysterious Mayan ruins. We can see all of these at the **Lamanai Outpost Lodge**, an isolated jungle lodge that offers a lot of on-site activities, with first-class accommodations and service. **Chan Chich** would be another excellent choice for a jungle getaway.

Someone from the lodge will meet us at the airport in Belize City and drive us to the little village of Tower Hill, where we'll board a boat for a beautiful ride up the river to the lodge. The whole trip takes about 2.5 hours from the airport. Get your camera out, because we'll be seeing crocodiles, turtles, herons, cormorants and all sorts of water birds as we motor along through the steaming jungle.

On arrival at the lodge, we'll be handed a nice cold drink, we'll take our shoes off, plop down in a hammock and enjoy doing nothing for a while. Once we've decompressed and adjusted to Belizean time, let's explore the **Lamanai Ruins**.

For centuries, Lamanai was a wealthy trading center with a population of over 35,000. It had a longer history than most other Mayan cities, and was still inhabited when the Spaniards arrived. The ruins of a Spanish

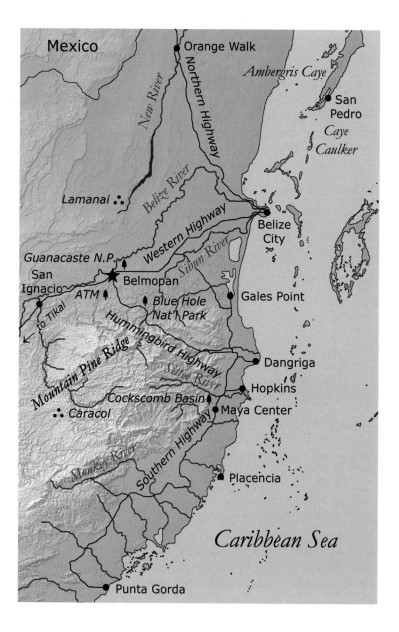

church bear witness to their vain attempts to convert the natives to Catholicism. The name Lamanai means "Crocodile," obviously a reference to the many crocs in the surrounding waterways. You'll see many representations of crocodiles here. Only about five percent of the 700 structures have been excavated. Some notable ones are the **Mask Temple** with its 13-foot stone carvings of Mayan gods, and the **High Temple**, one of the largest structures in the Mayan world. We can climb to the top for a spectacular view of the forest and lagoon. Finally we'll stop at the museum for a look at some fascinating carvings and other artifacts that have been found at the site.

After dinner, let's take a **cruise around the lagoon** on a pontoon boat to watch the sunset and spot even more animals and birds. Later on we can venture out at night with spotlights in search of some of the nocturnal residents. This is our best chance to spot an elusive ocelot or jaguar, to say nothing of owls and nightjars.

Day Two – San Ignacio
Every nature lover knows that early morning is the best time to spot animals and birds. Because we're right here on the spot, we can easily be in the woods or on the water in time for the dawn flighting. We can take a hike with one of the resort's resident guides, or paddle around the lagoon in a canoe in search of manatees, otters and crocs. A guide can point out some of the local plants that the ancient Maya used for medicines, some of the resident howler monkeys, or perhaps a few of the **over 400 bird**

species that live in the area. A dozen different herons and egrets, a dozen types of hawks, parrots, hummingbirds, trogons, toucans, motmots...and literally hundreds of LBBs (a technical birder term meaning Little Brown Birds).

We've got a long trip ahead of us today, so after an early lunch, it's time to say goodbye to Lamanai and head west. San Ignacio is not that far from here as the toucan flies, but the direct route leads across mountains and through roadless jungle. I suppose you could make it on a mule, but to get there via internal-combustion-powered vehicles will require a bit of backtracking. We want to see a lot in a short amount of time, so the best way for us to proceed from here is by rented car. We'll get out of Lamanai by the same way we came in, by boat to Tower Hill and then by van right back to the International Airport, which is the best and most convenient place to rent a car. There we'll pick up a vehicle and set out on the 2-3 hour ride to the Cayo district. As always, we've made a reservation at our lodge ahead of time, so we needn't worry about getting there a bit late, but we hope to stop in San Ignacio for a look around before heading to our lodge.

ALTERNATE PLAN
There are several ways to get around Belize. You could certainly do this itinerary by public transport, but you'd have a lot of hectic travel time (to get from Lamanai to San Ignacio by bus in one day would require a very early start). A more convenient but more expensive option would be to **hire a van and driver** for each leg of your trip. If you're traveling with a group of four or more people, this could be economical. The fastest and most expensive option would be to charter a small plane for each long travel leg. For example, if you stayed at Chan Chich, you could take a charter flight from nearby Gallon Jug to Flores, near Tikal, and proceed by van from there.

San Ignacio, also known as **Cayo**, is the largest town in western Belize and a major center of ecotourism. Located on the Macal River with the sister town of Santa Elena on the other bank, San Ignacio is a lively little town that serves as a transport hub, a place to stock up on supplies, and headquarters for the area's multitude of tour operators. Our first stop will be **Eva's Restaurant**, on Burns Street in the center of town, *the* gathering spot for visitors. Here we'll have a nice little dinner and a chat with owner Bob about the latest local news. The bulletin board overflows with brochures describing all the fun tours and activities in the region. *Info*: www.evasonline.com; Tel. 804-2267.

Where to stay? The **San Ignacio Resort Hotel** is the nicest of the hotels right in town, and it has a green iguana breeding center on-site, which is well worth a visit, especially if you are traveling with kids. Also nice, at a lower price, is **Cahal Pech Village Resort**, high on a hill above town, right next to the Mayan ruins of the same name. Cahal Pech was one of the earliest Maya settlements in Belize. The small site includes a 77-foot pyramid, two ball courts, an ancient carved stela and an awesome view of the Maya Mountains and the Belize River valley.

Most visitors to the area don't stay in town, but rather at one of the many jungle lodges in the region. I highly recommend the elegant **Hidden Valley Inn**, right in the middle of the Mountain Pine Ridge preserve. The eco-friendly **Du Plooy's** is another great choice. Wherever we stay, we can book tours through our lodge (convenient) or directly with the tour operators (cheaper). Most tour outfits will pick you up in their van, but the attractions in this region are spread out, so our rental car may come in handy.

Day Three – Mountain Pine Ridge
The sights in this region are endless. A trip to Caracol over Mountain Pine Ridge is our best chance to see a little of everything – rivers, caves, monkeys and Mayans. From Cayo, we'll head

south through the **Mountain Pine Ridge Forest Reserve**, Belize's largest protected area. The Caribbean pine trees that dominate this forests support a very different ecosystem from the broadleaf jungle found in most of the country. The backbone here is solid granite, which explains the large number of waterfalls and caves in the area. Looking at the pine trees, red clay soil and granite outcroppings, you might almost think you're in Georgia.

The wildlife, and especially the birds, are a little different than you'll see elsewhere. Rare orange-breasted falcons, Stygian owls and ocellated turkeys join more commonly-seen birdies such as toucans, parrots, hummingbirds and woodpeckers. Baird's tapir, pumas, jaguars and ocelots prowl at night.

This vast uninhabited area is traversed by a few graded dirt roads that are kept in pretty good repair and should be passable in an ordinary car, except during periods of heavy rain. A couple of hours' ride brings us to **Caracol**, the largest Mayan site in Belize. Caracol was planned on a large scale, with a radial street plan that covered some 65 square miles, and back in the seventh century AD it was one of the largest Mayan cities, with a population of over 140,000 people – twice the size of modern Belize City! Luxurious objects of jade and obsidian indicate that the residents of Caracol were especially prosperous. They were also doughty warriors, defeating the mighty city-state of Tikal in a famous battle in 562 AD.

The site is spectacular, at about 1,500 feet above sea level, with stunning views of the surrounding Maya Mountains. The high point of the city, both literally and figuratively is a complex of structures called **Caana**. The magnificent pyramid remains the highest man-made structure in Belize. We'll climb to the top to enjoy a spectacular view – nothing but uninhabited forest for miles and miles. *Info*: www.caracol.org.

On the way back from Caracol, we'll stop off at one or more of Mountain Pine Ridge's attractions. **Hidden Valley (or Thousand Foot) Falls**, the highest waterfall in Central America, is worth a quick look. **Big Rock Falls** is actually even more interesting, and there are nice pools where you can swim. On the grounds of **Five Sisters Lodge**, the falls of the same name are another beautiful place for a swim. The most popular stops of all, visited by every day tour group, are the **Río On Pools** and the nearby **Río Frío Cave**. Check out the lovely waterfalls and swim in the warm pools, then explore the large cave. The river running through the cave keeps things cool, and nurtures ferns and mosses.

Days Four & Five – Tikal
Tikal National Park, just across the border in Guatemala, is the world's largest excavated Mayan site. It's possible to visit Tikal on a day trip from San Ignacio, but it really deserves at least an overnight trip. There are three inexpensive but mediocre hotels adjacent to the park. If you dont mind staying about an hour away from the ruins, try one of the much nicer lodgings around Lake Petén Itzá (see *Best Sleeps*).

If we get here early enough, we'll drop by the visitors' center and line up a guide for tomorrow morning. Then it's time for a dip in the pool and a cold beer, then dinner at our hotel restaurant. There's no big nightlife scene around here, but the hotel bars often harbor some lively conversation among the visitors from all over the world.

The name Tikal means "Place of Voices." The voices of the ancient Mayans speak most clearly early in the morning, so we'll be there right at 6am when the gates open. Early morning mist rises from the jungle, revealing the huge stone heads of long-dead kings. Ceiba roots entwine the stones, flocks of colorful macaws flit about, and deer graze irreverently among the ancient palaces.

During the Maya's Classic Period (around 300-900 AD), Tikal was one of the largest and most powerful city-states in the Mayan world, a metropolis of over 100,000 residents that traded with cultures as far away as Teotihuacan in Mexico, and made war with neighbors such as Caracol and Naranjo. Rulers such as Dark Sun, Stormy Sky and Jaguar Paw built grand palaces, temples and monuments, and recorded their deeds in the Mayan glyphs on stelae (stone columns).

There are over 3,000 structures at Tikal, including six large pyramids, 250 stelae, several royal palaces, no less than seven ball courts and hundreds of small residential buildings. The center-piece is the **Grand Plaza**, where two pyramids, the Temple of the Great Jaguar and the Temple of the Masks, face each other with a large plaza in between, surrounded by dozens of stelae and altars. Around the corner is the complex called the **Lost World**, with a huge pyramid and other structures from several different historical periods.

Visiting Tikal is a good workout, as it is an enormous site. It's no place to visit with small children, or anyone who minds walking. The walk from the entrance to the Grand Plaza is almost a mile. For hardy hikers like us, the trails that connect the various parts of the site make for a pleasant stroll through the jungle. Parrots, toucans, spider and howler monkeys are common, and the par-tially cleared landscape makes spotting them easier than in the dense jungle.

When the midday heat starts becoming oppressive, we'll amble back to the hotel and cool off with a quick dip in the pool, then try one of the small *comedores* across from the visitors' center for an authentic Guatemalan lunch. After lunch, we'll visit the two small museums at the site. The Morley Museum, named for a colorful character who was one of the early explorers, displays beautiful ceramic and jade artifacts from the site. At the visitors' center, the most interesting of Tikal's stelae are protected.

In this climate, it makes sense to get up early, as we did, and do your walking around before it gets really hot. We might even indulge in that civilized Spanish/Latin American custom called a *siesta*, and nap for a couple of hours. In the evening, we'll go back into the park for another hour or so, perhaps seeing the **Palace of the Inscriptions**. *Info*: www.tikalpark.com. Tikal National Park is open daily 6am-6pm. Entry is $20, which includes the Morley Museum.

Day Six – Actun Tunichil Muknal
There's no finer experience on Earth than waking up in the jungle, to the sound of the birds and the monkeys. Early morning

is always the best time to spot birds and wildlife, so let's get up at daybreak and take another short hike around the site. After a leisurely breakfast including lots of fresh tropical fruit, we'll head back into Belize and along the Western Highway to the cave of **Actun Tunichil Muknal**. ATM was an important ceremonial center for the Maya. Here they sacrificed young virgins to the rain god Chac. During the Terminal Classic era, the Maya performed these ceremonies ever more often and ever deeper into the cave, as they strove to appease the gods and end the terrible droughts that finally did them in.

The cave was only discovered in 1989 and opened to the public in 1998, and all the artifacts have been left exactly where they were found. You can visit only as part of an organized tour, which you can arrange through your lodge or any of the tour operators in San Ignacio. It's a fairly strenuous tour. To get here, you ride 45 minutes from San Ignacio, and then hike 45 minutes through the **Tapir Mountain Nature Reserve**, crossing three streams on the way. Once you get to the cave, you actually have to swim a short way, and there are several more spots inside where you'll have to wade. And that water is cold! I recommend bringing a large Ziploc bag or two for your camera and a change of clothes. The site can be a bit of a circus during tourist season – there'll be lots of groups visiting and, unlike at large sites like Tikal, you don't have much room to spread out in a cave.

The wonders of ATM are many. There are beautiful stalagmites and stalactites, some of them carved by the Maya so that a light placed in the right spot casts the shadow of a human figure on the

wall. There are chambers strewn with ceramic pots and stoneware. There are altars where the Mayan elite performed blood-letting ceremonies, piercing themselves with stingray spines in order to talk to the gods. And of course, there are the macabre skeletal remains of 14 humans, which lie encrusted with calcium that dripped over the centuries. The most famous of these is the Crystal Maiden, the skeleton of a young girl that has become encased in sparkling calcite.

Day Seven – The Hummingbird Highway

Although we've only scratched the surface of what there is to see in Western Belize, it's time to head down south. We'll take the Western Highway back to Belmopan, where we'll hang a right and head down the Hummingbird Highway to the coast. We've got an easy four-hour drive to Hopkins, so there's time to make one or two stops along the way.

Guanacaste National Park, at the intersection of the Western Highway and the Hummingbird Highway, makes a very convenient place for a quick walk or a picnic lunch. This small park is named for an enormous guanacaste tree overlooking the river, a huge spreading old gentleman, covered with epiphytic bromeliads. Two miles of walking trails feature labels for many other native plants, and you may also spot a trogon, a red-lored parrot, a deer or a few enormous iguanas. The river is a nice place for a cooling swim. *Info*: www.belizeaudubon.org/parks/guanacaste.htm.

South of Belmopan, we'll pass right by Caves Branch, one of mainland Belize's biggest tourist draws. **Ian Anderson's Caves Branch Adventure Company** is a popular jungle lodge that offers a wide variety of spelunking and other tours in the area (www.cavesbranch.com; see *Best Sleeps*). Ian has ever more competition these days, as outfits are eager to cash in on the craze for cave tubing. Floating on an inner tube through the underground caverns on the Caves Branch River is perhaps the single most popular activity on mainland Belize, attracting day-trippers from the many lodges in the area, as well as huge hordes from the cruise ships. During the high tourist season, the masses of tubes jostling down the river seem more like a water ride at Disney World than the wilds of Central America. Of course, there are several other less-touristed caves in the region, including **Crystal Cave**, one of the largest caves in Belize and once a ceremonial center for the Maya.

At **Blue Hole National Park**, an enormous sinkhole that resembles the more famous Blue Hole offshore is a capital place for a swim. **St. Herman's Cave** is probably the easiest cave to visit in the country. The park also has five miles of well-marked hiking trails and several picnic areas. Residents include deer, agoutis, peccaries and over 200 species of birds. *Info*: www.belizeaudubon.org/parks/bhnp.htm.

Days Eight & Nine – Cockscomb Basin
Arriving on the southern coast, we'll choose a nice beachfront resort to make our base for three nights. The nicest areas to stay are around Hopkins and Placencia. Each has a good selection of lodgings in all price ranges, convenient to the forests of the interior and the coral reefs offshore. Near Hopkins, **Hamanasi** and **Jaguar Reef** are good choices in the luxury category. Travelers with lower budgets will like **Beaches and Dreams** or the **Hopkins Inn**. The Placencia region has a huge selection, including luxurious **Kanantik** and the **Inn at Robert's Grove**, as well as the excellent mid-price value **Laru Beya** (see *Best Sleeps*).

Hopkins is within easy day-trip range of Cockscomb Basin Wildlife Sanctuary, also known as the **Jaguar Reserve**. (Placencia is a couple of hours away by car). This is one of the largest and nicest wildlife reserves in Belize, and it's quite easy to visit. The 128,000-acre reserve includes some of the lushest rain forest in Belize, thick with orchids and bromeliads, and over 300 species of birds. It's home to all five of Belize's cat species, including 60-80 jaguars, the rare Baird's tapir, pacas, kinkajous and other beasts. Even here in the heart of jaguar country, your chances of seeing one of these shy nocturnal predators are slim, but on my most recent visit, we saw a margay, as well as jaguar pawprints and droppings.

The park features an excellent network of well-maintained trails of various levels of difficulty. You can hike along the river for an hour or two, enjoy one of the many lovely waterfalls, or even float down the river on an inner tube. One of the most popular medium-difficulty hikes takes you to **Ben's Bluff**, an overlook with a panoramic view of the undisturbed forest.

Before the establishment of the park, the area was home to a few dozen Maya families, who were relocated to a place called **Maya Center** near the entrance to the sanctuary. Today, the villagers support themselves by working as guides, providing lodging for visitors and selling their arts and crafts (instead of by clearcutting the rain forest to grow corn). This is a classic eco-tourism success story, but it will only work if the locals do make some money, so we're going to hire a local guide at Maya Center. The Chun Brothers are the best known, immortalized in the wonderful book *Jaguar*. We'll contact them ahead of time, and have them pick us up from Hopkins – or, if our budget is small, we could stay in one of the rustic rooms right here at Maya Center. *Info*: www.mayacenter.com; Tel. 520-3044.

Day Ten – Hopkins & Sittee River
The sleepy Garifuna fishing village of **Hopkins** has a nice long sandy beach. A couple of places in town rent windsurfers, kayaks and other watercraft, and two dive resorts just south of town run daily trips to the barrier reef and Glover's Atoll. Garifuna culture is thick here. We'll be sure to pay a visit to **Lebeha**, a drum school offering lessons by day, a bar with a kicking drum jam by night.

Just south of Hopkins is the estuary of the **Sittee River**. One of Belize's largest rivers, the Sittee has its source high in the jungles, and ends up here in a vast area of mangroves, marshes and lagoons. Whether you like birds or fish, you'll find them here. Local guide **Horace Andrews** can put you on to either or both. Anglers bag snook up to 26 pounds and

ALTERNATE PLAN
Placencia, a bit farther south than Hopkins, offers a bigger (but still relaxed) tourist scene, and boasts its own airstrip. South of town is the **Monkey River**, another splendid place for a jungle river cruise and/or a bit of tarpon and snook fishing. Several local guides run boat trips from the funky little village of Monkey River Town. *Info*: www.monkeyriverbelize.com.

tarpon from 10-70 pounds in the nearby Anderson and Boom Creek lagoons. River cruises are one of the very best ways to see wildlife. You're sure to see turtles, crocodiles and iguanas, and you may see any of the 200 species of birds that hang out around the river. Tiger herons, snowy egret, kingfishers, flycatcher, oropendola, seedeater, kiskadee, chachalaca, honeycreeper, tanager, trogon, parrots, hawks, kite, falcons, etc ... It's also easy to rent canoes or kayaks and poke about on your own. *Info*: www.belizebyhorace.com; Tel. 603-8358.

Days 11-14 – The Cayes
We've saved the "surf" part of the trip for last, but don't spend so much time in the interior that you run out of time for the islands, because they really are spectacular. At this point in the itinerary, we have two options: either spend our beach time here in the south near Hopkins or Placencia (see Chapter 7), or head back up north to **Ambergris** or **Caulker** (see Chapter 4). Either alternative will offer similar opportunities. The majority of tourists head for Ambergris, but the south has the same things to offer – great diving, a selection of nice resorts, and beaches that are every bit as good as those in the north.

Wherever you decide to spend your island time, make a snorkeling or dive trip your first priority. Even if you've never snorkeled before, the colorful coral reefs are simply too amazing to miss (they may not be around forever), and snorkeling is easy to learn. Spend the rest of your time on an ideal mix of fishing, kayaking and other water sports. Don't forget to leave plenty of time for lying around in a hammock doing nothing, and for eating grilled fish, *ceviche* and lobster!

9. BEST SLEEPS & EATS

Belize has a wide range of different types of lodgings, from luxurious resort complexes to funky backpacker crash pads. There are colorful jungle and oceanfront lodges dotted throughout the country, some of them very special places indeed (photo below from The Lodge at Chaa Creek: see page 194).

Belizean food is like the Belizean people: a mixture of influences in every possible combination. In addition to "traditional" Belizean fare, you'll find excellent Mexican food, good Chinese, and (in tourist areas), American favorites such as burgers and chicken wings. You'll also find plenty of the Caribbean/Latin American staple: beans and rice, more beans and more rice. By far the best thing going is the wide variety of fresh fish and seafood.

Hotels

Lovely settings and friendly service are the norm, but there are a few issues to warn you about. Belize is not exactly a budget travel destination. More upscale lodgings can be expensive, and some fail to come up to US/European standards, leading many visitors to call them overpriced. Remember that this is the tropics – you'll find the occasional bug or mildewy smell at even the best establishments. Hot water is often a problem, even at expensive places, and air conditioners may be old and cranky.

Lodging Prices

Prices quoted are for one double room.

$$$$$ Luxury: $200 +
$$$$ First-class: $125-200
$$$ Midrange: $60-125
$$ Budget: $25-60
$ Backpacker: $25 or less

Quoted prices may sound like great deals, but Belizean hoteliers are masters at tacking on nickels and dimes that can almost double the cost of a room. There's a government hotel tax of 9%, and many hotels add a 10-16% "service charge" or other mysterious fees. Upscale hotels accept major credit cards (sometimes with extra fees), but some cheap local places do not. Most places will gladly arrange transportation to and from the airport and tours of local attractions, but some will add extra charges for these services.

Eating Out

Vegetarian fare is easily available in tourist areas, but unheard-of in local eateries. The rice and beans are sometimes cooked with lard, sometimes with more appetizing coconut milk. Be wary of salads, which may have been rinsed in unclean tap water.

A **Belizean breakfast** consists of refried beans, scrambled eggs, and fry jacks (something like a deep-fried piece of pita bread). A fruit plate, with fresh papaya, pineapple, or whatever's in season, is often a good choice in the morning.

Belize City, San Pedro, Cayo and other tourist areas boast a good variety of restaurants, many of the best of them in the upscale hotels. On the cayes, seafood is fresh and served in an interesting variety of ways (how about fish fajitas, or lobster marinara?), although it's not always cheap. Caye Caulker is the place to go to gorge on **lobster** at a reasonable price. At the various island and jungle lodges, the cuisine tends to be a mix of local and international, geared to the tastes of  sophisticated travelers, and is often excellent. In Southern Belize, be sure to sample some **Garifuna** cuisine at a thatched beach restaurant. A typical meal includes cassava bread, conch soup and fresh fish grilled or cooked in coconut milk, with a side of *hudut*, a savory dish made of mashed plantains.

The most common local **beer** is Belikin, which comes in regular (lager) and stout varieties. **Wine** is, of course, not produced in the tropics, so Belize has no real wine-drinking tradition. Some of the finer eateries, however, have decent wine lists. Chilean wines are common, and may be the best value.

Throughout the tropics, the local liquor is **rum**, which is made from sugar cane. Belize produces a variety of rums, which run the gamut from cheap rotgut to fine sipping rums. By most accounts, the best is a brand called "One Barrel." The drink to have on the islands is a **panty ripper** (One Barrel and pineapple juice). Even the finest Belizean brands are inexpensive, at least if you buy them at a supermarket. Other liquors from around the world are available at higher prices. Another interesting local tipple is **cashew wine**.

Belize grows very good **coffee**, and some establishments serve an excellent brew. Alas, not all Belizeans appreciate a good cuppa – some cheaper places may serve you a generic cup of instant.

Whatever you eat in Belize, be sure to sample some of whatever **fruits** are in season. The mangos, pineapples, papayas, bananas, citrus and other tropical delights that grow down here are simply different fruits from the ones you buy at the supermarket back home: sweet, juicy and cheap. Quench your thirst with a *pipa*, a chilled green coconut with a straw inserted so you can sip the sweet milk. Kids love to chew on a stalk of sugar cane. Fresh-squeezed **juices** from a rainbow of exotic fruits are available everywhere. Don't be afraid to experiment.

THE NORTHERN CAYES

BEST SLEEPS ON AMBERGRIS CAYE

This slender island is Belize's most popular tourist destination, and it is rapidly growing into one of the Caribbean's major resorts. There are well over 75 hotels and guest houses, and more are under construction everywhere, especially in San Pedro, so don't be surprised if your hotel is located next to or near a noisy construction site.

When choosing a place to stay, location is key. There are plenty of places right in the town of San Pedro, mostly mid-price and budget options. A road south of town leads to many more lodgings, including a few upscale establishments. Most of the real luxury resorts are north of town, accessible by boat only. If you want to be in the middle of the party, stay in town. If you want a more secluded island experience, stay north or south of town. Any place on the island is fine for diving, as most dive operators will pick you up from your hotel's dock.

Both lodging and food are more expensive here than anywhere else in the country. Truly low-budget travelers should head for Caulker or Punta Gorda instead. If you're staying for a while, or are with a large group, consider one of the many places that offer suites with kitchens.

San Pedro

Being in town gives you easy access to a range of restaurants, night spots and dive shops. San Pedro is a party town, so rooms may be noisy, especially if you need to leave the windows open. The beach in central San Pedro is a narrow pedestrian thorough-fare; boats and watercraft of all descriptions race around madly, so it's not much good either for lounging around or for swimming.

Ramon's Village $$$$

This is one of the best-known lodgings on the island, and the only sandy-compound-thatched-hut-style place right by town (just a short walk south of the airstrip).  The cabanas are quaint, the grounds are lush, the beach is excellent and the staff are friendly. Some cabanas are by the beach, some are by the noisy road, so choose carefully. Ramon's has their own dive operation with seven boats, rentals and PADI instruction. They also do fishing tours and rent windsurfers, bikes and scooters. The food is only fair, but there are plenty of great eateries nearby. Across the street is the sister property, Steve & Becky's Cute Little Hotel, with little gingerbread cabins, access to all the facilities of Ramon's, and slightly lower prices. *Info*: www.ramons.com; Tel. 800/MAGIC 15 US.

Tradewinds Paradise Villas $$$$

These one-and two-bedroom villas on the north edge of San Pedro have central air and small kitchens. They're a good value for families. The palm-shaded compound includes a pool and has a laid-back feel. *Info*: www.belizeparadisevillas.com; Tel. 226-2822 or 800/451-7776 US.

Blue Tang Inn $$$$

This nice three-story building surrounds a shady courtyard in a peaceful location just north of San Pedro. The 14 newly-renovated suites have kitchens, AC and ceiling fans. Large windows let you enjoy the cool tropical breeze. The third-floor suites have Jacuzzi bathtubs and vaulted ceilings. There's a nice pool with a wooden deck. *Info*: www.bluetanginn.com; Tel. 226-2326 or 866/881-1020 US.

Sunbreeze Suites $$$$

Run by the same folks as the Sunbreeze Hotel (see next page), this resort (formerly Aquamarina Suites) is toward the north end of town. The large air-conditioned rooms have full kitchens and sitting areas. Some rooms overlook the ocean, some overlook the cemetery next door. There's a small pool, a nice beach and a gift shop. *Info*: www.sunbreezesuites.com; Tel. 226-4675 or 800/820-1631 US.

Sunbreeze Beach Hotel $$$$
This is a very nice motel-style place, two stories around a central courtyard. The location, across from the airstrip at the south end

of town, is not as noisy as it sounds, as the airstrip serves prop planes only, and most flights are during the day. The décor features nice tile and paintings by local artists, while the pleasant sandy compound lends a laid-back tropical feel. The 42 comfortable rooms each have two double beds, private bath with a large tiled shower, phone, TV, AC and ceiling fans. Premier rooms have Jacuzzi baths and refrigerators. The attractive pool and open-air restaurant and bar invite you to linger. Bartender Chris mixes a mean panty ripper and is a font of information about the local scene. *Info*: www.sunbreeze.net; Tel. 226-2191 or 800/688-0191 US.

Mayan Princess Resort Hotel $$$$
If you're here to dive and party, this would be a good base, right in the center of town in front of the Amigos del Mar dive shop and next to lively Fido's. The rooms have typical tile floors and rattan furniture, kitchenettes and oceanfront balconies. *Info*: www.mayanprincesshotel.com; Tel. 226-2778 or 800/850-4101 US.

The Palms $$$$
Just south of the airstrip, these 13 apartments have AC, full kitchens, TV, phones, and private porches. Nice local art graces the walls. There's a nice pool and lush grounds. *Info*: www.belizepalms.com; Tel. 226-3322.

San Pedro Holiday Hotel $$$
This small colonial-style place is great for the price. Managers Celi and Kim are longtime pillars of the local tourist industry. The 16 rooms are clean, the AC works fine and the staff is great.

Right here are the Bottom Time dive shop and Celi's, one of San Pedro's most popular restaurants. There's a nice little swimming area and some beach loungers for chilling out. *Info*: www.sanpedroholiday.com; Tel. 226-2014.

San Pedro

Hotel San Pedrano $$
This small central hotel is the nicest of the cheapies, basic but clean. All six rooms have private bath, and three have AC. They open onto a balcony with a bit of a sea view. *Info*: www.toucantrail.com/Hotel-San-Pedrano.html; Tel. 226-2054.

Other decent budget options on Front Street include **Ruby's** (www.ambergriscaye.com/rubys; Tel. 226-2063), which has rooms with or without private bath and AC; and the **Tomas** (Tel. 226-2061). The cheapest place to stay is **Pedro's Inn** (www.backpackersbelize.com; Tel. 226-3825), a nice little hostel just out of town, with dorm beds starting at $10.

North of San Pedro
These resorts are **accessible by boat only**. Most offer a free boat trip to town only upon arrival and departure, so you may have to pay for every trip into town. The idea is that you'll stay at your resort and chill out for your entire stay (except for a couple of dive trips from their private dock). There are no "things to do" up here, and boat rides back to town are expensive, as are drinks and food. That's Ambergris.

Capricorn Resort $$$$$
Capricorn is renowned as one of the finest restaurants on Ambergris, if not in all of Central America (see below). It also happens to be the perfect honeymoon getaway, with three air-conditioned beachfront cabanas. Each is beautifully decorated, with lovely hardwood floors, pastel walls, local art, a private porch and a shower made for two! *Info*: www.ambergriscaye.com/capricorn; Tel. 226-2809.

El Pescador $$$$$
As the name implies, this place caters to anglers, with a special emphasis on flats fishing for bonefish, tarpon and permit. They have what is probably the largest fly fishing shop in Belize. This

Timeshare Pitch Alert!

Sooner or later on Ambergris Caye, you'll be accosted by a pitchman who offers you a free weeklong stay at one of the island's best-known luxury resorts – a $2,000 US value – what a great deal! The catch? You must sit through a presentation that culminates in a high-pressure sales pitch for timeshare units (timeshares will not be mentioned until you've committed yourself to hearing the spiel). You may be tempted to endure the pitch in order to claim that free week's vacation, only to find that the "prize" is so hedged with conditions as to be practically worthless.

is no gaudy luxury resort, but the accommodations are first-class. Rooms in the colonial-style main lodge have AC and ceiling fans. All face the ocean and overlook the pool. There are also four three-bedroom villas in beautiful tropical style. You'll find a full range of amenities – three pools, an exercise room, free kayaks and bikes, wireless internet, a tour office and gift shop, and a restaurant serving fresh local fish on an outdoor deck. But the best feature of all is the family that runs the place. "We never say no" is their motto, and a steady stream of delighted guests can tell you that it's true. Divemaster Alonzo guides small groups on dream trips to the local reefs. *Info*: www.elpescador.com; Tel. 226-2398 or 800/242-2017 US.

Tranquility Bay Resort $$$$$
This luxury resort is the northernmost lodging on the island, a remote and relaxing getaway. The eleven beachfront cabanas have AC, comfortable beds and casually elegant furnishings. The restaurant features fresh seafood, and even offers a few vegetarian dishes. The resort has its own in-house dive operation, and a collection of kayaks, windsurfers and other watercraft. The reef is closer up here than elsewhere on the island, and some folks actually kayak out to the reef for a snorkel. *Info*: www.tranquilitybayresort.com; Tel. 220-5880.

Captain Morgan's Retreat $$$$$
This is the best-known resort on the island, the one that everyone talks about. It's a fully-equipped and well-run upscale resort

with 32 thatched-roof air-conditioned cabanas and all the expected amenities. Most visitors love it, but some hip travelers may be put off by the Disneyesque feel of the place – a trashy American TV show was filmed here, and smarmy salespeople hawk timeshare units. *Info*: www.belizevacation.com; Tel. 888/653-9090 US.

North of San Pedro

Belizean Shores $$$$$

Everyone loves this beachfront resort. The suites are large and luxurious, with full kitchens and dining areas, as well as private balconies, some with views of the sea. The grounds are green and peaceful, and the pool with its swim-up bar is a wonderful highlight. The Blue Moon restaurant has a panoramic ocean view and

serves a delicious mix of Caribbean and international cuisine. *Info*: www.belizeanshores.com; Tel. 226-4478 or 800/319-9026 US.

Journey's End Resort $$$$$

This resort offers hotel rooms, private cabanas and a three-bedroom house. The air-conditioned cabanas have wonderful beds, ceiling fans and minibars, but no TVs or phones. Cabanas 3 and 4 are quite nice, because you have a view of the sea from the bed. The Serenity Spa offers massages and exotic treatments such as seaweed wraps and mango baths right on the beach. There's a pool, tennis courts, game room, an on-site PADI dive facility, a tour desk and free wireless internet. If you tire of lazing about, try one of the free Hobie cats or kayaks. People come from all over the island to dine at the Luna Restaurant, a huge ocean-view palapa serving a fusion of local seafood and trendy modern cuisine. Kids will like the Smiling Toucan, where they can get pizza and burgers. *Info*: www.journeysendresort.com; Tel. 800/460-5665 US.

Mata Chica Beach Resort $$$$$

Rustic elegance and personal service are the pride of this well-known resort. The staff who pick you up at the airport greet you

North of
San
Pedro

South of
San
Pedro

by name, and call in a drink order on the way, so your favorite libation will be waiting as you step off the boat. The fourteen villas have AC and open floor plans with high thatched ceilings. Some have quirky touches such as hand-painted murals and open-air showers. Have a massage or a banana facial at the Jade Spa, or relax in the Jacuzzi or the palm-lined pool. The Mambo restaurant is exquisite. *Info*: www.matachica.com; Tel. 220-5010 or 220-5011.

South of San Pedro
The road south of town is lined with midrange-to-upscale lodgings. Staying in this area gives you the best of both worlds – you're out of the noise and bustle, but it's easy to take a bike or a golf cart into town when you want to. You can also walk along the beach and sample the restaurants and bars of the various resorts.

Victoria House $$$$$
This is the poshest of the resorts south of town, and many have called it the nicest on the island. The beautiful beach, luxuriantly landscaped compound and three swimming pools are kept immaculate by an army of groundskeepers. The 42 units offer a range of options, from second-floor State Rooms to thatched Casitas to the four-bedroom Casa Azul with its private pool. All have nice beds with mosquito nets, minibars and efficient AC, but most have no phones or TVs. The Ra*Info*rest Suite is especially nice, with charming tropical décor and French doors opening right onto the beach. The Restaurant Palmilla is probably the most expensive on the island. There's also more casual dining at the poolside restaurant or beach bar. Or, why not have your meal delivered to your own patio? Victoria House has their own Fantasea dive shop, offering

daily dive trips from their private pier. *Info*: www.victoria-house.com; Tel. 226-2067 or 800/247-5159 US.

Banyan Bay $$$$$
Each of these oceanfront suites has two bedrooms, two baths (one with a Jacuzzi tub), a full kitchen and a nice veranda. This is a good place for families, with a nice swimming beach and a huge pool including a kids' wading area. The on-site dive shop makes this a good choice for divers, too. Rico's restaurant serves a

splendid conch *ceviche*, and the staff is friendly and helpful. *Info*: www.banyanbay.com; Tel. 226-3739 or 866/466-2179 US.

Royal Caribbean Resort $$$$
This first-class resort is next door to Victoria House. The 42 thatched cabanas are spacious, with separate bedrooms and living areas, kitchenettes complete with coffee makers, TVs, phones, nice new air conditioners and ceiling fans. There's an enormous pool and a brand new restaurant and bar. The staff are doing an excellent job. This is a fantastic value for the price. *Info*: www.royalcaribbeanbelize.com; Tel. 888/400-3515 US.

Xanadu Island Resort $$$$
Located just a short way south of town, this elegant tropical resort has 19 suites with full kitchens, dining areas, central air, ceiling fans, and all the goodies. There's a nice pool with a wooden deck, a private dock and plenty of hammocks for lazing about. Repeat guests rave about the service and the peaceful atmosphere. Wedding packages are a specialty. They'll put on a complete tropical wedding for you, taking care of the license, a minister, flowers, a band and all the trimmings. *Info*: www.xanaduresort-belize.com; Tel. 226-2814.

Mata Rocks Resort $$$$
This small and friendly beachfront resort a mile south of town has eleven rooms arranged around a swimming pool, all with ocean views. Downstairs rooms open onto the pool deck; upstairs rooms have private balconies. All have private bath, AC, TV, and a small refrigerator. There are also six Junior Suites, each with full kitchenette. There are no phones in the rooms, but there's a phone in the office available for guests. There are also bicycles that are free for guests' use during daylight hours only (too many guests were taking the bikes to bars at night, then forgetting where they were). The daily happy hour at the Squirrel's Nest, the cool and breezy beachside bar, is a good time to compare notes on the day's adventures with your fellow guests. Canadian owners Terry and Liz embrace the casual Belizean lifestyle, and their excellent local staff will cater to your every desire. *Info*: www.matarocks.com; Tel. 226-2336 or 888/628-2757 US.

Exotic Caye Beach Resort $$$$
Just south of town. All rooms have AC, kitchens and sea views. There's a pool, an attractive beach and on on-site dive shop. Crazy Canuck's Beach Bar is one of the local hot spots, with occasional live bands. *Info*: www.belizeisfun.com; Tel. 226-2870.

Corona del Mar Apartment Hotel $$$
This is one of the best values on the island, a first-class hotel at midrange prices that gets consistent rave reviews. A short walk south of San Pedro are twelve rooms and four apartment suites with all mod cons. The AC works great (not always the case in Belize), the beds are comfortable, and there's even an elevator! Some rooms have balconies with splendid ocean views. They serve a nice breakfast on the beach, and keep a pitcher of free rum punch in the lobby all day. The staff are what really keep the guests coming back. Miriam, Pamela and Frank are friendly and attentive, and will get your tours and other activities set up in an efficient manner. Don't let Frank hustle you at horseshoes! *Info*: www.ambergriscaye.com/coronadelmar; Tel. 226-2055.

BEST EATS ON AMBERGRIS
Ambergris eateries range from elegant restaurants, perfect for a candlelit dinner for two, to casual sand-floor places and streetside

stalls where you can grab a quick burger. Several of the fancy places are located at resorts south or north of town, so you may have to take a boat or bike (and make reservations in advance), but the dining is often worth the effort. The variety of cuisines includes Belizean, Mexican, Italian, Chinese, Thai, Jamaican, and American. Seafood is naturally a specialty, and you'll find lobster prepared in a wonderful variety of ways, as well as snapper, conch and other delights. *Ceviche* (fish or seafood in a lemon marinade, served with chips) is an excellent choice for an appetizer.

Restaurant prices are not necessarily cheap. You can get a good Belizean or Mexican-style dinner at a bargain price, but seafood dishes can get spendy. San Pedro's favorite crustacean is still reasonably priced by US standards – expect to pay around $20 for a lobster dinner in one of the casual restaurants. Atmosphere is cheap: almost all of the restaurants listed below are oceanfront. Most restaurants offer food only during normal meal times, serving lunch from around 11am-2pm, then closing in the afternoon and opening again for dinner around 5pm. Most accept credit cards.

Upscale
Capricorn
Snazzy food mags have called this one of the best restaurants in Central America. The menu is a delightful fusion of Belizean and  Continental influences. When was the last time you had fresh stone crab claws with French crepes? The specialty of the house is a grouper filet stuffed with onions, peppers and cheese. Home-baked breads and desserts round out the picture. Capricorn is accessible only by sea. A moonlight boat ride and a table under the stars make the perfect romantic evening. *Info*: www.ambergriscaye.com/capricorn; Tel. 226-2809.

Rendezvous Restaurant & Winery
Also located north of San Pedro, this top-rated intimate (only 24

seats) restaurant specializes in Thai and French fusion cuisine. Offerings include classic Thai dishes (*phad Thai*), French specialties (*creme brulée, escargot*), and such unique creations as salmon mousse with basil and mint rolled in an almond crumble. The Rendezvous even produces their own brand of wines (from imported grapes, of course). *Info*: ambergriscaye.com/rendezvous; Tel. 226-3426.

Palmilla Restaurant

The restaurant at the Victoria House Resort is known to locals and tourists as one of the finest on the island, serving a unique

mix of island seafood and Continental cuisine. It's no surprise that excellent *ceviche* and lobster salad are on offer, but what say you to orange-scented seafood bouillabaisse, or shrimp salpicon with chipotle? *Info*: www.victoria-house.com; Tel. 226-2067.

Casual
Elvi's Kitchen

San Pedro's most famous eating spot. Elvi has had a restaurant here for over 25 years, and has won all kinds of awards for her Belizean cooking. Despite all the fame, Elvi's remains a casual place with reasonable prices. Seafood is the specialty, but the chicken wings and desserts have also won renown. On Fridays there's a Grand Mayan Buffet, one of the few places you can sample traditional Mayan cuisine. *Info*: www.elviskitchen.com; Tel. 226-2176.

Ambergris Delight

The menu at this casual spot on Middle Street ranges from seafood to Mexican to burgers and even pizza. You can dine on Belizean stew chicken for under ten bucks, or have a lobster tail or a stone crab dinner for around $20. Seafood is prepared in many delightful ways, from salad to soup to kebabs. My favorite? A simple but excellent grilled lobster tail. *Info*: Tel. 226-2464.

Cocina Caramba

Also on Middle Street, this place is only a few years old, but it gets rave reviews from locals. The main offerings are seafood and Mexican dishes, including burritos and fajitas with fish, shrimp or lobster, jerk fish and of course lobster served a variety of ways. There are several vegetarian offerings. There's a decent wine list and an array of cocktails, smoothies and fresh juices. *Info*: www.ambergriscaye.com/caramba; Tel. 603-1652.

JamBel Jerk Pit

Locals consider this the best medium-priced restaurant in town. The cuisine is JAMaican, with a BELizean touch (get it?). There are two locations: one in the Coral Beach Hotel, and one a bit further north, on the beach, with an open upstairs dining area (very nice, unless it's rainy). There's nothing fancy about this place (in fact, the beachfront location is pretty funky), but the food is excellent. The  menu includes jerk chicken, fish and seafood, served with beans and rice and I-tal vegetables. JamBel is also one of the cheaper places to have a lobster tail. Reggae music cranks for an Irie dining experience! *Info*: Tel. 226-2594 or 226-3514.

The Blue Water Grill at the SunBreeze Hotel (across from the airstrip) serves good seafood dishes and wood-fired pizza on a pleasant beachfront deck.

Caliente, in the Spindrift Hotel on Front Street, serves very good Mexican cuisine, including *enchiladas de mole, tacos al carbón*, and a particularly good *ceviche*. Vegetarians will dig the vegetable *quesadillas*.

Celi's Restaurant, on the beach next door to the San Pedro Holiday Hotel, is a local favorite, inexpensive and good. The best burgers in town are here, plus beach barbecues with live music.

Celi's Deli, on the main street side of the Holiday Hotel, has BLT, turkey, chicken and other sandwiches.

Lily's Restaurant (Tel. 226-2059) is on the beach, in the hotel of the same name. Lobster, shrimp and conch creole are just a few of the seafood specialties on the menu. Dine on the beachfront deck or inside.

The Grill At Fido's, on Front Street in the center of town, features a variety of dishes including inexpensive sandwiches. Fido's is also a local drinking hotspot, with live music every night.

The Stained Glass Pub (Tel. 226-4147), towards the north end of town, serves British burgers, fish and chips and other pub favorites. Despite the British theme, there are no UK beers on offer except for bottled Guinness (not their fault – imported beers aren't available in Belize).

Estel's, on the beach just north of the Spindrift, is casual even by San Pedro standards. The floor is sand, and it's no shirt, no shoes – no problem! The menu, chalked on the wall, consists of simple but hearty standards, filling but undistinguished. Estel's is one of the few San Pedro eateries where you can eat any time. Lunch is served all afternoon, and breakfast all day (from 6am). No credit cards.

If you're looking for a cheap snack, check out Ambergris Street, off Front Street on the beach side. There's a whole row of "fast food" stalls serving everything from burgers to fruit smoothies to (of course) beans and rice to locals.

Wine De Vine (www.winedevine.com; Tel. 226-3430), toward the south end of town, has an amazing selection of cheese, wines and spirits at the shop.

BEST SLEEPS ON CAYE CAULKER

Most of the lodging on Caye Caulker is basic and inexpensive, but there's a lot of new construction going on (maybe next to your hotel – better ask!), and the new guest houses are tending more towards the upscale. Prices are lower here than on Ambergris, with fewer sneaky fees, and hotel staff are very laid-back. In fact, there may not be anyone there when you show up – no problem – have a cold one and wait. Some of the smaller places close in the low season.

Iguana Reef Inn $$$$

This upscale inn is on the lagoon side, not the ocean side, but there's a pleasant beach and swimming area, the staff are super-friendly, and everyone who comes here seems to have a great time. The bright and airy rooms have tile floors, wicker furniture, pastel walls and artwork by local artists. Pleasant breezes keep things cool, but there's also nice cold AC (none of the rickety old window units you'll find at cheaper places). The pool is splendid. *Info*: www.iguanareefinn.com; Tel. 226-0213.

Seaside Cabanas $$$

This is also a splendid choice, a fairly new yellow masonry building right by the water taxi dock in the center of town. The 17 rooms are spacious and attractive, with private bath, AC, TV and refrigerators. Most of the rooms have private verandas, and a few have rooftop terraces with hammocks. There's a nice pool and free wi-fi. *Info*: www.seasidecabanas.com; Tel. 226-0498.

OASI $$$

In a quiet location amid lush grounds, a couple of minutes from the beach and center of town, these apartments have small kitchens, AC, ceiling fans and TVs. Guests rave about the comfortable rooms, and especially about owners Luciana and Michael. There are two dogs and a cat. *Info*: www.holidaybelize.com; Tel. 226-0384.

Caye Caulker Condos $$$

Eight nice newish units near the Split, all with private bath, kitchens, AC, safes and private verandahs. The rooms are pleasantly tropical, with tile floors and mahogany furniture, and the second-floor ones have excellent views. There are complimentary bikes for guests' use, a nice pool, and a rooftop *palapa* with hammocks. Miss Claudette can cook a Belizean dinner for you in your room. *Info*: www.cayecaulkercondos.com; Tel. 226-0072 or 600-8485.

De Real Macaw $$$

This friendly guest house has seven double rooms and a two-bedroom apartment. All have private bath, AC and ceiling fans, and some have nice porches with sea views. Pets are accepted, and there are lots of cats hanging around. Some guests don't like the fact that the hotel is adjacent to the boisterous street market. These folks also have some new one-bedroom apartments available by the week. *Info*: www.derealmacaw.com; Tel. 226-0459.

Auxillou Beach Suites $$$

These pleasantly decorated rooms feature porches, TVs, AC, and little kitchens for basic meals. Wendy Auxillou also has a three-bedroom, two-bath house on offer. *Info*: www.auxilloubeachsuites.com; Tel. 226-0370.

There are a number of newer apartments and condo-style accommodations in the middle price range, some of them pretty luxurious. Property manager Caye Caulker Accommodations offers a selection of these, including **Sailwinds Beach Suites** and **Seaside Villas Condos**, both new beachfront places with AC, kitchens and rooftop terraces. Seaside Villas even has a pool. *Info*: www.cayecaulkeraccommodations.com; Tel. 226-0381.

As we move into the middle and lower price ranges, many of Caulker's lodgings may appear a bit too rustic for the typical American tourist, at least from outside. But if you don't expect luxury, you'll find several places offering clean and comfortable rooms right on the beach, at nice prices.

Vega Inn & Gardens has been here since 1959, and has rooms with private bath and sea views for $75-130. A mangrove bird rookery right in front provides birding opportunities. *Info*: www.vegabelize.com; Tel. 226-0142.

Trends Hotel has some rooms on the beach and some a few feet away on Front Street. All have private bath and ceiling fans, and some have AC. *Info*: www.trendsbze.com; Tel. 226-0094.

Popeye's Beach Resort, on the beach toward the south end of town, has pretty nice air-conditioned rooms for $55-120. *Info*: www.popeyesbeachresort.com; Tel. 226-0032.

Tina's Backpackers Hostel is quite popular for the social scene and the bargain price (dorm beds for $10 per person, which includes use of the kitchen), but several guests have reported sanitary issues. *Info*: Tel. 206-0019. Several other cheap sleeps cluster near the water in the middle of the village. Ask around, and you should be able to find a basic but clean room for $20-30 double.

Caye Caulker

Maxhapan Cabanas $$
These three cabanas offer excellent value for the price, with private bath, AC, ceiling fans and TVs. Owner Louise Aguilar is an interesting character, and everyone who stays here seems to love it. *Info*: www.toucantrail.com/Maxhapan-Cabins.html; Tel. 226-0118.

Tropical Paradise Hotel $$
At the south end of the village, next to the old island cemetery, this is a classic tropical hideaway, wooden cabanas in a sandy beachfront compound. The rooms are nothing fancy, but they are clean and well appointed. The best is #14, which faces directly onto the beach, and has a nice porch, the perfect place to sit and write your masterpiece. Or, if you prefer, to do absolutely nothing. The restaurant serves Belizean specials at good prices (see below). The owners also operate the cheaper and less pleasant Tropics Hotel in town, as well as Star Tours, which offers daily snorkel tours from Tropical Paradise's private dock. *Info*: www.startoursbelize.com; Tel. 226-0124 or 226-0374.

Walking south past the Tropical Paradise, you'll find a string of beachfront lodgings, each funkier than the last. **Sea Beezzz** (www.seabeezzz.com; Tel. 226-0176), run by colorful expatriate Chuck Balfour, has units with private baths and ceiling fans for around fifty bucks. Open Nov-April only. **Tom's Hotel** (Tel. 226-0102) has austere but clean rooms with shared or private bath. **The Anchorage** (www.anchorageresort.com; Tel. 226-0304) has 18 rooms, all with private bath, AC, TV, refrigerator and balcony.

Caye Caulker

A new addition to the "strip" is **Barefoot Beach** (www.barefootbeachbelize.com; Tel. 226-0205), which has nice new rooms with private bath and AC starting at $50. **Ignacio's Beach Cabins** (Tel. 226-0175) are very rustic wooden cabins on stilts, starting under $20 for a cold-water cabin. **Shirley's Guest House** (www.shirleysguesthouse.com; Tel. 226-0145 or 600-0069), the southernmost lodging, has a nice sandy compound and decent little rooms starting under $50.

BEST EATS ON CAULKER

Caye Caulker's restaurants operate on island time. Shirts and shoes are optional, the floor may be sand, and both menus and opening times may be flexible. Prices for food are much better than in San Pedro or Belize City. If part of your ideal Belize vacation involves gorging on lobster, Caye Caulker is the place to do it. You can have your lobster in a wide variety of Caribbean, Oriental and Italian sauces, in a soup or a salad, or just steamed or grilled.

A good lobster dinner should cost you less than $20 (much less at one of the streetside barbecue stands). The **Tropical Paradise Restaurant**, located at the hotel of the same name, is a good sit-down restaurant, open for breakfast, lunch and dinner. Seafood and Belizean specialties are creatively prepared and reasonably priced. The lobster specials can be very special indeed, for example a huge portion of lobster in a tasty marinara sauce for $12.

Rasta Pasta, on the beach in the center of town, is a colorful spot even for Belize. Dine in the shady sand-floored dining room, or out on the beach. A delightful mix of Jamaican, Italian, Thai and Mexican, the menu features pasta, seafood, I-tal salads and plenty of choices for vegetarians, as well as inventive desserts and an assortment of herbal teas. If you are "impatient, picky or just plain mean," a sign behind the bar kindly advises you to "take your Ras elsewhere!" Open all day.

Syd's (Tel. 206-0294), toward the south end of town, is an institution, the place where the locals eat. It's nothing fancy (décor is chrome dinette and plastic), but the food is excellent and cheap, with main dishes starting around five bucks.

Habanero's serves delectable fajitas and firecracker prawns (made, of course, with habanero pepper). The menu has a Caribbean-Mexican vibe. At lunch here it's pizzas and salads only.

The Oceanside, in the center of town, offers excellent value, and is highly recommended. They serve curried lobster, pasta, and freshly caught fish, as well as tourist fillers such as omelettes, veggie burritos and burgers. Open for dinner only.

All along Front Street during the busy season, you'll see small improvised barbecue stands, sometimes consisting of nothing more than a bisected oil drum grill and a cooler full of drinks. This is the cheapest way of all to enjoy a grilled lobster tail, although some travelers may have misgivings about sanitary issues.

For breakfast, head for **Amor y Café**, on Front Street (formerly Cindy's). There's excellent organic coffee from Guatemala, as well as Chai, smoothies, homemade muffins, banana bread, fruit plates and other healthy treats. This is *the* morning hangout spot, a great place to swap stories with experienced travelers and find out what's happening on Caulker and beyond.

Cocoplum Garden Café, Spa and Gallery
(www.cocoplum.typepad.com), off the beaten path on the south end of town, is a culinary bright spot (photo at right). Owned by Dutchman Chris and his Belizean wife, CocoPlum offers healthful cuisine amid lush gardens, and is also a day spa where you can have a massage, a yoga class or even a Mayan spiritual bath.

The **Lazy Lizard**, at the Split, is a local hangout where you can swim in the clear, fast-moving water.

BEST LODGES ON THE SMALLER CAYES

Smaller
Cayes

If you really want to get away to a secluded Caribbean paradise, one of the smaller cayes could be the island of your dreams. There are a couple dozen little lodges dotted among the vast sprawl of tiny islands south of Caulker. Most exist for the purpose of diving and/or fishing, and most guests come on weeklong packages. If you're a hardcore sportsman, this could be the perfect option. The really hot diving and fishing sites are closer here than they are from San Pedro, and you can concentrate on the fishies with no distractions.

However, the remote island experience isn't for everyone, and it's probably not for parties that include non-diving spouses or kids. Most of these places are the **sole lodging and dining option on their respective cayes**, and there are few "things to do." The only access to most of these spots is by the resorts' private boats, so once you're there, you're there for the duration. Supplies also travel by small boat, so these places tend to be more expensive than their mainland counterparts, and occasional embarrassing shortages are a fact of life. Some of the cayes have beautiful beaches, but most are not world-class swimming spots, as the water tends to be shallow, with lots of sea grass and squishy mud rather than nice sand.

See the section on Southern Belize, below, for several more island lodge options.

Caye Chapel Island Resort $$$$$

The only thing on Caye Chapel is this upscale golf resort, the only really proper golf course in Belize. This "personal playground for the discriminating elite" features an 18-hole par-72 champion-

ship golf course, a deep-water marina and a private airstrip. Accommodations are in luxurious suites and beachfront villas. It's pricey, but the rates include unlimited golf. *Info*: www.cayechapel.com; Tel. 800/901-8938 US.

St. George's Caye Resort $$$$

The closest of the cayes to Belize City, St George's Caye has nothing but two lodges and a couple dozen private homes. This homelike dive lodge has cozy rooms in the main lodge, and six charming cottages built over the water, with thatched roofs. All have private bath and AC. These folks have been running a dive lodge for over thirty years, and it shows in the excellent dive operation, with first-rate facilities and personal service from some of Belize's most experienced divemasters. Diving possibilities include not only lots of nearby sites (the reef is only a half mile out), but also day trips to Turneffe or the Blue Hole (both much closer from here than from Ambergris or Caulker). After the diving, you can poke around in a kayak, windsurfer or jet ski, then join the other guests for a barbecue and a bonfire on the beach. *Info*: www.gooddiving.com; Tel. 800/813-8498 US.

Hugh Parkey's Belize Adventure Lodge $$$

This basic lodge on Spanish Lookout Caye consists of 12 rustic cabanas with private bath and ceiling fans, as well as dormitory-style lodging for student groups. There's a complete PADI dive shop, and various other water and land activities are on offer. *Info*: www.belizeadventurelodge.com; Tel. 223-4526 or 223-5086.

Turneffe Flats $$$

You can't get any closer to the fish than this. The Turneffe Islands are one of the best areas for diving in the country, and flats fishing

is also excellent. One of three lodges that comprise the only human habitation on this remote atoll, Turneffe Flats has pretty nice rooms with AC and private bath. Both diving and fishing guests give this place consistently good reviews. *Info*: www.tflats.com; Tel. 888/512-8812 US.

Gallows Point Resort $$

You don't have to spend a lot to enjoy the island hideaway experience. This basic little lodge on Gallows Point Caye is run by the same folks as the budget Hotel Belcove in Belize city. The six basic but clean rooms have private shower and fans. Meals are prepared on request, or you can use the kitchen to cook your own. Various diving and fishing packages are available. *Info*: www.belcove.com; Tel. 227-3054.

BELIZE CITY & NORTHERN BELIZE

BEST SLEEPS IN BELIZE CITY

Belize City is not that bad a place, but from a tourist's standpoint it can't compare to the jungle or the islands. Another reason not to spend the night is that the selection of sleeps is poor. The few first-class hotels tend to be second-class, and although there are plenty of lower-priced lodgings, most are in dodgy neighborhoods. Fortunately, frequent air connections mean you need never spend the night in the city. If you do, here are the best options.

Radisson Fort George Hotel & Marina $$$$

This historic landmark is the closest thing Belize City has to a first-class American- or European-style hotel, the place for business travelers and tourists who want a safe and clean haven from the city. Alas, the hotel has seen better days, and has been getting mixed reviews. Everyone enjoys the facilities – two restaurants, a bar, two pools, a fitness center, a full-service marina, tour and car rental desks, business center and 24-hour security. However, some areas are a bit dingy, and due for renovation. On my last visit, I found the rooms and most of the facilities to be clean enough, but there was a little mildew here, a little chipped paint there – the kind of thing that's hard to avoid in a tropical climate.

The rooms have all the goodies – AC, TV, phones, minibars, coffee makers and nice local paintings on the walls. The best (and most expensive) are the spacious Club Tower rooms, with marble floors and great views of the bay. The St. George's Dining Room is famous for their buffets, but the food here is good, not great. As at many Belize hotels, extra charges add up quickly. Internet access costs $10 per day. The convenient airport shuttle van is $10 per person. The tour desk is handy, but they tack on hefty fees for tours that you could easily book yourself. *Info*: 2 Marine Parade. www.radissonbelize.com; Tel. 223-3333 or 888/201-1718 US.

The Great House $$$$

This is a good place to stay in Belize City, a beautiful old mansion (built in 1927) with colonial-style charm. While it lacks the long list of amenities you'll find at the Radisson (across the street), the Great House does have most of the modern conveniences, including wireless internet. There are only twelve rooms, each with private bath, AC, ceiling fans, TV, phones, hair dryers, refrigerators, coffee makers and safety deposit boxes. Tile floors and rattan furniture lend a light and airy feel, as sea breezes blow through the wide verandahs. The Smoky Mermaid restaurant is a charming tropical patio with good grilled meats and seafood. *Info*: 13 Cork St. www.greathousebelize.com; Tel. 223-3400.

Villa Boscardi $$$

This may be the best of the mid-price options, a little B&B in a quiet residential area, a block from the water. The six rooms have AC, TV, phone, ceiling fans, hair dryers and desks. *Info*: 6043 Manatee Drive, Buttonwood Bay. www.villaboscardi.com; Tel. 223-1691 or 602-8954.

Fallen Princess

The **Princess Hotel & Casino**, a 181-room resort hotel once considered the second-finest in town, has fallen from her throne. For several years now, guests have been complaining of plumbing and AC problems, poor food, clueless staff and sanitary issues. It's a shame, because the hotel has a good view and wonderful facilities.

Hotel Mopan $$$

This venerable favorite is a classic old colonial house facing the water a few blocks south of the Swing Bridge. Though the neighborhood is dodgy at night, the hotel is clean and welcoming. The rooms are nothing fancy, but they have nice private bathrooms and TVs. It's worth the extra $10 for the Balcony Rooms, the only ones with really nice views. The owners are pillars of the local scene – stop in at the bar to get the skinny on what's happening around town. *Info*: 55 Regent St. www.hotelmopan.com; Tel. 227-7351.

Belcove Hotel $$

This is an okay hotel in a convenient but seedy location, on the river just around the corner from the Swing Bridge. The plain rooms have private bath and AC. It's run by the same people as the more relaxing Belcove Island Lodge on Gallows Point Caye. *Info*: 9 Regent Street West. www.belcove.com; Tel. 227-3054.

Most **budget lodgings** in Belize City are in neighborhoods that are dangerous after dark. Many have no AC, and some have little ventilation. The following are basic but clean. North of the Swing Bridge you'll find the homey **Sea Guest House** (18 Gabourel Lane. Tel. 223-6798 or 203-0043) and the spartan **North Front Street Guest House** (124 N Front Street. Tel. 227-7595). **Smokin Balam** is a funky but friendly riverfront hotel and drinking spot with a restaurant and a cheap internet connection (59 N Front Street. Tel. 223-3969 or 610-4510).

BEST SLEEPS OUTSIDE BELIZE CITY
Black Orchid Resort $$$

This fine hotel has 12 spacious rooms with AC and nice tile floors, as well as a pool, restaurant and gift shop. It's situated in a pleasant spot on the river near the village of Burrel Boom, 20 minutes from the airport. You can take a cruise on the river in a canoe, kayak or power boat. They also offer a full range of tours all over the country. If you want a comfortable lodging place not too far from Belize City, in a good spot to serve as a base for exploring the interior, this could be a good choice. *Info*: www.blackorchidresort.com; Tel. 225-9158.

Best Western Belize Biltmore Plaza $$$

This resort-style hotel is located just out of town, on the way to the airport, quite convenient if you're traveling by car. The pool and peaceful garden courtyard are a pleasant oasis, and the list of facilities is first-class: 24-hour security, free parking, laundry service, restaurant, two bars, room service, gift shop, tour desk, business center and small gym. The 75 air-conditioned rooms are well appointed, with phones, TVs, coffee makers, hair dryers and safe deposit boxes. *Info*: www.belizebiltmore.com; Tel. 223-2302.

Belize River Lodge $$$

This fishing lodge is located down a side road and across the river from the airport. The setting is remote and tropical, even though you're near Belize's metropolis. Most guests are here on weeklong fishing packages. *Info*: www.belizeriverlodge.com; Tel. 225-2002 or 888/275-4843 US.

Embassy Hotel $$

This hotel couldn't be more convenient for the airport – it's right across the parking lot. The 40 rooms have private bath and AC, and the place is reasonably clean and well run, though spartan. They also rent cars. *Info*: www.embassyhotelbelize.com; Tel. 225-3333 or 225-4444.

BEST EATS IN BELIZE CITY

The **Smoky Mermaid**, at the Great House, has grilled meats, seafood dishes and a special lobster menu with such delights as lobster quesadillas, a lobster burger and a plain old "naked" lobster. The pleasant plant-filled courtyard is a peaceful place for a cold beer or an umbrella drink. Or why not a bottle of wine? The Mermaid has a good wine list, including French bottles at reasonable prices.

Harborview Restaurant has nice harbor views and vaguely Continental cuisine. There's also a separate lobster menu and a fair wine list, mostly US and Chilean bottles. *Info*: next to the Tourism Village.

Chateau Caribbean has an upstairs dining room with nice views of the harbor. The cuisine is a mix of Caribbean, Asian and North American influences, and the service is good. There's also a cocktail lounge, in case you'd just like to have a drink and enjoy the view. *Info*: 6 Marine Parade.

Chef Bob is a very Belizean place, although the menu includes Italian and English favorites in addition to better seafood than you'll find in some other spots. Bob's is well known among both locals and tourists. *Info*: just down the road from the Princess. Tel. 223-6908).

There are plenty of places for cheap local chow. **Three Amigos** (2B King St) offers good Mexican and Belizean dishes. **Nerie's**, on Queen Street, is one of the best bets for Belizean cooking. Another popular local spot is **Big Daddy's**, on the top floor of the City Market.

For light fare, try the **Maya Café** (160 N Front St), which serves fresh fruit juices, good coffee and teas. **Super Subs Deli**, inside Brodie's Supermarket on Albert Street, is a good bet for a cheap lunch to go.

BEST SLEEPS IN NORTHERN BELIZE

Hiking, birding and river trips to the Lamanai ruins are the attractions in this region. All these lodges are fairly remote, with no other dining options or "things to do" nearby, so a package that includes meals and possibly some local tours will be your best bet.

Chan Chich Lodge $$$$$

This luxury ecolodge is located on Gallon Jug Estate in the northwestern corner of the country, in the middle of a vast forest area teeming with wildlife. The grounds are in the middle of an unexcavated Mayan site, a peaceful and lovely setting for 12 cabanas. From outside the cabanas look rustic – thatched roofs, louvered walls to let in the breeze, and porches with inviting hammocks. Once inside, however, you'll appreciate the tile floors, big comfortable beds, armchairs, plenty of closet space and huge bathrooms. High ceilings and fans keep things cool. There are several miles of marked hiking trails that are fantastic for spotting wildlife. Over 350 species of birds have been spotted, and wild cat sightings are not rare! Horseback riding, canoeing, and day trips to Lamanai are a few other possible activities. The pool and hot tub are really special, and the food is excellent. Gallon Jug has an airstrip about

15 minutes from the lodge, so you can get here via a 30-minute charter flight from Belize City. *Info*: www.chanchich.com; Tel. 223-4419 or 800/343-8009 US.

Maruba Resort Jungle Spa $$$$$

Some people find their dream vacation here, others just don't get it – but all agree that Maruba is unique. This all-inclusive resort and spa has mineral baths, two wonderful pools amid tropical greenery, and a full range of massages, multicolored mud baths and other New Age wellness treatments. There's even a Mayan seer on hand for psychic readings. Accommodations are luxurious, especially the suites. Honeymoon packages are a specialty. The location is convenient to many attractions in the region, and a range of tours is on offer. Some people absolutely love the atmosphere, and others find it Disneyesque (fittingly, day tour groups from cruise ships sometimes visit). The site is lushly landscaped, not virgin jungle, the exotic "tribal chic" décor – thatched ceilings, wild mosaics on floors and walls – is either really cool or really tacky, and the trance music that plays all over the resort is not for everyone. Don't go near Pancho the monkey! *Info*: www.maruba-spa.com; Tel. 225-5555.

Lamanai Outpost Lodge $$$$

Just a few minutes from the Lamanai Mayan site, the unpretentious and laid-back Lamanai Outpost gets a steady stream of rave reviews. There's a huge range of activities – visit the nearby ruins, tour the surrounding waterways by canoe or airboat, go fishing with the local fishermen, or go out tagging crocodiles with resident biologists. See how many of the 400 local bird species you can  check off your list. The waterfront grounds are lovely and peaceful, and the 20 cabanas are attractive and well appointed. Most don't have AC, but you probably won't miss it. The all-inclusive packages are the way to go. *Info*: www.lamanai.com; Tel. 672-2000 or 888/733-7864 US.

Bird's Eye View Lodge $$$

Birders love this place – it's directly on the water, and you can tour the adjacent Crooked Tree Wildlife Sanctuary (with its 250 bird species) by foot, horseback or canoe. You may even spot a wood stork or a kiskadee from your balcony. The lodge itself is not quite luxurious, but the 20 rooms were renovated in 2007, and all have private bath, AC, ceiling fans and nice tight screens. *Info*: www.birdseyeviewlodge.com; Tel. 203-2040 or 225-7027.

WESTERN BELIZE & TIKAL

BEST SLEEPS IN BELMOPAN

Most travelers visit Belmopan only to change buses – and you will too, if you take a bus to anyplace in the west or south of the country. There's no real reason to spend the night in the town, but there are a couple of special lodges in the immediate area.

Bull Frog Inn $$$

This is the best lodging in town, modern and clean. The 25 rooms all have private bath, AC, TV and phone. The restaurant is quite good, and the bar has live music on Friday nights. *Info*: 25 Half Moon Avenue. www.bullfroginn.com; Tel. 822-3425.

LODGES NEAR BELMOPAN

Banana Bank Lodge & Jungle Equestrian Adventure $$$$

If you love horses, this is the place for you. Banana Bank is an upscale jungle lodge located on the Belize River. The equestrian center is probably the largest in Belize, with about 100 head of quarter horses. There are miles of beautiful trails through the jungle. Other ways to spend your time include tubing and kayaking on the river, lazing around the pool, and visiting resident painter Carolyn Carr's studio and gallery. There are several different lodging options, with or without AC, at quite reasonable prices. *Info*: www.bananabank.com; Tel. 820-2020.

Ian Anderson's Caves Branch Adventure Co.
& Jungle Lodge $$/$$$$

If you love caving, this is the place for you. Oops! You say dad loves caves and mom loves horses? Not a problem. Ian's place is not far from Banana Bank – many visitors stay at one and take day trips to the other. This part of Belize has enough adventurous activities to keep you busy for months. There are dozens of interesting caves in the area, and Ian and his merry band of spelunkers know them better than anyone. However, even they haven't charted them all – you can visit in the off-season and help them scope out new ones. Cave tubing is especially popular – float down the river on an inner tube, rushing in and out of caves! There are accommodations here for all budgets, from $15 beds in the bunkhouse to luxurious treehouse suites. *Info*: www.cavesbranch.com; Tel. 822-2800 or 888/357-2698 US.

JB's Watering Hole
JB's is a piece of Belizean history. Years ago, it was the only watering hole between Belize City and San Ignacio. The restaurant is a popular pit stop off the Western Highway (at mile 32), and serves very good Belizean fare. JB's is well worth a visit just for the view, the atmosphere and a look at the murals by local artist Juan Esquivel. Internet access is available. There's one cabana available for overnight stays, with a few new ones in the planning stages. *Info*: www.jb-belize.com.

BEST SLEEPS AT MOUNTAIN PINE RIDGE
Blancaneaux Lodge $$$$$
One of two luxury lodges in Belize owned by Francis Ford Coppola, Blancaneaux sits on 50 acres of grounds on the Privassion River. The thatched cabanas, some riverfront, are well appointed and very attractive, with all kinds of quirky antiques and local art. There's a fully-equipped spa for massages and mango baths, a stable full of riding horses, and an organic garden and chicken

farm to provide fresh produce for the excellent
gourmet restaurant. This
is an international luxury
lodge, not a quaint local
establishment, and some-
times it feels as if you're
in Europe, not Belize (love
it or hate it – personally I
think it's a great mix). As
you'd expect at an estab-

lishment of this caliber, the rooms, food and wine are expensive, but the service is top-notch and very personal. *Info*: www.blancaneaux.com; Tel. 824-4912 or 800/746-3743 US.

Hidden Valley Inn $$$$
This beautiful lodge sits on a 7,200-acre private estate in the Mountain Pine Ridge preserve, home to 300 species of birds and animals and 76 species of orchid. The 12
rooms are bright, airy
and private, set in six
adobe-style cottages.
Luxuries include the
expected (large bath-
rooms, fireplaces,

large comfortable beds) as well as the unexpected but very handy (a shoe cleaning kit and a bottle of Skin-So-Soft bug-repellent oil). The lovely waterfall pool and hot tub is perfect for soaking tired feet after a day of hiking. The dining is excellent, with fresh-baked bread, a good wine list and delicious coffee grown and roasted right on the premises. Manager Flavien Daguise presides over a locally-recruited staff that caters to your every whim. There's also a resident naturalist and bird expert who leads tours. 90 miles of hiking trails lead you to idyllic waterfalls and clear pools deep in the jungle. You can hike all day without seeing another human, but luxury is only as far away as you want it to be. They'll lend you a handheld radio, so if your feet get tired, just call in to be picked up and driven back to the lodge! *Info*: Cooma Cairn Road. www.hiddenvalleyinn.com; Tel. 822-3320 or 866/443-3364 US.

Pine Ridge Lodge $$$
This comfortable little lodge is right in the forest on a nice little creek, and offers good prices and an eco-friendly outlook. The thatched cottages, decorated with local Mayan-themed art, are as romantic as you please. After dark, light is provided by kerosene lanterns, and the babbling brook lulls you to sleep. An organic garden and lots of tropical fruit trees provide goodies for the table. Jungle waterfalls with lovely pools for swimming are a short hike away. *Info*: www.pineridgelodge.com; Tel. 606-4557 or 800/316-0706 US.

Five Sisters Lodge $$$

This lodge, overlooking the beautiful waterfall of the same name, has 19 cute thatched cabanas with private baths, balconies and hammocks. There's plenty of birds and wildlife right on the grounds, and the location is great for exploring the sights of the area. *Info*: www.fivesisterslodge.com; Tel. 820-4005 or 800/447-2931 US.

Mountain
Pine
Ridge
___
San
Ignacio

BEST SLEEPS IN SAN IGNACIO

Hotel prices in San Ignacio vary according to the season, how full they are and, perhaps, how the owner likes your looks. Especially in the cheaper establishments, try bargaining for a discount.

San Ignacio Resort Hotel $$$$

This is the best of the hotels right in town. The 24 rooms have recently been renovated, and are well appointed, with AC, private bath, TV and phone. There's a pool, tennis court, hiking trails, tour desk, gift shop, business center, and laundry service. The Green Iguana Project is well worth a visit (especially with kids) even if you aren't staying here. The bar is something of a hangout for colorful US expats. *Info*: 18 Buena Vista Street. www.sanignaciobelize.com; Tel. 824-2125 or 800/822-3274 US.

Cahal Pech Village Resort $$$

This pleasant resort sits high on a hill above San Ignacio, right next to the Mayan ruins of the same name. There are 13 thatched cabanas, 14 rooms and five suites, all with private bath and AC. Some of the cabanas have much nicer views than others, so be careful which one you choose. There's a splendid pool, an open-air restaurant and beautifully landscaped grounds. But what everyone raves about is the staff, which provides excellent personal service. *Info*: www.cahalpech.com; Tel. 824-3740.

Martha's Guesthouse $$$

Martha's is another very nice option right in the center of town. The rooms are spotless, the beds are comfortable, and the pleasant patio restaurant is very good. The suites are fantastic for the prices, with mountain views from the private balconies, and kitchen facilities. *Info*: 10 West St. www.marthasbelize.com; Tel. 804-3647.

Midas Tropical Resort $$
This inexpensive lodge features rustic cabanas with private bath just outside of town in a pleasant setting on the Macal River. With seven acres of forest around, it feels secluded, yet it's only a five-minute walk from town. The restaurant serves tasty Belizean food at good prices. *Info*: www.midasbelize.com; Tel. 824-3172.

Burns Avenue, in the center of San Ignacio, has several economy hotels. You can get a double room with private bath and AC for under $35, or one with shared bath and fan for $15. Be sure to specify a room with a window! Some of these places don't have phones, much less web sites, so ask at Eva's Restaurant (see below).

Across the bridge in Santa Elena, the **Aguada Hotel** (www.aguadahotel.com; Tel. 804-3609) has 17 rooms with AC and private bath, starting around $35, a pool and a restaurant.

BEST EATS IN SAN IGNACIO
Eva's Restaurant serves breakfast, lunch and dinner. The menu covers a wide range, including steaks, chicken, curry, Mexican food and vegetarian dishes. Prices are cheap ($3-10 for a meal), and the food is pretty good. Eva's is the local tourist hangout, the place to go to find info on the region and compare notes with other travelers. Owner Bob Jones is a friendly British expat, and an encyclopedia of current information on lodging and tours throughout the Cayo area and beyond. If you're showing up in Cayo without lodging and/or tours already booked, make Eva's your first stop. *Info*: in the center of San Ignacio on Burns Avenue. www.evasonline.com; Tel. 804-2267.

Hode's (pronounced ho-dee's) **Place** (Tel. 804-2522) serves fine local dishes. It's a great place to bring the kids, as there's a playground and a game room. At night, the place to be is the **Cahal Pech** disco.

JUNGLE LODGES AROUND SAN IGNACIO
Most of these lodges are pretty secluded, but not that far from the Western Highway and San Ignacio. Most visitors come on all-inclusive packages – they'll pick you up from town, feed you each

night, and arrange tours and activities for you during the day. This is a good way to go, because there's no other way to get around the area on your own, unless you rent a car. Some lodges have plenty of hiking, birding and other opportunities right on the grounds, and all will gladly arrange excursions to the Mayan ruins, waterfalls, caves, nature reserves and other area attractions.

Near San Ignacio

The Lodge at Chaa Creek $$$$$

This is one of the most venerable ecolodges in Belize, open since 1981, and the recipient of many prestigious awards. Set in a 365-acre private reserve on the Macal River, the lodge offers plenty of opportunities for rain forest hiking, horseback riding, mountain biking and canoeing. The 23 thatched cottages are each uniquely decorated and lavishly appointed.  Some have private Jacuzzis. *Info*: www.chaacreek.com; Tel. 824-2037 or 877/709-8708 US.

Mopan River Resort $$$$$

This luxurious all-inclusive resort is on the Mopan River near the village of Benque Viejo, a short distance from the Guatemalan border. Everything is included here, even day trips to Tikal, Caracol, Caves Branch and other regional sights. The 12 cabanas and suites have every amenity – AC, minibar, hair dryers, safes, etc etc. The lodge is hooked up to city power and water, so there are none of the shortages you may encounter at more remote lodges. The grounds are lush, with a great pool, a birding tower, groves of tropical fruit trees and some nice hiking trails through the adjacent 78-acre private jungle reserve. The cuisine is an elegant mix of international influences, and has been written up in foodie magazines. *Info*: www.mopanriverresort.com; Tel. 823-2047.

Du Plooy's $$$$

Everyone loves this friendly ecolodge. The location couldn't be better, on the Macal River, with the Belize Botanic Gardens next

Near
San
Ignacio

door. It's one of the top birding destinations in the country, with 300 species hanging around and expert bird guides on staff. The rooms are spacious and comfortable, with all mod cons, the personnel are extremely friendly, and the food is great. Unlike at some lodges, you'll have three meal options each night, including a vegetarian one. Du Plooy's gets a big thumbs-up for their environmental awareness. There are no plastic straws or paper napkins, and no beef on the menu (did you know that cattle emit more greenhouse gases than all the cars and trucks in the world?). They have several rooms for larger groups that are actually quite cheap. *Info*: ten miles west of San Ignacio. www.duplooys.com; Tel. 824-3101.

Windy Hill Resort $$$$

This resort has a great location, on a hilltop with cooling breezes and nice views, in a central location that's convenient for day

trips around the region. The attentive staff and tasty food draw rave reviews. The wood-lined cottages have private bath and ceiling fans, and they are spacious and comfortable. Some have AC. There's a restaurant and bar, a fitness center, pool and gift shop. Several hiking trails begin on the grounds, and there are horses and birding guides on staff. *Info*: www.windyhillresort.com; Tel. 824-2017.

Maya Mountain Lodge $$$

Right in the jungle on lovely grounds, adjacent to a private reserve, are eight typical thatched cabanas, with inviting hammocks hanging from the eaves. They also have seven cheaper hotel rooms, but the cabanas have just been renovated, and are much nicer. All have private bath and AC. The pool is very cool, surrounded by greenery. *Info*: www.mayamountain.com; Tel. 824-2164.

Black Rock Lodge $$$

This eco-friendly lodge has a dramatic riverside setting, surrounded by mountains, rain forest and waterfalls. The 12 cabanas have large bathrooms and fine views of Black Rock Canyon and the Macal River. Power is produced by solar panels and a small hydroelectric plant. *Info*: www.blackrocklodge.com; Tel. 820-4049.

BEST SLEEPS NEAR TIKAL

There are three places to stay right at the Tikal ruins site, but all are mediocre at best. There's nothing particularly wrong with the rooms, which are comfortable enough for the price, but the staff are jaded from years of tour-bus tourists whom they know won't ever be coming back. The food is as poor as the service. There are a couple of local-style *comedores* across the street that are cheaper and a little better.

There are several nicer hotel options around Lake Petén Itzá and the town of Flores, but the ride to the ruins may take an hour or more.

Camino Real Tikal $$$
This is the nicest place in the immediate area, a lakefront resort with 72 first-class rooms featuring AC and other mod cons. Many of the rooms have balconies and a view of Lake Petén Itzá. There are two restaurants and a bar, a nice
pool, and kayaks for exploring the lake. It's about a 45-minute ride to the ruins. *Info*: www.caminoreal.com.gt.

The Tikal Inn $$
This so-so hotel, located adjacent to the ruins, has a nice pool, a big plus in this humid area. *Info*: www.tikalinn.com; Tel. (502) 7926-1917.

The Jaguar Inn $$
Next door to the Tikal Inn, the Jaguar has similar rooms at about the same price (50-60 bucks for a double room). *Info*: www.jaguartikal.com; Tel. (502) 7926-0002.

The Jungle Lodge $$
The third member of the Tikal rogues' gallery also has a pool, and is comparable to the other two. *Info*: www.junglelodgetikal.com; Tel. (502) 2477-0570.

SOUTHERN BELIZE

BEST SLEEPS IN GALES POINT
Manatee Lodge $$$
This remote little lodge has a spectacular location, right on the lagoon, adjacent to miles of deserted beach. The staff are great and the décor is cheery, but the eight rooms are a bit run down and due for renovation. Hang around with the manatees, look for sea turtles on the beach, or fish in the lagoon for snook and tarpon. *Info*: www.manateelodge.com; Tel 220-8040 or 877/462-6283 US.

BEST SLEEPS AROUND DANGRIGA
Dangriga, the largest town in Southern Belize, has several mostly budget lodgings right in town, and there are some nice resorts in the surrounding countryside.

Thatch Caye Resort $$$$
This place opened in 2008, and has already earned several prestigious awards, as well as rave reviews from guests. Owners Steve and Travis took eight years to build it by hand, bringing everything by boat. On my visit, I found a very well-run upscale

resort that may soon be spoken of as the best island lodge in the country. Casitas have every amenity you could want, including refrigerators, ceiling fans and rooftop hammocks. They also have AC, but to date, no one has needed to use it. The main lodge features beautiful wood-work and amazing artistry in rattan. Divemasters Ian, Emily and Chico (who has been diving in these waters for 17 years) lead snorkeling and diving trips to the barrier reef, a short boat ride away, or only slightly farther, to Glover's Reef, perhaps the most pristine dive site in Belize. Flats fishing for bones, tarpon and permit is also on offer. This is a very eco-friendly lodge – sun and wind provide electricity, and rainwater fills the cisterns for showers. But every luxury is here, including wireless internet. Thatch Caye isn't just for well-heeled travelers – you can camp here too, and enjoy the dining, diving and fishing. *Info*: www.thatchcaye.com; Tel. 603-2414 or 800/435-3145 US.

Mama Noots Backabush $$$$
This relaxed jungle lodge is located in Mayflower Bocawina Na-tional Park. Millions of birds race about, and hiking trails lead to picture-perfect waterfalls surrounded by greenery. The cabins are on the rustic side, but they are clean and comfortable. Best of all are the warm and friendly owners and staff, who seem to win the hearts of everyone who visits. It's a very eco-friendly lodge, pow-ered by hydro and solar electricity. *Info*: www.mamanoots.com; Tel. 670-8019.

Isla Marisol $$$$
Located on a tiny caye on Glover's Reef just off Dangriga, this rustic resort draws high praise from serious divers and fishers, who come on weeklong packages. The reefs in the area are spectacular and pristine, and there's excellent fly fishing on the flats. As I discussed above, these remote island getaways aren't for everyone. The boat leaves once a week, so once you're here, you're here. The cabanas have private bathrooms and AC, but they are no luxury chalets. *Info*: www.islamarisolresort.com; Tel. 522-0235, 610-4204 or 866/990-9904 US.

Blue Marlin Lodge $$$$
This lodge on South Water Caye, near Dangriga, has a couple of lodging options – the best are the new beach cabins, which have AC and nice Caribbean décor. A variety of weekly diving and fishing packages are on offer. This place is nothing fancy (the management themselves describe it as "rustic" and "funky"), but it's comfort

Dangriga

able, and the staff are great (don't believe them when they say there are no sand fleas, though). *Info*: www.bluemarlinlodge.com; Tel. 522-2243 or 800/798-1558 US.

Bonefish Hotel $$$

The Bonefish, located in the center of Dangriga, is the sister hotel to the Blue Marlin Lodge. The seven rooms are funky but clean, all with AC. There's a view of the sea from the lounge. *Info*: www.bluemarlinlodge.com/bonefish.html; Tel. 522-2243 or 800/798-1558 US.

The **Riverside Café**, right by the boat docks, serves good Belizean fare. There are a few little thatched beach spots that serve grilled fish and other Garifuna goodies. For a super-cheap and tasty meal, hit one of the little improvised streetside barbecue stands.

BEST SLEEPS AROUND HOPKINS

This peaceful little Garifuna village is not known as a tourist hotspot – yet. But the area does have a wide variety of accommodations, including a couple of luxury lodges and several decent low-budget spots.

Hamanasi Adventure and Dive Resort $$$$$

Everyone loves this small and intimate resort. The staff remembers your name, and goes above and beyond to make sure you have a great vacation. From the shady, bird-infested grounds to the flowers strewn on your bed, to the candlelit dinners of seafood fresh from the dock, all the elements of a dream vacation or honeymoon are here. The rooms are spacious and luxurious, with AC, private porches, elegant hardwood furniture and comfortable beds. Phones? TVs? Bah! Don't need 'em. The beachfront rooms are nice, but the most popular are the treehouses, freestanding cabanas 12 feet up in the air, with colorful birdies to sing right outside your window in the morning. Naturally, a full range of diving and other tours can be arranged, but this isn't a hard-core dive lodge. *Info*: www.hamanasi.com; Tel. 520-7073 or 877/552-3483 US.

Jaguar Reef Lodge $$$$$

This isolated and intimate resort does a great job of delivering that relaxing Caribbean vacation. It's especially popular for weddings and honeymoons. The highlights are the long and lovely sandy beach, and spectacular fishing and diving. Beachfront cabanas and poolside suites are spacious, clean and at-

Near Hopkins

tractive, with tile floors and local art on the walls. Fishing opportunities include snook and tarpon on the Sittee River; flats fishing for bonefish and permit; and reef trips for barracuda, kingfish and wahoo. Amenities include two swimming pools and a Jacuzzi, a restaurant and bar on a pleasant beachfront patio, high-speed internet access, and free use of sea kayaks and mountain bikes. *Info*: www.jaguarreef.com; Tel. 520-7040 or 800/910-7373 US.

Kanantik $$$$$

This remote luxury resort offers a bit of European flair in the Central American jungle. The 25 air-conditioned cabanas are spacious, private and lovely, with rich wood floors and Mayan-themed décor. The beach is long, sandy and palm-shaded, and the pool is cool. There's a complete dive operation on site. The dining is a highlight. Everyone loves the pizzas made in a real wood oven, and the coffee from a real Italian espresso machine. Garifuna dancers entertain weekly. The owner is a real character – most guests love him. *Info*: www.kanantik.com; Tel. 520-8048 or 877/759-8834.

Belizean Dreams $$$$

These luxurious oceanfront villas have beautiful kitchens and large verandahs overlooking the sea. The immaculate grounds include an infinity pool and a beautiful beach. A friendly concierge is on hand to book tours and see to your every need. The poolside Woven Palm restaurant serves up a gourmet fusion of Belizean and Mediterranean cuisine. *Info*: www.belizeandreams.com; Tel. 523-7272 or 800/456-7150 US.

Hopkins Bay Resort $$$$

The sister property to Belizean Dreams offers the same level of luxury, with an infinity pool, concierge service and even in-room massages. The villas have one, two or three bedrooms, each with full kitchens, AC, wi-fi and every luxury amenity. The Orange Grove Caribbean Café presents trendy island fare. *Info*: www.belizeandreams.com; Tel. 523-7272 or 800/456-7150 US.

Beaches and Dreams Seafront Inn $$$

This basic but friendly little resort is on the beach in Hopkins. There are only four cabanas, all with private bath, clad in hardwood with cheerful Caribbean décor. Great fishing trips leave from the private dock. The restaurant is a local favorite. *Info*: www.beachesanddreams.com; Tel. 523-7259 or 888/304-2735 US.

Sir Thomas' at Toucan Sittee $$$

This lodge is on 18 acres of jungle on the banks of the Sittee River. The quaint bungalows put you right in the middle of the forest, but have mod cons including fridges and wi-fi. Birders and wildlife enthusiasts will love this place. *Info*: www.sir-thomas-at-toucan-sittee.com; Tel. 523-7039.

Hopkins Inn $$

Right in Hopkins, this modest inn has beachfront cabanas with private bath, refrigerators, coffee makers, fans and small verandahs. Nothing fancy, but spotlessly clean, and the owners are wonderful. You can have breakfast in your room, and other meals at one of the nearby restaurants. The beach bar next door is a blast. *Info*: www.hopkinsinn.com; Tel. 523-7283.

Glover's Atoll Resort $$

This tiny island on Glover's Reef has basic accommodations for every (low) budget: quaint thatched cabins over the water, dorm beds and a campground. There's limited electricity and no running water, but there is a dive center and a little restaurant, and all the coconuts you can eat or drink are free! The boat goes every

Sunday from Sittee River, and is included in the price of a week's stay. *Info*: www.glovers.com.bz; Tel. 520-5016.

Hopkins is becoming a bit of a hip backpacker spot, and budget lodgings are sprouting up. Two nice beachfront ones are **Tipple Tree Beya** (www.tippletree.com; Tel. 520-7006) and the **Seagull's Nest** (Tel. 523-7015).

The main hangout in Hopkins is **King Kasava's**, a restaurant and bar located right in the center of town where the buses stop. Cheap meals, stout drinks and colorful characters. **Lebeha** is a drum school that also has a restaurant and bar, and the locals slap the skins until the wee hours.

BEST SLEEPS AROUND PLACENCIA
Placencia town is located at the end of a long peninsula, an hour's drive on a bone-rattling dirt road from the Southern Highway. Right in town, there are lots of budget and midrange lodgings, perfect for those who want to be part of the scene. The upscale resorts are located just north of town, most of them a medium walk or a short taxi ride away. Farther north, around the village of Maya Beach, are a few more resorts in various price ranges. Some guests like the seclusion up there, but others feel trapped, and don't dig the tedious (and expensive) ride into town.

The Inn At Robert's Grove $$$$$
This is my favorite place in Placencia, a true luxury resort located just north of the airstrip. There's a lovely beach, kayaks and windsurfers, an in-house dive shop, two restaurants, three pools, rooftop Jacuzzis, a tennis court, a full-service spa and a well stocked gift shop. The 42 rooms and suites have attractive décor, large comfortable beds and every luxury

amenity – AC, TV, fridge, hair dryer – the works. Those who are tired of beans and rice will delight in the excellent dining. The Seaside Restaurant offers a large selection of local and American favorites, while over on the lagoon side, the more casual Habanero serves great Mexican food. Start the day with the wonderful (included) Continental breakfast, or peruse the menu for the full compliment of bacon and egg dishes. Saturday night is the famous poolside barbecue. The staff are very professional and very friendly, and there are even two dogs and a cat. *Info*: www.robertsgrove.com; Tel. 523-3565 or 800/565-9757 US.

Blancaneaux's Turtle Inn $$$$$

One of Francis Ford Coppola's two properties in Belize, this beachfront resort is one of the most luxurious in the country.

There's a variety of accommodations, from seaview cottages to huge seafront villas. All are sumptuously appointed and decorated in Oriental style. Some have large private verandahs and outdoor garden showers. The food is splendid, with great Italian and Belizean cuisine, wonderful wine and coffee. *Info*: www.blancaneaux.com; Tel. 523-3244, 824-4912 or 800/746-3743 US.

The Placencia Hotel and Residences $$$$$

This place is just a couple of years old, part of a big modern complex that includes a hotel, condos and houses for sale. There's a huge pool, tennis courts, three restaurants and all that you'd expect at a major luxury resort. It's a good ride north of Placencia, so it's for those who want a secluded luxury experience, and don't mind paying. *Info*: www.theplacencia.com; Tel. 520-4110 or 800/746-3743 US.

Chabil Mar Villas $$$$$

These luxurious bougainvillea-wreathed villas draw consistent rave reviews from guests. Most are two-bedroom units, and all have full kitchens with all the modern gadgets, dishwashers, washer/dryers, TV with DVD player, free wireless internet, and on and on. There are beauti-  ful tile bathrooms and colorful local art on the walls (including a jaguar mural in my room – a sure way to guarantee a good review). There's no dining room, but there's a full menu and bar – all delivered wherever you like – in your room, on the beach, by the pool…in fact everything can be handled right in your room, even checking in and out. Iguanas roam the lush grounds, the two infinity pools are refreshing, and the sandy beach is neatly raked. The staff know their jobs well, and always have a friendly hello. Luxury and privacy are the watchwords here (although it's a short walk into Placencia). For a romantic getaway or a family trip, this is my top choice. *Info*: www.chabilmarvillas.com; Tel. 523-3606 or 800/819-9088 US.

Near Placencia

Laru Beya Resort $$$
This beachfront resort is next to Robert's Grove, and it also offers private elegance. There's a variety of rooms and villas, all with ceiling fans, AC and full kitchens. The nicest ones, such as the Penthouse Villa, which features a private rooftop Jacuzzi, are predictably pricey, but if you choose one of the cheaper rooms, you can stay here at an amazingly good price for a first-class resort. There's a large pool with a wooden deck, and the beach is nice for swimming or for messing about in one of the complimentary catamarans, windsurfers or kayaks. *Info*: www.larubeya.com; Tel. 523-3476 or 800/245-2495 US.

Maya Beach Hotel $$$
If you don't mind staying at Maya Beach, a good ride north of Placencia, check out this popular mid-price spot. Simple but nice

rooms, all with private bath, AC and ceiling fans. Guests rave about the service and the peaceful vibe. *Info*: www.mayabeach.com; Tel. 520-8040 or 800/503-5124 US.

Green Parrot Beach Houses And Resort $$$
Also in Maya Beach, here are a couple of thatched cabanas and six larger beach houses with kitchenettes, good value for families. There's a restaurant, a gift shop, and the usual beach toys. *Info*: www.greenparrot-belize.com; Tel. 523-2488.

Ranguana Lodge $$
Right in Placencia Town, five cozy cabanas on the beach, with private bath, AC, ceiling fans, fridges, coffee makers and micro-waves, as well as nice little porches with hammocks. *Info*: www.ranguanabelize.com; Tel. 523-3112.

Sea Spray Hotel $$
Another nice little budget hotel on the beach in the middle of the village. All rooms have private bath and ceiling fans. Some have AC and kitchenettes. *Info*: www.seasprayhotel.com; Tel. 523-3148.

One World $$
This guest house is run by a Swiss lady and, not surprisingly, is neat as a pin. It's one of the few lodgings that isn't on the beach, but the amenities, including AC, TV, fridges, make it a bargain for the price. *Info*: www.oneworldplacencia.com; Tel. 523-3618 or 620-9975.

Manatee Inn $$
This fairly new two-story inn has nice wood furnishings and a verandah with an ocean view. *Info*: www.manateeinn.com; Tel. 523-4083 or 607-0202.

Serenade Guest House $$
Nine bright, cheery rooms with a sea view from the porch, and a pleasant restaurant next door. The same folks run the Serenade Island Resort, on one of the Sapodilla cayes, a few miles offshore. *Info*: www.belizecayes.com; Tel. 523-3380.

Paradise Vacation Hotel $$
Located at the southern tip of the peninsula, this pleasant place
has 12 rooms and a two-bedroom suite, all recently renovated,
with private bath and AC. *Info*: www.paradisevacationbelize.com;
Tel. 523-3179.

There are lots of apartments and small guest houses for rent, and
this is a more economical way to go if you're staying more than a
few days, or if you're with a larger group. See www.placencia.com
for a comprehensive listing of lodgings in all categories.

BEST EATS IN PLACENCIA
The area has a great selection of eating places in all price ranges.
Most of the hotels have restaurants. The **Inn At Robert's Grove**
offers elegant dining at the Seaside Restaurant, and good Mexi-
can fare with a nice water view at Habanero. For a luxurious
fusion of Continental and Caribbean cuisine, make a reservation
at **Blancaneaux's Turtle Inn**.

There are several casual sand-floor-and-thatched-roof joints on
the beach, serving up Caribbean-style seafood dishes and um-
brella drinks. The most popular are **De' Tatch** (Tel. 503-3385) and
the **Cozy Corner** (Tel. 523-3540). For authentic Belizean food,
visit **Wendy's**, down by the docks (no relation to the barfsome
chain of the same name).

Maya Beach has a couple of beachfront places that serve nice
Belizean/international fusion with fresh local ingredients: the
Green Parrot (Tel. 523-2488) and the **Maya Beach Hotel Bistro**
(Tel. 520-8040).

There are plenty of little bars where locals and tourists mingle,
and expats go to seed. The **Pickled Parrot** serves American bar
food, cold beer and the dreaded "parrot piss." The **Barefoot Bar
at the Tipsy Tuna** is a fun beachfront spot that has a weekly
schedule of live music.

BEST SLEEPS & EATS NEAR PUNTA GORDA
Cotton Tree Lodge $$$$
This is a special place, loved by all who visit. It's located on the

lovely Moho River – they'll pick you up by boat from the airstrip. The cabanas are elegantly rustic, and tightly screened. You'll be serenaded to sleep by the crickets, and wake up to a symphony of birdsong – partially cleared jungle sites like this support an incredible variety of bird species. There's also a jungle house, way back in the forest, where you may see howler monkeys from the porch. Owner Chris is very environmentally conscious – solar cells provide electricity, and composting toilets fertilize the bananas. Vegetables and eggs come from the on-site organic gardens, and there's a vast variety of tropical fruit trees, including cacao. You can watch how they turn these into delicious chocolate, and even try doing it yourself. There are plenty of activities in the immediate area – kayak on the river, hike or ride a horse through the forest, swim by a lovely waterfall, or visit one of the nearby Mayan villages for a fascinating cultural experience. Meals are served in the central lodge, where Buddy the dog and Mister Miss the cat entertain. *Info*: www.cottontreelodge.com; Tel. 670-0557 or 866/480-4534 US.

Machaca Hill $$$$
This new upscale eco-lodge (actually a completely refurbished lodge, formerly El Pescador) sits on a breezy hilltop within the 11,000 acre Laughing Falcon Reserve. The location offers wonderful views of the rain forest canopy. The 12 cabanas are first-class, with AC, ceiling fans, mini-fridges, hair dryers and even wi-fi. There's a pool, a small spa and a gift shop, and all kinds of tours to the local wonders are on offer. *Info*: www.machacahill.com; Tel. 722-0050 or 672-0050.

The Lodge at Big Falls $$$$
About 20 minutes from town, on the Rio Grande River, this excellent lodge has comfortable cabanas, great food and an especially helpful

staff. The cabanas have river views and nice décor with tile floors and verandahs with hammocks. Swim in the pool or the river, or take a kayak or a mountain bike for a ride. The food here is especially good. *Info*: www.thelodgeatbigfalls.com; Tel. 671-7172.

Coral House Inn $$$
The nicest of the places right in town, this remodeled old house is on the beach at the very southern end. The four rooms have private bath, AC and wireless internet, and there's a nice little pool. *Info*: www.coralhouseinn.net; Tel. 722-2878.

Sea Front Inn $$$
Another pretty nice seaside inn with good prices, located at the north end of town. This family-run inn has 14 hotel rooms and six apartments, all with private bath and AC. Some have large verandas with fine views. *Info*: www.seafrontinn.com; Tel. 722-2300.

Hickatee Cottages $$
These three pleasantly-furnished little cottages are set in a nice jungle area about a mile south of Punta Gorda. There's a well-maintained hiking trail for you to check out the orchids, toucans, hummingbirds and a resident troop of howler monkeys. Owned by a British couple, this humble establishment consistently gets rave reviews. The low prices include transfers from the airstrip or bus station, internet access and bikes. *Info*: www.hickatee.com; Tel. 662-4475.

Local watering holes include **Earth Runnin's Café**, an internet café with a Reggae vibe, and beachfront **Waluco's**, where you're likely to catch some local Garifuna drumming and partying.

10. BEST ACTIVITIES

Belize offers **good shopping**, especially wood carvings and crafts of various kinds; **great outdoor sports and recreation** possibilities, from sunning yourself on a beautiful beach to diving, snorkeling, swimming, fishing and other water sports; and (on occasion and in the right spot!) **fun nightlife**, particularly in the Cayes but in a few other spots as well.

We steer you to the best activities in this chapter, with our focus on what Belize does best: the great outdoors. Enjoy!

SHOPPING

Belize produces some very nice handicrafts, from wood carvings to leather to clothing and jewelry. You'll find crafts on sale throughout the country, especially tourist staples such as hammocks and small Mayan-themed carvings. **Jade**, sacred to the ancient Maya, is a favorite material for upscale artworks. You may also be offered black coral, but be aware that it is an endangered species, subject to the Convention on International Trade in Endangered Species. Except for fossils, coral is generally illegal to buy or remove from the country.

Belize has many excellent **visual artists**. Most of them take the natural wonders and colorful people of the country as subjects, and many of them paint in the charming Caribbean Primitive style. Oils, watercolors and sculptures are often reasonably priced.

Coffee and **rum** make good cheap gifts for the folks back home. Both are best purchased in a local grocery store. The duty-free shop at the airport is not any cheaper. Prices in tourist shops around the country are usually higher. Consumer goods of all kinds can be very expensive in Belize, so stock up on things like film, spare batteries and other travel items before you go.

The Cayes

Like all tourist towns, San Pedro has any number of shops selling t-shirts, fridge magnets, and "handicrafts" that may or may not have anything to do with Belize. There are some very nice carvings, paintings and clothing to be had, but the good stuff may be hard to find among the tourist junk.

Ambergris Maya Jade Store and Museum is a classy shop with many beautiful Mayan jade items, some of them replicas of artifacts from the classical Mayan era. It's also a mini-museum, with exhibits about jade and its significance to Mayan culture. *Info*: Tel. 226-3311. Front Street.

Belizean Arts, located inside Fido's Courtyard, is an excellent art gallery that's well worth a visit, even if you don't plan to buy. The highlight is the huge collection of oil paintings by Belizean artists, several of whose works can be seen in local hotels. Other local galleries include **Island Originals** on Front Street and **Isla Bonita Gallery** just south of the airstrip. *Info*: www.belizeanarts.com; Tel. 226-3019.

On Caye Caulker, **Caribbean Colors Art Gallery** has some nice paintings by local artists. **Chocolate**, of Manatee tour fame, has a gift shop well stocked with imported dresses and postcards, toward the north end of the village. *Info*: www.caribbean-colors.com.

Belize City
The Fort George neighborhood has several shops selling crafts and other gift items. The best of these is the **National Handicraft Center**, which has much more than just handicrafts, all of it Belizean: charming paintings, coral, slate and wood carvings, baskets, jewelry, bottled herbs and sauces, Belizean music, postcards and t-shirts. It's a one-stop shopping center for Belizean souvenirs. Among the benefits: it's air-conditioned, they take credit cards, and you can buy coral items without worrying about whether they're legal. *Info*: Tel. 223-3636. 2 South Park Street.

The many shops at the **Fort Street Tourism Village** mostly sell overpriced crapola that has nothing to do with Belize, but there is a nice little art gallery there. **North Front Street** is lined with vendors aggressively hawking wood carvings (and other less respectable products). Be sure to stop in at the **Image Factory**, a local art cooperative that has rotating exhibitions of Belizean visual art, as well as a shop selling fine crafts and books. *Info*: www.imagefactory.bz. Open Mon-Fri 9am-5pm.

Western Belize
On your way out to San Ignacio, don't fail to stop at **Caesar's**

Place, at Mile 60 on the Western Highway. This is about the best craft shop in the country, with all kinds of carvings, artwork, clothing and gift items from Belize and neighboring countries, as well as a good selection of CDs and tapes by Belizean musicians. There's also a small restaurant and an internet café.

At **Maya Center**, on the Southern Highway just south of the turnoff to Hopkins, you'll find a nice craft shop, run by a cooperative of village women. This is jaguar country –the men guide tours in the nearby Jaguar Reserve, and the women carve the cats' images in wood and stone.

NIGHTLIFE & ENTERTAINMENT

If you want to party, San Pedro is the place to be. There are no glitzy discos, but the beach bar scene is very cool. More laid-back, hippyish scenes take place on Caulker, around Cayo and in Placencia. Belize City has a moderately lively scene going on, but the most authentic locales tend to be unsavory, and the streets are not safe at night. If you want to experience Belizean music, head down south to Dangriga or Punta Gorda, where Punta and other regional styles of music were born, and where the Garifuna keep the tradition of native drumming alive.

Punta & Garifuna Music

Most of the traditional folk music of Belize is a product of the Garifuna culture. The **Garifuna** (or Garinagu) live all along the Caribbean coast from Belize down to Nicaragua, and their music is popular throughout the region.

The most popular genre of Garifuna music is called **Punta**. As are other Afro-Caribbean styles such as Reggae, Calypso and Salsa, Punta is descended from a mixture of African and European influences, with a uniquely Caribbean flavor. Drums and other percussion instruments are central to the sound. Traditional Punta is played on locally-made instruments such as the *garawon* drum, rattles, turtle shells and sometimes wind instruments made of conch shells. A typical Punta song pits male against female, with sexually-charged dialogue and energetic dancing that involves shaking the buttocks at incredible speeds!

Popular Punta artists include Andy Palacio, Chico Ramos, Mohobub and Supa G. A related musical genre is **Paranda**. The most famous Paranda artist is Paul Nabor, who hails from Punta Gorda. Many call his song *Naguya Nei* the unofficial Garifuna national anthem.

Punta Rock is a modern version of Punta music that adds electric guitars and synthesizers to the traditional instrumentation, and often has socially-conscious lyrics. The acknowledged founder of Punta Rock is **Pen Cayetano**, from Dangriga. Since its origins in the early 1980s, Punta Rock has grown to become the most popular musical style on the Caribbean coast of Central America. Cayetano is also a talented painter, and he has a studio in Dangriga that you can visit, but it's usually open only in November, during the festivities around Garifuna Settlement Day. You're likely to hear the infectious rhythms of Punta at any nightclub or disco in coastal Belize, but if you really want to get into the music, head for Dangriga or Punta Gorda (see Chapter 7). *Info*: www.cayetano.de; www.stonetreerecords.com.

Belize City Nightlife

Tourist-oriented nightlife centers around the **Princess Hotel**. Their casino has cheesy live entertainment and a free midnight buffet. The **Calypso Club**, out on a dock over the sea, is a pleasant place for a drink and some seafood. Afterwards, you can step over to the **Vogue Bar**, which has DJs and dance bands on the weekends. In the neighborhood around the Princess are a couple of local nightspots and several places offering late-night eats, but they tend to go in and out of business, so ask the bartender at the Calypso Club where everyone goes these days.

There are a couple of hip local nightspots on **Queen Street** with DJs spinning dance music – again, places come and go. This is a dodgy neighborhood, so use caution and *take a taxi*. Several of the hotels, including the **Fort George** and the **Bellevue**, have live music from time to time. For a mellower scene, you can swap stories with other budget travelers over drinks at **Smokin Balam** on North Front Street, or the bar at the **Hotel Mopan** (see *Best Sleeps*). I said it in Chapter 5 and I am repeating it here: in Belize City, absolutely take a taxi, especially at night!

Nightlife on the Cayes
Belize's biggest tourist hotspot, Ambergris Caye, has plenty going on after the sun goes down. The classic local drink is called a **panty ripper**, and consists of fresh pineapple juice with a generous shot of the country's finest rum, a brand called One Barrel. Of course, plenty of ice-cold Belikin and the usual selection of fruity tropical drinks flow freely.

Fido's, an open-air thatched compound on Front Street in the center of San Pedro, has live music every night (photo on right). **Cannibal's**, a beachfront bar and restaurant located next to the water taxi pier, has semi-live music several times weekly. The **Crazy Canuck**, located just south of town at the Exotic Caye Beach Resort,  is a good local nightspot, and has live bands every Monday night.

The closest thing to a nightclub in San Pedro is the **Jaguar**, in the center of town, which has DJs spinning dance music every night. **Wet Willy's** sees a huge turnout for ladies' night every Wednesday. **Big Daddy's** is an after-hours club where the locals get crazy (and I mean very crazy) until dawn. The **Pier Lounge** is popular with sports fans, as The Game (including Monday Night Football) is shown on a huge plasma TV. The bar at the **Holiday Hotel** is another good place to watch sports on TV.

On Caye Caulker, the place to go to watch the sunset is the **Lazy Lizard**, at the north end of town. Ask around there to find out where everyone's going after happy hour is over. Several spots have live music from time to time. Be sure to check out the **I&I**

Reggae Bar, on the side street just inland from the Tropical Paradise Hotel, where rootsy Reggae music cranks at all hours, and you might just smell some herbs that aren't on the menu.

Down south in Placencia, the **Barefoot Bar at the Tipsy Tuna** is the place to go after dinner, with live music every week. On my last visit, a punta rock band was playing, the *pantyrippaz* were flowing, and hips were shaking. Several of the resorts have a weekly beach barbecue, sometimes with live bands.

SPORTS & RECREATION

When it comes to outdoor activities, Belize really does have something for everyone. Water sports naturally happen on the Cayes and the southern coast. Enjoying the forest and wildlife on foot, by boat or on horseback is a favorite activity anywhere in the country. World-class spelunking and other adventure sports mostly happen in Western Belize. San Ignacio (Cayo) is headquarters for fit adventurers.

Scuba Diving & Snorkeling

Belize is arguably the finest destination for diving and snorkeling in the Western Hemisphere. The **world's second-longest barrier reef** (after the Great Barrier Reef in Australia) parallels the shore from north to south. Belize also has three of only four coral atolls in the hemisphere (an atoll is a large ring of coral reefs surrounding a shallow lagoon). Belize's relatively low population density means that most of the reefs are in good shape, and the country has wisely protected many of the most sensitive areas as marine reserves.

Visibility is usually excellent, and you'll see plenty of live coral in all the colors of the rainbow – brain coral, staghorn, elkhorn, and the stinging fire coral – to say nothing of gigantic barrel sponges and waving sea fans. You'll see plenty of fish large and small. Colorful reef fish include gobies, blennies, sergeant-majors, tangs, angelfish and parrotfish, which crunch coral with their strong beaks, digest the animal matter and poop out sand. Larger predators include barracuda (fearsome to look at, but not dangerous), snapper and grouper. If you're lucky, you may see snook, tarpon or sharks. Sea turtles and stingrays are frequent reef visitors.

The reefs are accessible to everyone, not just scuba divers. Snorkeling is very easy to learn, and some of the most beautiful reef structure is quite shallow. There's a fascinating other world just a short boat ride offshore so, even if you've never tried it before, do not pass up the chance to go snorkeling before you leave Belize.

Planning Your Dive Vacation

Each of Belize's regions has its own pros and cons for divers. **Ambergris Caye** has the largest variety of dive operators (well over a dozen at last count), and plenty of nice sites just a short boat ride away. There are some excellent resorts where you can stay in luxury and still concentrate on diving, and there are activities for non-diving companions. On the other hand, Ambergris has crowds of other divers and the highest prices in the country. It's a long boat ride north of the Blue Hole and Turneffe. The more pristine reefs are far from the bubble-blowing hordes on Ambergris, for obvious reasons.

Caye Caulker is smaller (only three dive operators), more laid-back, cheaper and a little closer to the action. If you re-

Snorkeling Safety

What's the biggest danger to snorkelers? Sting rays, eels, sharks, fire coral? Nope. None of those things will hurt you if you don't touch them, but **the sun can hurt you badly** if you aren't careful. Always wear a t-shirt when snorkeling. You'll be spending most of your time face-down floating on top of the water, with your back exposed to the broiling sun. You may also want to consider some waterproof sunblock for your neck and legs. And remember, the tropical sun can burn you even on cloudy days.

Coral Reefs

Coral is a communal organism. The colorful formations you see are colonies of thousands of tiny animals, which filter food from the water. The calcium they secrete builds a coral reef over hundreds of years. The coral attracts tiny fish and crustaceans, which attract larger predators, and so up the scale. A living reef is a very complex ecosystem, which provides habitat for many important fish species. Like rain forests, reefs worldwide are slowly disappearing. Pollution, sedimentation, overfishing – all chip away at the reefs as a worldwide catastrophe waits in the wings. Rising sea temperatures are killing reefs in many areas and, worse yet, scientists now fear that, as absorbed carbon dioxide changes the chemistry of sea water, corals' very ability to produce calcium could be impaired. Whatever the future holds, Belize's reefs are beautiful now, so get out and enjoy them!

ally want to get away from it all and dive dive dive, consider one of the dive lodges on the tiny islands. **The St. George's Caye Resort** is even closer to the flagship sites, and there are a couple of lodges on the Turneffe Islands and in Southern Belize that I highly recommend, especially for divers (see *Best Sleeps & Eats*). Some resorts run their own in-house dive operations, while others have a quasi-independent dive shop on the premises. Any and all hotels in Belize will gladly arrange dive trips for you, or you can book dives directly with a dive shop. In either case, most operators will pick you up and drop you off at your hotel's dock. Most dive shops also arrange snorkeling and fishing Most shops offer a range of scuba instruction (almost all are PADI shops). A PADI Open Water Certification course will cost you $400-475. Some shops also offer Advanced, Divemaster, Rescue and Nitrox courses. If you aren't a certified diver, but you really want to blow some bubbles, you can take a resort course, which gives you some brief instruction and a supervised ocean dive, for about $150. Another option for earning your certification is a referral course (around $300), which means that you do your classroom and swimming pool instruction at home, and your certification dives in Belize.

All dive operators offer diving gear for rent, but serious divers will want to bring their own gear. Don't plan on buying dive equipment here, as selection is limited and prices are high.

Belize is often featured in the various dive magazines. Check out either of these sites:
• www.skin-diver.com
• www.scubadivingbelize.com

Dive Sites
Hot dive sites are found from north to south, on the barrier reef or one of the three coral atolls. Belize's most popular spot for short snorkel and dive trips, visited by every dive shop on Ambergris and Caulker, is **Hol Chan Marine Reserve**, a few miles south of San Pedro. This section of the barrier reef includes the fish and coral-rich Hol Chan Channel and **Shark Ray Alley**, where you can swim with enormous nurse sharks and Southern stingrays in water only a few feet deep – it's a fine place for novice snorkelers, and an unforgettable wildlife encounter even for seasoned divers. *Info*: www.holchanbelize.org.

Lighthouse Reef Atoll is the location of the **Blue Hole**, Belize's Eiffel Tower (when you get back home, everyone will ask you if you saw it). Cavern formations open up into the sheer walls of this enormous round sinkhole, and you can swim through vast limestone cathedrals, accompanied by sleek sharks. It's a unique place, but some divers find it disappointing. It's a deep dive, so you only get to spend a few minutes admiring the sights, and there isn't a whole lot in the way of fish and other sea life.

However, the atoll has no shortage of great dive sites. Out here in the open ocean the visibility is superb, and you may catch a glimpse of some large pelagic fish. At **Half Moon Wall**, you can see a wide variety of underwater habitats in a small area, at moderate depths (30-70 feet). Large sharks, eagle rays and manta rays are frequent visitors.

Turneffe Atoll, the largest of Belize's three coral atolls, is 25 miles east of Belize City. This huge ring of reefs is dotted with over 200 tiny mangrove islands. Here you'll find a variety of great sites suitable for all skill levels. The western edge of the atoll has lots of shallow reefs, perfect for beginning divers and snorkelers. Intermediate divers enjoy some of the finest wall dives in the Caribbean, as well as the wreck of the **Sayonara**. One of the most impressive advanced dive sites in the country is the **Elbow**, a wall that drops off into a deep channel where strong ocean currents sweep around the south end of the atoll. This is an excellent drift dive, and perhaps the best place to see really big fish such as lemon, blacktip and hammerhead sharks, manta and spotted eagle rays, green and hawksbill turtles, and bottlenose and spotted dolphin.

Glover's Reef Marine Reserve protects the most remote of Belize's three coral atolls (about 35 miles southeast of Dangriga), and it has some of the most pristine dive sites in the country. Glover's has sites for all skill levels, from snorkelers to advanced divers. The outside of the ring has some excellent walls, and within the lagoon are over 700 patch reefs. How do **Long Caye Wall**, **Grouper Flats** and **Shark Point** sound? See the destination chapters for more details of dive sites.

Whale Sharks
The largest fish on the planet are members of the shark family but, unlike their more rapacious relatives, they are filter feeders, eating a variety of tiny fish and other sea life, and therefore not dangerous to humans (but I wouldn't advise getting too close). Whale sharks frequent Southern Belize from March-June, especially around full moon nights. Snapper spawn around Glover's Reef Atoll in vast numbers around that time, and the whale sharks come to feed on the eggs. The sight of thousands of

snappers spawning in a huge ball while giant whale sharks swim overhead slurping up the eggs is the dive experience of a lifetime. Whale shark encounters are much like dolphin encounters – your boat cruises around in likely-looking areas while your eagle-eyed skipper looks for the tell-tale boil in the water that indicates the presence of whale sharks and the small fish that accompany them. When they are located, snorkelers and scuba divers plop over the side and, hopefully, swim quietly while the giant fish lurk around.

Whale sharks are usually slow swimmers, but may not show much interest in visitors. Sometimes they'll circle around a little, but often they will just keep on swimming in the direction they were going. The trick is to observe the whale sharks from the boat to determine which direction they are swimming in and then drop the tourists in the water a little ahead of their path. Be sure to take an underwater camera along on this outing.

Ambergris Caye Dive Shops

Ambergris has a passel of dive operators, as well as the country's only decompression chamber. A few of the resorts have their own dive shops, and there are a dozen more on the beach in downtown San Pedro. Many of the hotels have arrangements with certain dive operators, but most dive outfits will pick you up from any hotel dock. All the shops offer equipment rental and PADI instruction, all make trips to Hol Chan, and most go to the Blue Hole, Turneffe and other favorite sites. A two-tank dive will cost you $70-80, a day trip to the Blue Hole around $250. There are only a couple of places on the island to buy dive and snorkel gear: **Island Diver Supplies** downtown, and **Captain Shark's** near the airstrip.

Ramon's Village, an upscale resort just south of San Pedro, has a dive operation that's one of the largest and best in the country. Ramon's and Protech are the only PADI 5-star IDC Gold Palm shops in Belize (hardcore divers will know what that means).

They have seven boats including a splendid 42-footer for Blue Hole trips, and offer a full array of instruction and rentals. *Info*: www.ramons.com; Tel. 601/649-1990 or 800/MAGIC 15 US.

Protech is a highly professional operation and an especially good choice for advanced divers. Owner Peter Jones is very experienced in both recreational and technical diving, and offers probably the most extensive range of courses in Belize, all the way up to Advanced Nitrox Diver. They have all sorts of nifty gear, including rebreathers and scooters. They're located south of town at the Belize Yacht Club. *Info*: www.protechdive.com; Tel. 226-3008.

Ecologic Divers is a new shop, located toward the north end of town. They are well financed, with five nice new boats, nice new gear and some good instructors, a couple of them Protech alumni. *Info*: www.ecologicdivers.com; Tel. 226-4118.

Amigos del Mar Dive Shop is the biggest dive outfit on the island, with eight or nine boats, including a wonderful 48-footer that they use for long trips to the Hole and Turneffe. On the way back home, they break out the beer and rum and everyone has a ball. Owner Changa is one of the top dive gurus in Belize. This excellent shop is especially good for novice divers. Their divemasters will get your gear set up and handle every detail for you. *Info*: www.amigosdive.com; Tel. 226-2706.

Patojo's Scuba Center is a respected shop run by Elmer "Patojo" Paz, Changa's brother and a PADI Instructor with 17 years of experience. He and his wife also own the adjacent Tides, a nice midrange hotel with a pool and AC private-bath rooms for around $125 double. Patojo offers a full range of diving, snorkeling and fishing trips, instruction and rentals. *Info*: www.ambergriscaye.com/tides; Tel. 226-2283.

Ambergris Divers, located on the beach near the Spindrift Hotel, is a highly professional shop offering a wide variety of trips from their fleet of six boats, plus the usual menu of instruction and rentals. *Info*: www.ambergrisdivers.com; Tel. 226-2634.

Bottom Time Dive Shop is the oldest outfit on Ambergris. Several of the owners of other shops started off as divemasters here. Their shop is on the pier at the San Pedro Holiday Hotel. They have nice new boats and a good staff. *Info*: www.sanpedroholiday.com/dive.html; Tel. 226-2014.

Aqua Dives, another local operator of long standing, is located at the excellent SunBreeze Hotel at the south end of town. *Info*: www.aquadives.com; Tel. 226-3415 or 800/641-2994 US.

Resorts that have in-house dive operations for their guests include **Victoria House** (www.victoria-house.com), **Portofino** (www.portofinodiving.com), **El Pescador** (www.elpescador.com) and **Journey's End** (www.journeysendresort.com).

Ambergris Caye Snorkeling
A snorkel trip will run you about $35 per person including mask, fins, and snorkel. Most snorkeling trips from San Pedro go to the Hol Chan Marine Reserve, which costs you an additional $10 admission fee. You can arrange a snorkeling trip through your hotel or through any of the dive shops on the beach.

Unlike scuba diving, which requires certification, if you can swim, you can learn to snorkel in a few minutes. Much of the underwater beauty off San Pedro is in shallow water, so snorkeling may be just as spectacular as diving. You do need a boat, however – nowhere on Ambergris is the coral reef near enough to shore for you to swim out to it.

Caye Caulker Dive Shops
There are only three, all with good reputations. Prices are a tiny bit lower here than on Ambergris. The Blue Hole is closer, so you should be able to do a 3-tank trip for $200 or less. A PADI certification course runs about $300.

Look, Don't Touch!

Never touch any coral, ever. In fact it's wise not to touch anything out on the reef. Bright orange fire coral can cause a nasty burn, and there are sharp sea urchins and other nasties awaiting unwary fingers. But the pain that fire coral might cause to your little pinky is nothing compared to what you'll do to the coral. Touching coral tends to kill the little organisms. It's even worse with gloves, which is why some dive shops discourage wearing them.

Belize Diving Services, at the northwest corner of the village by the soccer field, has been in business since 1978. Their 38-foot boat accommodates 14 divers, and their 28-footer takes eight, with a maximum of four-five divers per divemaster. They offer trips to a wide variety of little-visited sites, and a full range of instruction, including over 24 different courses. *Info*: www.belizedivingservice.com; Tel. 226-0143.

Frenchie's Diving Services is a fine shop has been in business for twelve years. Their five boats go to all the usual sites, and they offer a full roster of courses. *Info*: www.frenchiesdivingbelize.com; Tel. 226-0234.

Big Fish Dive Center, on Front Street near the south end of town, offers trips to all the usual spots, and a full range of courses. *Info*: www.gocayecaulker.com/members/bigfish.html; Tel. 226-0450.

Caye Caulker Snorkeling & Boat Excursions

Unlike in San Pedro, snorkeling trips are not generally booked through the dive shops, but rather through any of a dozen tour operators. A snorkel trip should cost you about $30 or $45 for trips to the Hol Chan Reserve). A couple of the best-known outfits are **Star Tours** (Tel. 226-0374; www.startoursbelize.com) and **Raggamuffin Tours** (www.raggamuffintours.com), which also offers sunset sailing trips. Any of the larger hotels will be happy to arrange any tour your heart desires.

One of the most popular trips on Caulker is to see the manatees on nearby Swallow Caye. Several local operators now run manatee-watching tours, but **Chocolate's Manatee Tours** (Tel. 226-

0151; E-mail chocolateseashore@gmail.com), run by Caye Caulker resident Lionel Heredia, is still the best. The tour lasts all day (9am-4pm) and also includes a stop at Sergeant's Caye, a tiny island right on the barrier reef with a beautiful white sand beach and a splendid snorkeling area. Cost is $60 apiece including snorkel gear. *Info*: www.swallowcayemanatees.org.

Cayes Dive Resorts

Hard-core divers should consider staying at one of the dedicated dive lodges on one of the small cayes. You'll be close to the dive sites and among like-minded souls, but lodgings are usually short of luxury, and there are no "things to do" for non-diving companions (see *Best Sleeps*).

Just a short boat ride from Belize City, **The St. George's Caye Resort** on St. George's Caye is close to dozens of barely-touched dive sites. The reef is only half a mile out, and Turneffe and the Blue Hole are both much closer from here than from Ambergris or Caulker. This homelike lodge has cozy rooms, and six charming thatched cottages built over the water. The 30 years of experience shows in the excellent dive operation, with first-rate facilities and personal service from some of the country's most experienced divemasters. After the diving, you can use a kayak, windsurfer or jet ski, then join the other guests for a bonfire on the beach. *Info*: www.gooddiving.com; Tel. 800/813-8498 US.

You can't get any closer to the fish than one of the three lodges on the Turneffe Islands. **Turneffe Flats** has pretty nice rooms with AC and private bath. Both diving and fishing guests give this place consistently good reviews. *Info*: www.tflats.com; Tel. 888/512-8812.

At the **Turneffe Island Resort**, decent rooms with AC and private bath, and three great dives scheduled every day, await you. *Info*: www.turnefferesort.com; Tel. 713/237-7739 US.

The **Blackbird Caye Resort** (see photo on next page) in the Turneffe atoll offers oceanfront air-conditioned cabanas with private porches and hammocks, and dives on over 70 dive sites,

most no more than 12 minutes from the dock. *Info*: www.blackbirdresort.com; Tel. 888/271-3483 US.

Gallows Point Resort, a basic and cheap little lodge on Gallows Point Caye, is run by the same folks as the budget Hotel Belcove in Belize City. Various diving and fishing packages are available. *Info*: www.belcove.com; Tel. 227-3054.

Belize City Dive Shops
Most divers head for the islands, but it's quite feasible to take dive trips from Belize City, and the boat rides to some of the most popular sites aren't much longer.

Hugh Parkey's Belize Dive Connection is a full-service dive operator with a shop on the dock at the Radisson Fort George Hotel, as well as a lodge on tiny Spanish Look-Out Caye, 8 miles southeast of Belize City. The lodge has 12 cabanas built over the water with ceiling fans and private baths, as well as a dormitory for student groups. They also have a place where you can swim with penned dolphins. Both the dive operation and the "private island" cater to the cruise ship business. *Info*: www.belizediving.com; Tel. 223-5086 or 888/223-5403 US.

Sea Sports Belize on North Front Street offers dive trips to the usual spots, as well as a range of instruction, gear rental, repairs and sales. They also do snorkeling and fishing trips. *Info*: www.seasportsbelize.com; Tel. 223-5505.

Dangriga Area Diving
Thatch Caye Resort is an upscale resort with a small but excellent dive operation. Divemasters Ian, Emily and Chico (who has been diving in these waters for 17 years) lead snorkeling and diving trips to the barrier reef, a short boat ride away, or only slightly farther, to Glover's Reef, perhaps the most pristine dive site in Belize. *Info*: www.thatchcaye.com; Tel. 603-2414 or 800/435-3145 US.

Blue Marlin Lodge, on South Water Caye, near Dangriga, has a couple of lodging options and a variety of weekly diving and fishing packages. *Info*: www.bluemarlinlodge.com; Tel. 522-2243 or 800/798-1558 US.

Placencia Area Diving

There's excellent diving on the barrier reef offshore, and this region sees far fewer divers than the reefs around Ambergris and Caulker. Many divers come here to commune with the whale shark, the largest fish in the sea.

Located in the center of Placencia, **Seahorse Dive Shop** is a full-service dive operator that specializes in whale shark dives. *Info*: www.belizescuba.com; Tel. 523-3166, 523-3466 or 800/991-1969 US.

Splash Dive Shop, established in 2000, does dive and snorkeling trips, as well as inland tours. *Info*: www.splashbelize.com; Tel. 523-3058, 523-3080 or 620-6649.

There are also several resorts in the area that have their own in-house dive operations:

The Inn at Robert's Grove, an upscale resort, has a good dive outfit with several boats. *Info*: www.diverobertsgrove.com; Tel. 523-3565 or 800/565-9757.

Blancaneaux's Turtle Inn, a luxury resort, has an in-house dive operation. *Info*: www.blancaneaux.com; Tel. 523-3244, 824-4912 or 800/746-3743 US.

Live-Aboard Dive Boats

For the serious diver, this is the ultimate trip. You'll moor directly at the finest dive sites and dive until you shrivel up like a Greek olive. Two different live-aboards currently operate in Belize. All of them sail from the dock behind the Radisson Fort George in Belize City, and both do weeklong trips leaving every Saturday.

Peter Hughes Diving features the 138-foot Sun Dancer II, with nice staterooms with AC and picture windows. Dive sites include the Blue Hole, Half Moon Caye Wall and the Elbow. Weeklong trips start around $2,700. *Info*: www.peterhughes.com; Tel. 800/932-6237 or 305/669-9391 US.

The **Belize Aggressor III** is also a nice boat, offering six days of diving around Turneffe and Lighthouse. A week of total immersion starts around $2,600. *Info*: www.aggressor.com; Tel. 800/348-2628 US.

Fishing

The fishing in Belize is spectacular, but the charter fishing scene is surprisingly low-key, especially compared to the diving action. You won't see marinas full of sleek sport-fishing boats, as you do in Florida, Mexico or Costa Rica. Most fishing charters are run by freelance boat captains, and you can book a trip either through your hotel or through any of the dive operators. Fishing charters may cost up to double what dive trips cost, because they take fewer people and use more gas. Expect to pay in the neighborhood of $250 for a full-day trip to the flats or the reef, $400 or more for a deep-sea trolling trip.

Anglers come from all over the world to enjoy Belize's world-class **flats fishing**. With vast expanses of shallow flats in and around the cayes, Belize is one of the world's top saltwater fly-fishing destinations. You might even have a shot at a Grand Slam: a bonefish, tarpon and permit in a single day. The biggest tarpon cruise through the area in Spring and early Summer. The **Turneffe Islands** are perhaps the top spot in Belize for flats fishing. All three of the lodges there cater to anglers as well as divers (see *Diving*, above). The rivers and estuaries harbor snook, tarpon and cubera snapper. On the reefs, grouper, snapper, jacks, barracuda and other reef species are plentiful. On the seaward side of the reef, ocean depths plummet steeply to thousands of feet, and anglers troll for kingfish, dolphin, wahoo, tuna sailfish and marlin. The best months for billfish are April and May.

Captain Van's **Action Belize** is a tour operator that's been in business since 1979, and specializes in fishing tours. *Info*: www.actionbelize.com; Tel. 888/383-6319 US.

Belize River Lodge is located near the airport, and runs weeklong fishing packages aboard the Christina live-aboard yacht. *Info*: www.belizeriverlodge.com; Tel. 225-2002.

El Pescador is a first-class lodge on Ambergris Caye that caters to flats anglers, and has what is probably the largest fly fishing shop in Belize. The best feature of all is the family that runs the place. "We never say no" is their motto, and a steady stream of delighted guests can tell you that it's true. See *Best Sleeps*. *Info*: www.elpescador.com; Tel. 226-2398 or 800/242-2017 US.

The Turneffe Islands have vast expanses of flats, as well as easy access to the ocean depths. Of the three lodges on the atoll, **Turneffe Flats** is the most fishing-oriented, but **Turneffe Island Resort** and **Blackbird Caye** also offer fishing trips (see *Cayes Dive Resorts*, above). *Info*: www.tflats.com; Tel. 888/512-8812 US.

Whipray Caye Lodge is a place for the serious angler. Basic accommodations on a tiny island 11 miles off Placencia. Owner Julian Cabral is an expert at wade-fishing for permit on the flats. Tarpon, bonefish, snapper and grouper are also around. *Info*: www.whipraycayelodge.com; Tel. 610-1068 or 608-8130.

Tarpon Caye Lodge is another private island lodge near Placencia. Another of the numerous Cabral clan guides anglers to 30-pound permit, baby (up to 100 pound) tarpon, bonefish and snook. *Info*: www.tarponcayelodge.com; Tel. 523-3323.

Thatch Caye Resort, just off Dangriga, is surrounded by fishy flats, and they offer regular guided trips and a good selection of gear, including fly rigs. *Info*: www.thatchcaye.com; Tel. 603-2414 or 800/435-3145 US.

Kayaking & Canoeing
Sea kayaking is possible almost anywhere there's a coast. It's an

especially nice way to explore the offshore atolls. Most beachfront resorts have kayaks available for rent or even free for guests. In the inland lagoons, a kayak may be the very best way to navigate the winding mangrove waterways and silently sneak up on shy wildlife.

Slickrock Adventures (www.slickrock.com; Tel. 800/390-5715 US) specializes in sea kayaking, and has a private island off Glover's Reef. **Sea Kunga** (www.seakunga.com; Tel. 800/781-2269 US) offers adventure kayak tours at several locations. **Toadal Adventure** (www.toadaladventure.com; Tel. 523-3207), in Placencia, does both reef and jungle trips.

Belize Explorer (www.belizex.com; Tel. 624-8071) is one of several operators in San Ignacio that offer canoeing and kayaking on the Macal, Mopan and Belize rivers. Ask at Eva's for famous bird expert Tony of **River Rat Tours** to arrange tours or canoe rentals on the Macal River. **Ian Anderson's Adventures in Belize** (www.adventuresinbelize.com; Tel. 822-2800 or 866/822-2278 US) offers river and sea kayaking trips among their huge menu of tours, as do most of the tour operators listed in the *Practical Matters* chapter.

Other Water Sports
The beach in San Pedro often resembles a busy train station more

than a peaceful vacation spot, as people tear around on all manner of watercraft. **SailSports Belize**, at the Caribbean Villas Hotel (www.sailsportsbelize.com; Tel. 226-4488) offers all things with sails, from windsurfers to Hobie Cats to Lasers to kitesurfing, the latest extreme sport.

On Caulker, **Star Tours** (Tel. 226-0374; www.startoursbelize.com) and **Raggamuffin Tours** (www.raggamuffintours.com) offer all manner of ocean excursions. No list of boat trips would be complete without **Chocolate's Manatee Tours** (Tel. 226-0151; E-mail chocolateseashore@gmail.com). And sailors should check out www.belize-sailing-charters.com.

Spelunking

The porous limestone that lies under much of Western Belize is home to the **Chiquibul** cave system, one of the most extensive in the hemisphere. There are endless opportunities for both beginning and expert cavers. Every tour operator in the west offers cave trips, but the big daddy spelunker is **Ian Anderson**, a Canadian who began exploring the caves and caverns of Belize in the early 1990s, and now presides over an empire of adventure travel that includes a jungle lodge and a wide variety of tours in the area (www.cavesbranch.com; see *Best Sleeps*).

Birding

Belize is a birder's paradise. The variety of birds is simply amazing (over 550 species). As this small country has more bird species than some continents, birders (or *twitchers*, as the English call them) have plenty of opportunities to add species to their *life lists*. The jungles harbor parrots, toucans, hummingbirds, chachalacas, trogons, woodpeckers, kiskadees, tanagers and oropendolas. At night, you may see one of the many stately species of owls. Coastal regions teem with majestic herons (including the rufescent tiger heron), egrets, limpkins, ibises, spoonbills, cormorants, ducks and other shore birds. **Crooked Tree Wildlife Sanctuary**, in the north, is home to flocks of the rare jabiru storks.

Birders will find some action almost anywhere in the country. To maximize your sightings, visit both mountain forests and coastal wetland habitats. The unique ecosystem of **Mountain Pine Ridge** is home to some species that you won't see elsewhere. Many jungle lodges in the region, including the **Hidden Valley Inn**, have resident bird experts. Some of the remote cayes afford the opportunity to see rare species that are all but extinct on the mainland. Another offshore highlight is the **Half Moon Caye Natural Monument,** a bird sanctuary for the rare red-footed booby.

Yes, your chances of seeing something really rare are better in one of the very remote parks of the interior. However, don't overlook more mundane locations. Mayan archaeological sites can have a surprisingly large number of birds, which may be easier to see at such partially cleared sites than they are in the deep forest.

A boat ride is almost always one of the best ways to spot birds. The mangrove islands around Ambergris and Caulker, the **New River Lagoon** and **Crooked Tree** in the north, and the **Sittee and Monkey Rivers** in the south are especially prime for "boatin n birdin."

A few companies specialize in birding tours. Check out **Paradise Expeditions** (www.birdinginbelize.com; Tel. 824-2772), **Victor Emmanuel Nature Tours** (www.ventbird.com; Tel. 800/328-VENT) and **Exotic Birding** (www.exoticbirding.com).

Hiking

A day hike in one of Belize's national parks or wilderness reserves is a fine thing – if that's all you have time for, then don't fail to take one. But to get the full experience, spend at least one night in the rain forest. The best time to see birds and other wildlife is always early in the morning, and you won't be there early in the morning if you have to spend a couple of hours getting to the park from a hotel in town. Plus, there's simply something

magical about waking up to the sounds of water dripping, birds singing and maybe a troop of howler monkeys baying in the distance. Most of the jungle lodges listed in *Best Sleeps* fit this description, so there's no need to rough it to be in position for the best hiking and birding.

Horseback Riding

Several lodges have equestrian centers on-site, including **Mountain Equestrian Trails** (www.metbelize.com) and **Windy Hill Resort** (www.windyhillresort.com) near Mountain Pine Ridge, **Banana Bank Lodge** (www.bananabank.com) near Belmopan. Horseback tours are available almost everywhere – ask any local tour operator.

Golf

Belize is not a major golf destination. The only world-class course in the country is the exclusive **Caye Chapel Island Resort**, which occupies an entire small island a short way offshore from Belize City. This "personal playground for the discriminating elite" features an 18-hole par-72 championship golf course, a deep-water marina and a private airstrip. Accommodations are in luxurious suites and beachfront villas. Prices start around $200 per person per night, and go way up from there, but the rates include unlimited golf. *Info:* www.cayechapel.com; Tel. 800/901-8938 US.

11. PRACTICAL MATTERS

GETTING TO BELIZE

AIRPORTS/ARRIVALS
Belize's only international airport is **Philip Goldson International Airport** at Belize City (BZE). Several US carriers fly there from hubs such as Atlanta, Charlotte and Houston. Belize City also has a smaller airport, known as the **Municipal Airstrip**, which is used for some domestic flights.

Web-based travel search engines such as **Expedia** (www.expedia.com), **Orbitz** (www.orbitz.com) and **Travelocity** (www.travelocity.com) are useful for researching flight schedules and prices. Personally, I never actually book travel through these third-party sites, because it's just as easy to book directly with the airlines, and the third-party sites impose extra fees and more restrictive change policies.

If you can find a knowledgeable travel agent, she or he may be able to find you a better deal than you'd get directly from the airlines. It's also well worth considering buying your airfare as part of a package tour (see below).

All departing air passengers are supposed to pay a **departure tax of US $40** per person (!), which is not included in the price of your airplane ticket. On my last trip, however, no one asked me to pay, and I didn't complain.

CRUISES
Over a dozen major cruise lines now visit Belize. They do not dock in the country, but anchor out in the channel, and use

tenders to ferry passengers to the new cruise terminal in Belize City (see Chapter 5) and other locations. A wide variety of shore excursions and tours is offered to cruise passengers.

The major cruise lines are offering ever-more ambitious day trips in Belize, from snorkeling and diving to lounging on "private islands" to inland visits to the Mayan ruins and nature reserves. However (inevitable with thousands of passengers on a ship) mainstream cruise-ship tours are rushed and impersonal, with little chance to really get the flavor of the country. For a more Belizean cruising experience, try **American Canadian Caribbean Line**, which offers an 11-night itinerary that visits several of Belize's isolated cayes, as well as Guatemala and the Bay Islands of Honduras. *Info*: www.accl-smallships.com; Tel. 800/556-7450 US.

TOUR OPERATORS
Guided tours are a big part of the scene in Belize. On the coast it's diving, fishing and boat rides, inland it's trips to the nature reserves (by foot, horseback or boat) and the Mayan ruins. Spelunking and cave tubing are also popular activities. The tour business is a complex web of larger and smaller operators. Wholesale tour companies subcontract with local tour guides, hotels, van drivers, etc. A tour can mean anything from hiring a local fisherman for a boat ride to a door-to-door package that includes airfare, hotels, ground transport...and a boat ride with that same local fisherman.

If you're the independent type, you can get around perfectly well on your own by bus, small plane or rented car. However, you will probably still want to hire a guide at one point or another. I highly recommend visiting the forests and Mayan ruins in the company of a local guide. You'll see much more, and learn more about the area, than you would on your own.

There are several other reasons why **using a local guide is a good idea**. Although traveling in Belize is safer, and public transport more reliable, than in neighboring countries, it's still the developing world, and all kinds of unexpected delays can rob you of your hard-earned vacation time. A good tour operator can meet you at the plane with a nice new air-conditioned van, and take you where you want to go quickly and comfortably.

Perhaps most importantly, hiring local guides is a good way to help the local economy. If the rain forests and coral reefs of Belize are to survive, the locals need to be able to make more money showing them to wildlife lovers than they would by clear-cutting the trees and stripping the reefs of fish. The struggle to protect the world's natural wonders for future generations is an ongoing battle, and your dollars can help support the right side.

There are three ways to go about arranging tours:

1) You can book tours over the web with a Belizean tour operator, or through your local travel agency, before you even leave home. If you wish, you can get a package that includes flights, hotels, meals and guides. If you want to visit one of the more remote regions, and have limited time, this is a good option, though it won't be the cheapest. The more independent-minded can simply book a tour with a local operator in each place that they visit.

2) Most hotels are familiar with the local tours that are on offer, and will be happy to help you make arrangements (they may tack on an extra fee). Quite a few have their own in-house tour agencies. Some hotels and restaurants (for example, Eva's in San Ignacio) are well-known clearinghouses for local tour guides, and are excellent places to find reputable guides.

3) In the more touristed areas, freelance tour operators hang around the beach or the main street and offer their services. The best guides are licensed by the Belize Tourist Board (see below). Use your judgment.

Note that all of the larger hotels, and most dive operators, can arrange tours to any part of the country, and most will let you put together a custom package of tours, transportation and lodging. Beacause the country is small, and tour services are well-developed, it's feasible to stay in one location and take tours to different areas. For example, if you'd like to stay on Ambergris Caye and go diving one day and take a mainland jungle tour the next, it's no problem, man.

The **Belize Tourism Board** (BTB) has an excellent database of tour guides on their web site . You can search for a company by region or by desired activities (fishing, diving, kayaking, etc), and find contact information for scads of BTB-certified tour companies. *Info*: www.travelbelize.org/tourguide.html.

Here are the best of the reputable tour companies:

• **Toucan Trail** is a "socially-responsible, environmentally-sound" outfit that represents 100 small hotels offering rooms for US $60 per night or less. *Info*: www.toucantrail.com.

• **International Zoological Expeditions** offers ecotourism, educational and adventure travel. Highly recommended. *Info*: www.ize2belize.com; Tel. 800/548-5843 US.

• **To See Belize** is a very good tour company owned by Ellen Howells, an old Belize hand whose family runs the Lamanai Outpost Lodge. *Info*: www.toseebelize.com; Tel. 877-222-3549 US.

• **Paradise Expeditions** specializes in birding tours. *Info*: www.birdinginbelize.com; Tel. 824-2772.

• **Victor Emmanuel Nature Tours** specializes in birding tours. *Info*: www.ventbird.com; Tel. 800/328-VENT.

• **Star Tours**, on Caye Caulker, does snorkeling tours and runs two budget lodgings. *Info*: www.startoursbelize.com; Tel. 226-0374 or 226-0124.

• **Caribbean Tours**, a new tour outfit based in Placencia. *Info*: www.ctbelize.com.

- **Ian Anderson's Adventures in Belize**. Mr. Caves now runs a travel agency and tour company. *Info*: www.adventuresinbelize.com; Tel. 822-2800 or 866/822-2278 US.

- **Belize Explorer Travel** is a package tour operator located at Cahal Pech Village Resort in Cayo. *Info*: www.belizex.com; Tel. 624-8071.

- **Yute Expeditions**, based in Cayo, has twelve modern vans and 4x4s, and offers transportation throughout the country. *Info*: www.inlandbelize.com; Tel. 824-2076.

- **C&G Tours**, based in Dangriga, runs tours all over the country, especially Cockscomb and Mayflower. *Info*: www.cgtourscharters.com; Tel. 532-3641.

- **Tide Tours**, in Punta Gorda, is associated with TIDE, a conservation group that manages several local national parks and reserves. Hiking, horseback riding, canoeing, fishing, diving, snorkeling, kayaking, you name it. *Info*: www.tidetours.org; Tel. 722-2129

- **S&L Travel and Tours** offers half-day to weeklong tours all over the country. *Info*: www.sltravelbelize.com.

Also check out the searchable database of tour guides at www.travelbelize.org/tourguide.html.

GETTING AROUND BELIZE

BY AIR
There are two domestic airlines: **Maya Island Air** (www.mayaislandair.com; Tel. 223-1140), and **Tropic Air** (www.tropicair.com; Tel. 226-2012 or 800/422-3435 US). Both offer several flights per day from Belize City to San Pedro, Caye Caulker and Corozal in the north; and Dangriga, Placencia, and Punta Gorda in the south. Charter flights are available from both Goldson International Airport and the Municipal Airstrip. Flights

are frequent enough that it's easy to connect with international flights and avoid spending a night in Belize City.

Other than Goldson International in Belize City, the country's airports are little more than landing strips with few or no facilities. Some of the smallest are nothing but a reasonably level field of grass. Little boys with sticks drive the cows off before each landing.

CAR RENTAL

Renting a car offers the maximum in flexibility, and driving in Belize is generally safe and easy. Well-maintained paved highways connect the major regions of the country, and decent dirt roads lead to most of the places you'll want to go. Some of the smaller roads are dodgy, especially in the rainy season, so if you plan to get off the beaten track, choose something with high ground clearance, and perhaps four-wheel drive. Most rental agencies have a good selection of 4WD vehicles, from cute little Subarus to hulking SUVs.

Driving in Belize is not the death-defying adventure that it is in other Central American countries, but do use extra caution. Many locals are terrible drivers, and are especially fond of passing on blind curves. Because of unlit vehicles and animals on the roads, you may want to think twice about driving after dark. Never leave anything of value in a parked car, and be very careful where you park in cities. In fact (and I give this advice to travelers everywhere in the world) I strongly recommend that you don't drive in Belize City at all.

The only real possibility is to rent your car at the international airport, where a large selection of companies (international chains and small local agencies) compete for your custom, offering nice new vehicles. There is one agency in Placencia, **Barefoot Rentals**, which I emphatically do not recommend (decrepit cars, snotty staff).

If you plan to rent from a chain, it's more convenient, and much cheaper, to reserve a car online before leaving home. A small local outfit may just give you a better price however, especially if you want to rent for a longer period, or if you want to hire a car and driver. Rentals in Belize are overpriced. Prices start around $60 per day and go up.

• **Crystal Auto Rental**. This is the largest of the local companies, with a fleet of over 150 vehicles, including vans and pickups. *Info*: www.crystal-belize.com; Tel. 223-1600.

• **Pancho's**, one of the oldest outfits in Belize, has a nice range of SUVs and vans. *Info*: www.panchosrentalbelize.com; Tel. 225-2540.

• **Budget Rent a Car**. *Info*: www.budget-belize.com; Tel. 223-2435 or 223-3986.

• **Vista Auto Rentals**. *Info*: www.vistarentalsbelize.com; Tel. 225-2292.

• **Euphrates Auto Rental**. *Info*: www.ears.bz; Tel. 227-5752.

• **Jabiru Auto Rental**. *Info*: www.jabiruautorental.bz; Tel. 225-3630 or 610-2454.

• **Hertz Auto Rental**. *Info*: www.hertz.com.

• **Thrifty**. *Info*: www.thrifty.com.

TAXIS
Taxis are reasonably priced, convenient and easily recognized by their **green license plates**. After dark in Belize City, a taxi is the only safe way to get around. A taxi can also be an affordable way to get to rural destinations, or just to take a tour around the countryside, especially if you're with a group. Fares to the most common destinations are fixed, but elsewhere they may be negotiable. A word to the wise: any time you take a taxi in the developing world, be sure to agree on a fare *before* riding anywhere.

BUSES
Buses run hourly from Belize City along all the major highways, with service to major towns in Belize, as well as Chetumal, Mexico and Melchor, Guatemala. There are also less frequent

express buses. The former monolith, **Novelo's Bus Line**, has recently split up into smaller regional companies. Finding the right spot to catch a bus to your destination can be a project, so ask for the latest info at your hotel.

Many buses are old American school buses, and are less than comfortable. The regular buses also make frequent stops, so it's well worth paying the extra price for an express bus. Belize's buses are reasonably punctual and reasonably safe, but do try to keep your eye on your luggage.

If traveling to or from Mexico, you'll find a wealth of information on bus services at www.travelyucatan.com/trans-4.htm. Current bus schedules are available at www.ticketbus.com.mx.

BOATS

Caye Caulker and Ambergris Caye are served by scheduled passenger boats operated by the **Caye Caulker Water Taxi Association**. They depart from the Belize Marine Terminal, located at the north end of the swing bridge in Belize City. The fare is $10 per person each way to San Pedro, and $7.50 to Caye Caulker. Boats can drop passengers at other islands on the way, such as Caye Chapel, Long Caye, and St. George's Caye, and you can arrange for pickup by phone. *Info*: www.cayecaulkerwatertaxi.com; Tel. 223-5752 or 226-0992.

International ferries run from Punta Gorda to Puerto Barrios, Guatemala (Requena's Charter Services, daily; www.belizenet.com/requena; Tel. 722-2070), and from Placencia and Belize City to Puerto Cortés, Honduras (weekly; www.belizeexpress.com; Tel. 663-5971 or 523-4045).

If you're going to one of the lodges on a remote caye, the lodge will arrange for a boat to take you to and from the mainland.

BASIC INFORMATION

BANKING & CHANGING MONEY

The Belizean dollar is fixed at an exchange rate of **two Belizean**

dollars to one US dollar. Both US and Belizean currency are accepted interchangeably, so there's no reason to change money. Belizean dollars are not convertible outside the country, so remember to change any leftover cash back to greenbacks before leaving, or squander it in Jet's Bar at the airport.

Most towns have at least one ATM, but many accept only Belizean bank cards, and will not work with your ATM card. As of this writing, there are a couple of usable ATMs on Ambergris, and one on Caye Caulker (Atlantic Bank). Credit cards are now pretty widely accepted, at least in tourist areas. Some places tack on an extra fee for using cards (this is technically against the rules, but they do it anyway). Most banks will do cash advances on credit cards.

Prices in this Book

In Belize, prices may be quoted in Belizean or US dollars. In order to make it easy for you to see how much things cost, this book quotes all prices in US dollars.

BUSINESS HOURS
Most businesses are open from around **9am to 5 or 6pm Monday through Friday,** and perhaps Saturday morning. Hours tend to be longer in larger cities and tourist areas. Many businesses and offices close for two hours at lunchtime. Most banks are open Mon-Fri 9am-4pm, but banks in small towns may have more limited hours. Most non-tourist-oriented businesses are closed on Sunday.

CLIMATE & WEATHER
Belize has two main seasons. The **dry season** lasts from November through May, and is the main tourist season. The **rainy season** lasts from June through October, and sees far fewer tourists. Most areas of the country do get a lot of rain during this season, and some remote regions can become almost inaccessible by road. However, prices can be lower at this time of the year, and the crowds are gone.

CONSULATES & EMBASSIES
• **US embassy**. *Info*: in Belmopan. www.belize.usembassy.gov.

• **British High Commission.** *Info*: in Belmopan. www.britishhighcommission.gov.uk.

• **Belize Embassy** to the US. *Info*: in Washington, D.C. Tel. 202/ 332-9636 US.

ELECTRICITY

Belize uses **110-volt AC, the same as in the US,** and the plugs are the same. Grounded (three-prong) plugs are not common, and the general level of electrical safety is low. Cheaper lodgings may feature "suicide showers," little electric heaters attached to the showerhead, sometimes with poorly insulated connectors (we've heard no reports of anyone actually being killed by one of these contraptions, which are also known as "widow makers," but *do not touch them*). Remote lodges get their power from generators, which may be turned off at night, and may deliver dodgy voltage.

EMERGENCIES & SAFETY
Crime

Belize is more prosperous than her Central American neighbors, and enjoys a far lower crime rate. Muggings and violent crime against tourists are rare here. However, you do need to be on your guard. Belize City in particular has a high crime rate. **Follow these rules** and you should be fine:

• It is absolutely, positively not safe to walk around the streets of Belize City after dark. *Always take a taxi.* Some areas are dodgy during the day as well, so don't wander aimlessly.

• Never, ever leave any valuables in parked cars. In fact, it's probably unwise to park anywhere other than a watched hotel parking lot.

• Be on the alert for pickpockets in any crowded situation, especially at airports, bus stations and such places. Not only cities, but heavily-touristed parks and attractions have their share of thieves.

• In some parks, walking alone on isolated trails is not recommended. Always check in at the ranger station, and hike in groups, preferably with a local guide. Also be careful about walking alone on isolated beaches.

• In crowded tourist areas, be on the alert for common scams: the "fellow American" who's been robbed and needs some money to get home, the fake fight or other disturbance, the "accidentally" spilled drink, the friendly stranger who offers you food (which may be drugged), the crowd of cute little kids who mob you and lighten your pocket, etc etc *ad infinitum*.

• Petty theft is not the only type of crime to watch out for. **Con men** run various investment scams on tourists and retirees. If you're doing any kind of business, buying real estate or investing in the country, be extra careful to deal only with reputable firms, and, most definitely, seek advice from a local third party such as a lawyer or accountant before signing anything or parting with any dough.

One of the saddest things about crime is that it can discourage you from making friends with locals. So remember, not every Belizean who approaches you is out to rip you off. They're friendly people in general, and many are simply eager to speak with a foreigner. It would be a terrible shame if you allowed your fear of crooks to make you keep every local you encounter at arm's length. You must use your own judgment about the people whom you meet on your travels.

I highly recommend a **money belt**. *Not* the external "fanny-pack," but a small flat belt that goes around your waist (there are similar things that go around your neck) *under your clothes*. With your passport, plane ticket and main cash stash zipped up out of sight, you can relax and enjoy your trip (keep a small roll of walking-around money in a pocket, so you never have to pull out your money belt in public). Money belts are available at any good luggage shop or (much cheaper) at discount stores.

As for those fanny-packs, they're famous around the world as magnets for thieves and con artists. Even if you don't plan to keep any valuables in it, I strongly urge you to leave it at home. A fanny pack shouts "opportunity!" to people whom you'd rather not meet. The sight of a fanny pack to a street hustler is like the sound of a can opener to a hungry cat.

Unlike some tropical vacation destinations, Belize is not particularly tolerant of **marijuana** or **drugs**. While the cops are not zealous about busting joint-smokers, they can and will put you in jail if you get on the wrong side of them. You will be offered *ganja*, especially in party-hearty centers such as Ambergris and Caye Caulker, but buying on the street exposes you to many dangers, including being ripped off or turned over to the authorities. I strongly advise against buying grass (or anything else) from street hustlers. As for coke and other drugs: Don't!

On the roads, you may occasionally pass through a police checkpoint. Have your passport and the car's papers available.

Prostitution is technically illegal in Belize, and therefore unregulated. The business is quite sleazy, with muggings and druggings a regular part of the scene. AIDS is quite common. Having sex with anyone under 18 is strictly illegal.

Info: for the latest Consular Information Sheets and Travel Warnings from the US State Department, go to www.travel.state.gov.

HEALTH
Belize's health care system is not so great. Larger cities have public hospitals and clinics, but you'll get better and quicker service from a private doctor or clinic, which you can find in the phone book. **In an emergency, dial 90 or 911 for the police.**

The health hazards here are the same ones you'll encounter in any tropical country. Be very careful about exposure to the sun: it can hurt you even on cloudy days. Some tap water is safe, some isn't. The folks at your hotel will tell you if the water in the bathroom is for washing only (and provide a jug of nice clean drinking water, as well). No matter how careful you are, it's not unlikely that a bit of Montezuma's revenge will be part of your Belizean adventure. Experienced travelers swear by Imodium AD, so bring some with you.

Malaria, a nasty disease that's spread by mosquitoes, is present in the southern regions, though it's usually a threat only to those who spend a long time in remote areas. Chloroquine drugs are effective preventatives. These are prescription drugs that you should start taking before your trip. These are very strong drugs, and some people report side effects such as digestive problems, headaches and very bizarre dreams. Some recommend a drug called Malarone, which is bit more expensive but is said not to have any of the unpleasant side effects.

Take stringent precautions against mosquitoes. Cover up with socks and long-sleeved pants and shirts (mosquitoes' favorite place to bite is your ankles). Light long pants such as linens or khakis really are the best choice for tropical travel. Skeeters, fleas and other insects are most active right around dawn and dusk. Some ecolodges have mosquito nets to drape over the beds at night – use them! If you do get sick, chloroquine drugs are also available at pharmacies in Belize.

Tiny little insects called **sand fleas** are a major problem in beach areas. Different people have different reactions to the little buggers: some people aren't bothered at all, some are mercilessly bitten, and some have dangerous allergic reactions. Most travelers agree that a liberal coating of Avon's Skin-So-Soft is effective against the sand fleas. It won't impress the mosquitoes however, so pack *plenty* of maximum-strength **insect repellent**, with DEET, for them. A tube or two of cortisone-based anti-itch cream is also a good thing to have.

No shots are required for travel to Belize, but you should definitely be up to date on your routine vaccinations. The **US Centers for Disease Control** (CDC) recommend malaria pills if you're going to a high-risk area. Dysentery, cholera and other diseases caused by poor sanitation are present. You can check with the CDC for the most recent health advisories and immunization recommendations. *Info*: www.cdc.gov/travel/index.htm; Tel. 877/394-8747 US.

AIDs is common in Belize. If you choose to have sex with a prostitute or anyone else, be absolutely sure to use a condom.

Poisonous snakes are common throughout the country, but snake-bites are rare. When hiking in the forest, watch your step at all times, and don't stick your hand in anywhere it doesn't belong. A stout pair of hiking boots is a very good idea for several reasons. Slipping in the mud and spraining your ankle is more likely than getting bit by a fer de lance, and it could ruin your holiday.

Travelers with special health concerns should note that remote jungle lodges have limited ability to evacuate you in a medical emergency: if something happens to you, it could be hours before you get to a hospital.

ETIQUETTE

Belizeans are great ones for politeness – when they meet, there's a great deal of handshaking, "How's the family?" and so forth, before any business gets discussed. Peoples' concept of time is different in Central America than it is in the US and Northern Europe. Public transport and other services are generally quite punctual, but individuals are not. Don't get too upset when people show up fashionably late.

Even though you're in the tropics, please don't dress as if the whole country is a beach. At coastal resorts and tourist towns, beach bum attire is fine, but in places like banks and stores, you'll notice that the locals wear long pants, shirts, and even jackets and ties, just as we do at home. Walking around in shorts, flip-flops and a baseball cap marks you instantly as a tourist.

LAND & PEOPLE

Belize is located in Central America, on the Caribbean Sea. Her neighbors are Mexico to the north and Guatemala to the west and south. Much of the country is flat, swampy coastal plain, rising to the Maya Mountains in the west and south. The country is divided into six *districts*: Corozal, Orange Walk, Belize, Cayo, Stann Creek and Toledo.

Belize is one of the most prosperous countries in Central America, but it is still poor compared to the US, with a per-capita Gross Domestic Product of $8,400 (compared with $41,600 for the US).

Some 33% of the people live below the poverty line. Rates of literacy (77%) and life expectancy (69 years) are only fair.

Belize is a very ethnically diverse country. About 49% of the people are **Mestizos** (of mixed Spanish and Native American descent), 25% are **Creoles** (of mixed British and African descent), 11% are **Maya**, and 6% are **Garifuna** (descendents of Caribs and African slaves, most of whom live along the southern coast). The remaining 10% includes East Indians, Chinese, Lebanese, Europeans and North Americans. About 50% of Belizeans are Roman Catholic and 27% are Protestant.

Who's a Creole?

The word **Creole** has many different meanings, and it means different things in different parts of the world. In Belize, the term (also spelled *Kriol*) refers to the people who form one of the country's main ethnic groups and to the dialect of English that they speak. The Creoles of Belize have a mixed ancestry of indigenous peoples, African slaves and British settlers.

Tourism is Belize's main economic activity, followed by agriculture (22.5% of GDP) especially bananas, cacao, citrus, sugar and farm-raised shrimp. Industry (15.2% of GDP) mostly consists of clothing production and food processing.

INTERNET ACCESS

Belize is getting wired up rapidly. Internet cafés are common in large cities and tourist areas. Many larger hotels offer internet service (with the exception of the more remote wilderness lodges, which may be out of reach of the telephone network). See the list of Belize-oriented internet directories and search engines at the end of this chapter. Belize's internet suffix is .bz.

LANGUAGE

Belize was a British colony until 1981, and the official language is **English**. Most locals speak a melodious local dialect, which is called **Creole** (or Kriol). **Spanish** is also widely spoken, especially in certain areas, including San Pedro and the area around San Ignacio. Many Belizeans are bilingual. There are several ethnic groups that speak their own indigenous languages, including **Garifuna** and three different **Mayan** dialects. Some of the traditional Mennonite groups speak **German** among themselves.

NEWS MEDIA
Belizeans are a literate lot. I highly recommend a look at some of the national and local papers to get a feel for the country before your visit. Check out www.belizenews.com, which has links to all the country's major news media.

National
• www.amandala.com.bz
• www.reporter.bz
• www.belizean.com
• www.guardian.bz
• www.channel5belize.com
• www.7newsbelize.com
• www.belizefirst.com
• www.belizemagazine.com

Regional
• www.sanpedrosun.net
• www.ambergristoday.com
• www.sanpedrodaily.com
• www.cayecaulkerchronicles.com
• www.placenciabreeze.com

PASSPORT REGULATIONS
Except for cruise ship passengers, all visitors to Belize need a passport to enter the country (drivers' licenses, etc, are no longer valid). Visas are not required for citizens of the US, Canada, British Commonwealth or European Union.

Visitors are permitted to stay in Belize for up to 30 days. To stay longer, you must get a visitor's extension from one of the district offices, and pay $50 per month. For more information, contact the Belize Immigration and Nationality Department (Tel. 822-2423) or the Belize Embassy in Washington DC (Tel. 202/332-9636 US). All visitors must pay a departure tax at the airport, currently $40 US per person.

POSTAL SERVICES
Belize's postal service is less than efficient (although some of the stamps are very pretty). You can expect mail from Belize to the States or Europe to take at least two weeks, if it arrives at all. When contacting hotels or tour operators in Belize, use email or fax if at all possible.

TELEPHONES
The telephone system is also a little on the crummy side, but serviceable. Cell phones are common, and you can even rent one for your visit – try the car rental agencies.

The country code is 501. To call Belize from the US, dial: 011 501 [local number].

To call the US or Canada from Belize, dial: 001 [area code and number].

Most phone booths use **phone cards**, which you can buy at grocery stores and newsstands. Phone cards are a bargain, and offer the cheapest way to call North America. Try to avoid making calls from hotels, which love to add a hefty markup to the price.

You can also dial the direct access number for your long-distance company and use your calling card:

• **AT&T Direct**: 555 (hotels), 811 (pay phones)
• **MCI**: 557 (hotels), 815 (pay phones)
• **Sprint**: 556 (hotels), 812 (pay phones)

Many remote lodges are far from phone lines or cellular coverage, so the only option may be to use a satellite phone, which is quite expensive.

You can send faxes at most post offices and hotels.

TIME
The time in Belize is the same as **US Central Standard Time** (six hours behind Greenwich Mean Time, one hour behind Eastern

Time). However, they do not recognize Daylight Savings Time. The length of the days and nights doesn't vary much here in the tropics. It gets dark about 6pm every day, year round.

TIPPING

Restaurants often add a "service charge" automatically, so examine your bill. If a service charge has been included, there's no need to do more than round up to the next even amount, unless service is exceptional. Taxi drivers don't usually expect tips. Porters should receive a little something. Many tour guides have come to expect tips, especially in tourist-swamped regions, but you really needn't give them anything extra unless they go above and beyond the call of duty.

When checking out of a hotel, I always leave a buck or two in the room for the housekeeping staff. Remember, that loose change that seems like a nuisance to you is a substantial amount of money to them!

You may occasionally be approached by freelance porters, usually young kids (in a former age, they would have been called "blackguard boys"), who hang around tourist areas and offer to carry your bags, guard your car while you're away, help you through the intricacies of buying a bus ticket, or other small services. Use your discretion as to whether they are to be trusted. If your tip is too small, they'll let you know.

TOURIST INFORMATION

The **Belize Tourist Board** has a lot of information on their web site at www.travelbelize.org. Brochures and tourist maps are available at pretty much every hotel.

WATER

Tap water is said to be safe to drink, especially at upscale hotels, which have their own large-scale filters. I drank the stuff on my last trip with no problems, but bottled water is easily available in case you're worried. Do whatever you feel safe doing.

WEIGHTS & MEASURES

Belize and the US are the only two countries in the world that do not officially use the metric system. You'll find the same familiar feet, miles, pounds and gallons that you're used to at home. However, as the metric system is used by all the neighboring countries, and by the large number of European visitors, Belizeans are familiar with metric measurements, and you'll sometimes see both systems used side-by-side.

WEBSITES

Be wary of information you find on the web. Many companies never update their sites. You'll find sites for hotels and tour operators that closed years ago. Always call for the latest schedules and prices.

- www.travelbelize.org, the site of the **Belize Tourism Board**, has lots of good info, including a searchable database of tour guides.
- The **Belize Chamber of Commerce** (www.belize.org) has info about doing business in Belize.
- **Amandala** (www.amandala.com.bz) is a weekly newspaper covering the whole country.
- www.belizenews.com has links to all the country's major newspapers.

Belize-based Search Engines
- www.belize.net
- www.belizesearch.com
- www.belizegateway.com

Regional Sites
- www.ambergriscaye.com has a great collection of info and links, not just about Ambergris Caye, but all over the country.
- www.sanpedrosun.net is the site of the San Pedro Sun, Ambergris Caye's local newspaper.
- www.goambergriscaye.com
- www.gocayecaulker.com
- www.belizedistrict.com has lots of info about Belize City and the north, including a searchable database of hotels.
- www.northernbelize.com
- www.southernbelize.com

- www.stanncreek.com
- www.placencia.com
- To learn more about Garifuna culture, see the web hub www.garinet.com and the site of the National Garifuna Council at www.ngcbelize.org.

Ecotourism

- www.ecotourism.org is the site of the International Ecotourism Society, and includes lists of environmentally friendly lodges and tour operators.
- www.planeta.com has lots of information about ecotourism in Belize and the world.
- www.ran.org is the site of the Rainforest Action Network, which has several projects in Belize.
- www.bzecotourism.org

General Info

- www.belizetourism.net
- www.belizeexplorer.com
- www.belizenet.com
- www.belizeit.com
- www.mayabelize.ca
- www.belizemagazine.com
- www.mybelizeadventure.com
- www.planetbelize.com
- www.toucantrail.com has a searchable database of budget hotels, and much other good info.
- www.tripadvisor.com and www.virtualtourist.com have comments from fellow tourists about various attractions, lodgings and restaurants.

A SHORT HISTORY

Belize's recorded history begins with the **Maya**, who built an advanced civilization of independent city-states that stretched from Mexico to Honduras. Their knowledge of astronomy, their calendar and their written language were unparalleled among ancient peoples. Scholars divide the Mayan era into three periods. Most of their cities were built during the Classic Period, which lasted from around 300-900 AD.

Belize has many important Mayan sites, including the earliest known community in the Maya world, **Cuello** in the Orange Walk District, which is believed to have been settled as long ago as 2000 BC. The Mayans built enormous cities – the largest in Belize, **Caracol**, had more residents than Belize City does today – with majestic temples, palaces and plazas. They recorded significant events in their history on pillars of stone called stelae. Around 900 AD, the construction of monuments and stelae stopped, the cities were abandoned, and the Mayan people reverted to a scattered race of subsistence farmers. Today there are several distinct groups of Mayan people living in Belize, speaking their own indigenous languages. See Chapter 6 for more about the ancient Maya.

After 1492, the Spanish began settling Central America, but they didn't have a monopoly on the area for long. With its many islands, reefs and shallow sand flats, Belize proved a perfect place for British privateers ("pirates" to the Spanish) to hide out and launch raids against the Spanish treasure ships that carried the riches of the New World back to Spain. Later, as the era of piracy wound down, some of these swashbucklers settled on the mainland and set about cutting logwood and mahogany. As you may imagine, these settlers, who became known as the **Baymen**, were a rowdy, hard-drinking bunch. According to popular legend, they built Belize City on a base of wood chips and rum bottles.

Conflict between the Baymen and the Spanish went on throughout the 1700s, culminating in the 1798 Battle of St. George's Caye, in which the Spanish were defeated and ceded control of the region to Britain. In 1871 it became the Crown Colony of **British Honduras**.

Logging was the mainstay of Belize's economy for many years. Unlike in other colonies in the region, large-scale sugar cultivation never developed here. The British began to import African slaves in the 1720s. However, the need for labor in the forests was far less than on the sugar plantations, one of the reasons why

Belize today has a far lower population density than neighboring countries.

Over the years, several other ethnic groups joined the British and the Africans to create the diverse patchwork of today's Belize. In 1832, a large number of **Garifuna** arrived in Southern Belize from the island of Roatan, where they had been exiled by the British (see Chapter 7). Around 1847, the Caste War in neighboring Yucatan, in which the native Mayans revolted against their Spanish and Mestizo overlords, sent thousands of refugees (**Mestizo** and **Maya**) into Northern Belize. Beginning in 1958, small groups of **Mennonites**, members of a pacifist Anabaptist sect, began to settle in the Orange Walk and Cayo districts (see Chapter 5).

In 1961, Hurricane Hattie caused a lot of damage in coastal areas, so the government decided to move the capital from low-lying Belize City to a new site at the geographic center of the country. Construction of the planned city of **Belmopan** began in 1970, and today it is the country's capital, although Belize City remains the business and economic center. British Honduras became a self-governing colony in 1964. The country gained full independence, and changed its name to Belize, in 1981.

INDEX